Goethe's *Faust*

GOETHE'S

𝕱𝖆𝖚𝖘𝖙

The German Tragedy

JANE K. BROWN

Cornell University Press

ITHACA AND LONDON

First published 1986 by Cornell University Press.

International Standard Book Number (cloth) 0-8014-1834-8
International Standard Book Number (paper) 0-8014-9349-8
Library of Congress Catalog Card Number 85-17149
Printed in the United States of America
Librarians: Library of Congress cataloging information
appears on the last page of the book.

The paper in this book is acid-free and meets the guidelines for
permanence and durability of the Committee on Production Guidelines
for Book Longevity of the Council on Library Resources.

This book is for Marshall

So sind wir nicht am rechten Ort
Und ziehen unseres Weges weiter fort.

Contents

Illustrations

Preface

No masterpiece of the European tradition has received more lip service and less real understanding than *Faust*. Especially now, when American awareness of German culture is at the lowest level it has reached since Goethe's death, in 1832, the most common reaction to this extraordinary text is not simply puzzlement but the conviction that it is overrated. William Hazlitt's critique of 1818 may stand here for that of many later readers as well: "Goethe's tragedies are . . . constructed upon the second or inverted manner of the German stage, with a deliberate design to avoid all possible effect and interest, and this object is completely accomplished. He is however spoken of with enthusiasm almost amounting to idolatry by his countrymen, and those among ourselves who import heavy German criticism into this country in shallow flat-bottomed unwieldy intellects."[1] Excerpts from *Faust* are dutifully included in anthologies of world literature, but not always in recognizable forms and rarely, one senses, with much conviction that Goethe truly ranks among the giants of our tradition. The dearth of books on Goethe written in English for a general audience testifies mutely but eloquently to the current invisibility of *Faust* in this country.

This book attempts to rectify the situation. It is intended not only to be an original reading of *Faust* but also to present the text to students and scholars of literatures other than German. Let me emphasize,

[1]*The Complete Works of William Hazlitt*, ed. P. P. Howe, 21 vols. (London and Toronto: Dent, 1930–34), 6:363.

9

however, that it is not an introduction to the historical and biographical backgrounds to the text, nor is it intended to replace a commentary. It is an interpretation, a reading of both parts of *Faust* in the context of European romanticism and in terms of the many texts that Goethe's play exploits and responds to.[2] I am concerned less with the provenance of motifs or figures than with the implications of their use in *Faust*. Goethe mines earlier texts deliberately, I argue, in order to situate German literature in the European tradition rather than in its own national tradition and in order, finally, to show that all literature is by its very nature allusive.

My goal has been to make *Faust* accessible to the modern reader first by clearing away understandable and widespread but mistaken expectations about the kind of play *Faust* is. It will then be easier to see how the play defines itself and what its place in the European tradition, and indeed the German tradition, may be. As a result, the discussion is organized around three basic topics, which will recur intertwined and in variations. These topics are (1) the genre of *Faust*—the kind of play it is; (2) the fundamental structure of *Faust*—the basic problem that it deals with over and over; and (3) the way in which *Faust* locates itself in the European cultural tradition.

In posing these questions, I am aware that I do not directly address what have traditionally been the central issues of *Faust* scholarship and that I assume without discussion positions still considered controversial in some quarters. I do so because it seems to me that the kinds of questions a largely non-German audience brings to this text are often different from those of an audience trained in the German tradition. Recent developments in critical theory have demonstrated above all that an interpretation is neither absolute nor universal but conditioned by the context—historical, social, philosophical, political—of the interpreter. Because of the political and social conditions involved in the late emergence of Germany as a nation-state in the nineteenth century, because of Goethe's particular conspicuousness as a recent giant in a literary tradition rather shorter than the English or French tradition, and because *Faust* was recognized even before its comple-

[2]Commentary in English and background materials may be found in the Norton Critical Edition of *Faust*, trans. Walter Arndt, ed. Cyrus Hamlin (New York: Norton, 1976). Condensed historical and biographical background in English may be found in the introduction to the school edition of *Faust* by R.-M. S. Heffner, H. Rehder, and W. F. Twaddell (Lexington, Mass.: Heath, 1954).

tion to be the masterpiece of German literature, both Goethe and the play have unavoidably been the bearers of the national heritage—whether as epitomes or antitypes—in a way that no single text of the English tradition has ever had to embody the entire culture. Wilhelmian Germany, Weimar Germany, republican West Germany, and socialist East Germany have all in their turn exhibited a powerful need for a compatible reading of Goethe's *Faust* to embody their own cultural and social ideals. Not only does the scholarship offer us, then, multiple avatars of Goethe's hero, but more important, it has firmly focused discussion of the play on the character of Faust—his nature, his ethics, his development, his achievement—and what he represents—whether Germany, Western man, modern man, romantic man, or whatever. Similarly, it has focused perhaps undue attention on the end of the play, certainly much more on the end than on the beginning. Here the question turns on the salvation of Faust. Is he seriously saved (the so-called perfectibilist position), and if so, for what reason, or is the end in some way ironic or invalid (the "nihilist" position)? This emphasis has led to the play's being read more in pieces than as a whole. Those who, for whatever reasons, see Goethe as the youthful vitalist seek the essential *Faust* in the Gretchen tragedy and some of the rest of Part I. Admirers of the classical Goethe focus on Act III of Part II, taking Act II as a kind of prologue to it. For those who see Goethe as an ethical thinker, the play consists in essence of Part I, the first scene of Act I in Part II, and Act V through the death of Faust.

All of these modes of reading have their validity in their respective contexts, and they continue to be important today to the extent that their contexts persist. Nevertheless, the context of the reading in this book is substantially different, and I have tried to adjust the questions asked accordingly. Americans reading *Faust* today tend to confront the play in the context of world literature or of romantic literature, and that is the context of my discussion. To the extent that the weight of emphasis in German scholarship has been on the psychological, ethical, and social dimensions of the text, I hope that this reading will offer an alternative perspective to specialists.

Because I have tried to formulate new basic questions about the play, I have avoided a running polemic with the scholarship both in the text and in the notes. My notes are intended rather to register connections to other, less expected contexts or to offer specific guidance to the reader unfamiliar with the German tradition. For the same reason I have consistently chosen the more common and general terminology over the specific vocabulary of Goethe scholars. It is common to speak, for example, about "polarity and enhancement" (*Polarität und Steigerung*) in Goethe but not about a dialectic, to see Goethe as a classicist rather than a romantic, to talk about "renunciation" but to deny Goethe any sense of tragedy. Except for the term *source* I have avoided the traditional terminology of Goethe scholarship. As I define the questions on which this reading is focused, I will try to indicate more specifically where my approach relates to and diverges from more familiar readings of the play.

This book emerges from fifteen years of teaching *Faust* in both German and English; in the process I have accumulated many debts to students and colleagues. The first is to my students at Mount Holyoke College, the University of Virginia, and the University of Colorado for their interest, enthusiasm, and perplexities, and above all for their patience with me. The responsiveness of these students, especially those who took the courses in English, convinced me that this book should address a broader audience. I have also received considerable help and encouragement from colleagues at Virginia and Colorado. My sense of Goethe and of *Faust* has been decisively influenced by Stuart Atkins and Cyrus Hamlin, though I am sure there are many points in my argument on which we differ. Cyrus Hamlin has been particularly generous, both as teacher and as friend, in sharing unpublished material and in offering criticism. I have also received generous and patient criticism from Neil Flax and helpful suggestions from Clark Muenzer. I have been particularly fortunate in my relatives. My mother, Gertrude Kurshan, read the manuscript with an eye to its accessibility to the lay reader. I cannot begin to catalogue what my husband, Marshall, has contributed to this book, from criticism, bibliographical help, and ferocious editing to love, support, and encouragement. As colleague and husband he has given me the best of both worlds.

Chapter 10 has appeared essentially unchanged in the *Yearbook of the Goethe Society of North America*, volume 2 (1984); I am grateful for permission to use it here.

JANE K. BROWN

Boulder, Colorado

Goethe's *Faust*

1

Introduction:
The Problem of *Faust*

Faust poses not one but three different, equally important problems: its genre, its structure, and its place in the European tradition. Why each of these issues is a problem with regard to *Faust* will constitute, I think, the clearest introduction to my reading of the play.

The Genre of *Faust*

Goethe subtitled his play *A Tragedy*. Since the later seventeenth century this term has been generally understood in the European literatures in terms of Aristotle's description in the *Poetics*, largely as that definition was interpreted and reinterpreted by neoclassical theorists. Thus the term immediately evokes a series of categories that are still in common use: hero, innocent suffering, fate, tragic flaw, guilt and repentance, reversal, catastrophe. Even where these specific categories may be seen not to apply, neo-Aristotelian theory has left a substratum of assumptions about the nature of drama and particularly of tragedy, namely that it deals with individuals confronting profound moral, emotional, and psychological issues, that psychological consistency is necessary to make a drama "believable," and that some kind of believability (neoclassical "verisimilitude") is the ultimate criterion of validity in literature.[1] It is possible to read Shakespearean

---

[1]Even a brief survey of introductions to freshman drama anthologies currently in print amply confirms this observation. Variation is to be found mainly in the degree of explicitness with which Aristotelian categories are presented.

15

tragedy in this mode, but its real advent is with the neoclassical tragedy of passion beginning with Racine.[2] Only with this new psychological focus does love emerge as the great subject for tragedy.[3] *Faust* contains, without doubt, such a tragedy of passion in the Gretchen sequence; but what is strange is that *Faust* contains so much besides that is often difficult to connect to this quintessential love tragedy, not least the ultimate salvation of the hero. From the vantage point of the later eighteenth century, neoclassicism had substantially narrowed the meaning of *tragedy*, for at least in Germany and England through the seventeenth century it had referred to any drama with an unhappy outcome or even, as Jacob Steiner has pointed out, simply to a stage play.[4] This recent change in meaning suggests that *tragedy* stands in the title not as a term to be taken for granted but as one to be questioned and defined by the play.

Goethe offers a clearer indication of the genre of his play in the two prologues. At the end of the "Prelude on the Stage" the director calls upon his people to pace out on the narrow stage the whole circle of creation and to move from heaven through the world to hell. This is a call for "world theater," for the cosmic drama that prevailed in Europe from the late Middle Ages through the seventeenth century. Played on the streets or in theaters with names like the Globe, such drama placed human beings in the largest possible context of their relations to the totality of society and to the divine order. These plays, in which supernatural figures, including God, appeared freely on stage—as in the "Prologue in Heaven," which follows immediately on the director's speech—took many forms: morality, mystery, or Corpus Christi play; masque; the Spanish Golden Age dramas of a Lope de Vega or a Calderón; opera and operetta; even, in many respects, Shakespearean comedy, tragedy, and romance. They were superseded—indeed, vigorously suppressed—in the late seventeenth and early eighteeth cen-

[2]Ernst Robert Curtius succinctly formulates the way in which neoclassical drama constitutes a major watershed in his section on theatrical metaphors in *European Literature and the Latin Middle Ages*, trans. Willard R. Trask (New York: Pantheon [Bollingen], 1953), 142.

[3]Jean H. Hagstrum has recently elaborated in impressive detail the broader implications of this obvious generalization in *Sex and Sensibility: Ideal and Erotic Love from Milton to Mozart* (Chicago: University of Chicago Press, 1980).

[4]Jacob Steiner, *Erläuterungen zu Goethes "Faust I"* (Stockholm: Natur och Kultur, 1959), 17. Steiner argues the term still had this neutral meaning in Goethe's informal usage in the 1790s.

turies by the character-oriented neoclassical drama and theory of the Enlightenment.[5] Thus if *Faust* is conceived in the tradition of world theater, which developed independently of the revival of Aristotle's *Poetics*, it should be read in terms of a different poetics.

Before outlining a poetics of world theater, however, it might be helpful to establish some historical basis for Goethe's relation to this mode. To begin with, Goethe respected Aristotle but not French neo-Aristotelianism. "By the introduction of misunderstood ancient doctrine and nice propriety," he wrote, "the French have so limited their poetry that it will finally disappear altogether, since it cannot even be translated into prose anymore."[6] In a ferocious segment of his autobiography (later deleted and published posthumously as the essay "German Theater") Goethe identifies police, religion, and "morally purified" taste as the main persecutors of the theater through history. "In France," he says, "the pedantry of Cardinal Richelieu subdued [the theater] and squeezed it into its present form"—the "present form" being, in this context, the theater of Corneille and Racine![7] In Germany, Goethe continues, the theater was taken over by "shallow incompetents," who turn out to be the leading exponents of French

[5]The consistent and increasingly effective rejection of Spanish Golden Age drama by French and Spanish theorists from the seventeenth to the nineteenth century has been documented in detail by Werner Brüggemann in *Spanisches Theater und deutsche Romantik* 1, Spanische Forschungen der Görres Gesellschaft, ser. 2, vol. 8 (Münster: Aschendorff, 1964), 2–99. Just a decade before Goethe reestablished Calderón's reputation as a major dramatist by his production of *The Constant Prince* in Weimar (1811), a junta to improve the Spanish theater banned several plays of Lope and Calderón and proposed as a model for the new Spanish drama the popular but vapid comedies of August von Kotzebue, Goethe's archenemy. A good sense of the ambivalence of English neoclassicists toward Spanish drama and toward their own Elizabethan heritage can be gained from John Loftis, *The Spanish Plays of Neoclassical England* (New Haven: Yale University Press, 1973), 3–23. Fielding parodies the neoclassical purification of the stage in England in *Tom Jones*, bk. 12, chap. 5. Gloria Flaherty has documented the neoclassical hostility to opera in Germany in *Opera in the Development of German Critical Thought* (Princeton: Princeton University Press, 1978). Gottsched's formal expulsion of the harlequin from the German stage is a cliché of German literary history.

[6]From "Urteilsworte französischer Kritiker [I]" (French critical terminology [I]), in *Über Kunst und Altertum* (1817), 1:3; Goethe, *Gesamtausgabe der Werke und Schriften in zweiundzwanzig Bänden*, 15 (Stuttgart: Cotta, n.d.), 928 (translation mine). Although this is a late formulation, such a position was already popular among avant-garde literati in Goethe's youth, and could be documented equally well for the Goethe of the 1790s.

[7]"Deutsches Theater [1813]," *Gesamtausgabe*, 15:591 (translation mine).

17

neoclassicism in Germany. Goethe, by contrast, wants to turn the devil loose on stage again and to restore the harlequin, both of whom, as standard figures in the world-theater tradition, had been driven from the stage by those same "shallow incompetents." The devil and the clown reappear combined in Goethe's own Mephistopheles. Despite the prominence accorded to *Iphigenie* and *Tasso*, the most neoclassical of Goethe's plays, the largest proportion of his dramatic output consisted of masques, libretti for operettas, allegorical festival plays, and of course *Faust*. Goethe's activity as director of the Weimar theater from 1791 to 1817 reflects similar concerns. He produced the plays of Terence, for example, in masks so that the interest would focus on types rather than individuals; he was the first to produce a play by Calderón in original form on the German stage. His major contribution to the history of theater was to train his company to work as an ensemble; the stage was to provide the spectator with total pictures, like masques. He staged Shakespeare's *Julius Caesar* because he was intrigued by the mob scenes; he adapted *Romeo and Juliet* as a kind of operetta. Even this cursory overview shows clearly that Goethe's conception of drama was not the tightly unified, psychologizing neo-Aristotelian tragedy but rather the episodic thematic drama of the world-theater tradition.

Two of Goethe's occasional dramas programmatically state his view of himself as this kind of dramatist. The first is a prelude written for the opening of the Weimar company's new summer theater in 1802, called *Was wir bringen* (What We Offer). The playlet begins as a comic genre piece in which the set evokes a painting by Adam Elsheimer of Jupiter and Mercury visiting Baucis and Philemon. An elderly couple is visited here by a group of allegorical figures, who for all practical purposes transform the couple into Baucis and Philemon. The couple ultimately realize that they are actors and that their cottage, which is transformed into a theater, was never real. In a later continuation (1814) Goethe added a full-scale operatic finale with figures from various Mozart operas. Evidently what Goethe thought he offered was what we have identified as world theater. A later work, *The Masque of 1818*, denies the application of the traditional neoclassical genres to *Faust*. Here major works by Weimar authors are introduced and discussed by Epic, Tragedy, Comedy, and the river Ilm (the *genius loci*). *Faust*, however, is introduced rather by Mephistopheles, and as everyone in the audience knew, Mephistopheles was played on this occasion by Goethe himself. The only other work introduced by Mephistopheles is the plotless masque *Wallenstein's Camp*, with which Schiller introduced his famous trilogy. Finally, we must discuss Goethe's admiration for Calderón, whom he came to see as the greatest exponent of this tradition after he read A. W. Schlegel's translation of *The Adoration of the Cross* in 1802. His first response is reported to have been effusive—most unusual for Goethe in this period—and remained genuinely enthusiastic to the end of his life.[8] When he said, as he did much later to Johann Peter Eckermann (May 12, 1825), that Calderón had had no influence on him, he can only have meant that he found in Calderón a sense of the nature of drama to which, by age fifty-three, he had already arrived in ignorance of the Spanish master. As we shall see, Goethe did not scruple to borrow motifs extensively from him. Goethe's assessment of Calderón's greatness may stand here as a summary of the entire tradition of world theater, or, as it can also be called, nonillusionist drama.

He does not provide an actual *view of nature* at all; he is rather thoroughly *theatrical*, indeed *stagy*. What we call *illusion*, especially the kind that arouses emotion, is completely absent. The plan *lies clearly before our understanding;* the scenes follow one another according to necessity, in a kind of *ballet*, which satisfies by its *artifice* and suggests the techniques of our contemporary *comic opera*. The principal motivations are always the same: conflict of obligations, passions, restrictions derived from the *contrast of characters*, from the particular circumstances.

[8]His first response was reported to Schlegel by Friedrich Schelling; see Brüggemann, *Spanisches Theater und deutsche Romantik*, 190. A full analysis of Calderón's long-term impact on Goethe may be found in Swana L. Hardy, *Goethe, Calderón und die romantische Theorie des Dramas*, Heidelberger Forschungen 10 (Heidelberg: Winter, 1965). Stuart Atkins repeatedly documents Calderonian motifs and techniques in *Faust* in *Goethe's "Faust": A Literary Analysis* (Cambridge: Harvard University Press, 1964), *passim;* and in his article "Goethe, Calderon, and *Faust: Der Tragödie zweiter Teil*," *Germanic Review* 28 (1953): 83–98. Goethe appears not to have known anything by Calderón before 1802, when Part I of *Faust* was essentially completed. Nevertheless, Brüggemann documents (99–168) that five of the plays had been available since 1770 in poor translations from the French and that information about the Spanish baroque theater was available from discussions by Lessing and others, as well as from imitations and adaptations by Carlo Gozzi and many others. Henry W. Sullivan has extensively documented the anonymous influence of Calderón on eighteenth-century German drama in *Calderón in the German Lands and the Low Countries: His Reception and Influence, 1654–1980* (Cambridge: Cambridge University Press, 1983).

The main plot runs its great poetic course; the interludes, which move in graceful *minuet-like figures*, are rhetorical, dialectical, sophistical. All aspects of humanity are exploited, and so, finally, even the *fool* is included, whose homely understanding threatens—immediately, if not sooner—*to destroy whatever illusion* may raise claims to sympathy and acceptance.

Now with a little consideration we realize that human conditions, feelings, events cannot be brought onto the stage in their original state of nature; they have to be worked over, prepared, *sublimated*. And so it is the same here: the poet stands on the threshold of higher culture, he presents a *quintessence* of humanity.[9]

The essential difference between world theater and Aristotelian drama is that the first is not mimetic.[10] The action is not an imitation of anything but rather a game or play that consistently observes certain given conventions, as the very word *play* suggests. The frequency of the play-within-the-play motif in Shakespeare, Calderón, and *Faust* reflects the extreme self-consciousness of such texts with regard to this trait. Costumes and sets tended to be extremely stylized, either toward schematic simplicity in religious drama or toward ornate elaboration in masque and opera. Medieval drama was so little concerned

---

[9]From a review of *Die Tochter der Luft* [The daughter of the air] in *Über Kunst und Altertum* (1822), 3:3; *Gesamtausgabe*, 15:1138 (translation and emphasis mine). A complete translation of this essay into English is available in *Goethe's Literary Essays*, ed. J. E. Spingarn (New York: Ungar, 1964), 208–11.

[10]There are no texts that may be called a poetics of this form, such as abound for neoclassical tragedy. It must, rather, be deduced from the plays themselves. There is an excellent account of this sort for the Corpus Christi cycles in thirteenth-century England in the first two chapters of V. A. Kolve, *The Play Called Corpus Christi* (Stanford: Stanford University Press, 1966). For further discussion of medieval drama and its theatric and dramatic presuppositions, see Glynne Wickham's definitive *Early English Stages*, 1 (London: Routledge & Kegan Paul; New York: Columbia University Press, 1959), esp. 149–57. The equivalent book for the Spanish tradition is N. D. Shergold, *A History of the Spanish Stage from Medieval Times until the End of the Seventeenth Century* (Oxford: Clarendon Press, 1967). Pp. 415–78 deal with the conditions of production of Corpus Christi drama in the seventeenth century. Stephen Orgel has provided important accounts for Stuart masque in the first chapter of *Inigo Jones: The Theatre of the Stuart Court*, with Roy Strong (London: Sotheby Parke Bernet; Berkeley: University of California Press, 1973), and in *The Illusion of Power: Political Theater in the English Renaissance* (Berkeley: University of California Press, 1975). Perhaps the paradigmatic text for this tradition is Calderón's *Great Theater of the World*, in which human life is portrayed as a drama played before God. Much of Goethe's dramatic practice in *Faust* can be seen in schematic adumbration in this seventeenth-century text, even though there is no evidence of specific influence.

with realistic portrayal that the prompter appeared on stage and designated who was to speak. This stylization kept the spectator always aware of the illusion as something to be interpreted and understood. The religious dramas presented sometimes abstruse points of doctrine, which would be explained either by *raisonneurs* in the play or by expositor figures. Shakespeare continued to use choruses, allegorical figures, and narrators sporadically over the whole span of his career. Even in Renaissance court masque, for which the techniques and equipment of the modern illusionist proscenium stage were developed, the focus was on the almost magical capacity to evoke illusions rather than on the realism of the illusion. Similarly, the conditions of performance—whether in the street, a converted banqueting hall, a court theater, or an Elizabethan outdoor theater—always reminded the spectators in some way of their place in society and thus metaphorically of their place in the larger cosmic structure in which the play defined itself. The illusion on the stage was thus not understood to be illusion or imitation of reality, a room with the fourth wall removed, but rather a game that revealed the illusoriness of reality in the face of a larger context and a higher truth.

The nonmimetic nature of this dramatic mode has important effects on character and plot, the two categories that dominate both Aristotelian poetics and our current language for discussing drama. E. R. Curtius saw the development of neoclassical drama as a shift from theocentric to anthropocentric theater, that is, from drama focused on our relations to the divine and cosmic to drama focused on our relations to ourselves and other people.[11] This distinction makes it easier to see why nonillusionist drama often has no hero at all; when there is one, the hero is typical and readily universalizable rather than individual. Think, for example, of the readiness with which Goethe's Faust is seen to represent Western man or modern man. And in general, characters tend to be allegorical, to embody qualities, powers, principles, or social roles, rather than to be rounded individuals. Typically such characters do not engage in individualized personal relationships with one another, nor is there necessarily much concern with psychological analysis or even consistency. Even when dramatists show great psychological insight, the movement of the drama will depend more on what characters are than on their moti-

[11]Curtius, *European Literature and the Latin Middle Ages*, 142.

vations or the interaction of personality and circumstance. Goethe's Faust, for example, is placed by the "Prologue in Heaven" into a larger cosmic structure in which erring is made the necessary condition for salvation. To ask, then, how Faust develops, what he learns, how his relationship to the devil evolves, is hardly meaningful, for if he ever learns not to err, he will not be human. Faust is instead a static character who repeatedly destroys other lives in his haste to realize ideals. At best Faust learns to understand and even manipulate the significance of his errors, but he never learns not to err. It is the spectator or reader, who does not identify with Faust, who truly learns and develops in response to the play. Similarly, the issue in the so-called Gretchen tragedy is not the morality or immorality of the seduction; it is what Gretchen represents for Faust and for us, her relationship to earlier and later manifestations of the ideal in the play.

Faust scholars have long recognized the importance of the "Prologue in Heaven" for the moral structure of the play, but that has not prevented extensive discussions of Faust's character, of his development, of the moral optimism or pessimism of the conclusions of the two parts of the play. Even Stuart Atkins, who has done so much to uncover Goethe's non-Aristotelian roots, reads the play as a drama of character.[12] It would be absurd to pretend that *Faust* is devoid of sophisticated psychological insight; my point is rather that by the nature of the play such insight is not central or organizing.

In the same way, plot structure does not involve the standard Aristotelian categories of peripety (or reversal), catastrophe, or unity. Not only the unities of time and place but also the more fundamental unity of action are frequently ignored. Such drama is, in other words, episodic, and the connection between episodes is more at the level of theme than at the superficial level of story line. Opera, Golden Age drama, and indeed Shakespearean comedy and romance—all tend toward plots based on Renaissance romance narratives, which are by nature episodic and meandering. Masque has no mimetic plot at all; the interest lies in interpreting a series of images rather than imitating reality. The episodic nature of *Faust* is immediately apparent. As one example of the implications of this view, let us consider the function of magic in the play. Mephisto's magic cloak or the potion in the "Witch's Kitchen" seem rather arbitrary ways to move the plot from

[12]Atkins, *Goethe's "Faust,"* vi.

one point to the next. Indeed they are arbitrary and ought to be recognized as such, but for Goethe's audience in 1808 this episodic mode was already the exception. The arbitrariness of Mephisto's magic thus emphasizes the lack of neoclassical verisimilitude in the apparent unity of the plot and calls attention to the fact that the play operates according to different generic principles. Magic is entirely symbolic in the play. It represents the attempted shortcut to transcendent knowledge that Mephistopheles seems to offer to Faust in the same way that it offers shortcuts from one part of the play to the next. The focus is on interpreting the significance of what is visible, not on the Aristotelian category of invisible causality.

The episodic nature of the play has troubled readers of *Faust*, the more so since the play was written over a period of sixty years, with some substantial interruptions.[13] Much energy has gone into defending the unity of the play, though readings of the play as an entirety are still rare, and there is no consensus that the play should be read as a unified text. There is a distinguished history of defenses of the unity of the play in conceptual or thematic terms, but rarely has it been defended in dramatic or theatrical terms and never, to my knowledge, in consistently generic terms.[14] The generic context I have been outlining offers a historical grounding for the discontinuities in the plot and seems to justify taking the disconnectedness of the text as a generic sign. *Faust*'s episodic plot is not disunified, but merely unified differently from neoclassical plots. Ultimately the best test of that assumption will be the coherence and cogency of the interpretation to which it leads.

Once sensitized to the non-Aristotelian aspects of *Faust*, the reader can readily see that the text is full of miniature non-Aristotelian forms.

[13]The Norton Critical Edition of *Faust*, 349–55, includes an analytical table giving the dates of composition segment by segment. A recent study in English of Part I in genetic terms may be found in John Gearey, *Goethe's "Faust": The Making of Part I* (New Haven: Yale University Press, 1981). The classic study of Part II in genetic terms, taken in the broadest and most abstract sense, is Wilhelm Emrich, *Die Symbolik von "Faust II": Sinn und Vorformen* (Frankfurt am Main and Bonn: Athenäum, 1964).

[14]As recently as 1966 Wolfgang Streicher denied the play dramatic unity in *Die dramatische Einheit von Goethes "Faust." Betrachtet unter den Kategorien Substantialitä und Funktionalität* (Tübingen: Niemeyer, 1966). Streicher's problem, like that of most scholars, is the total avoidance of historical categories for his discussion. Atkins is the great exception among those who consider dramatic unity, for he does actually regard *Faust* as a real stage play.

23

Act I of Part II contains a Renaissance masque; Act III contains an opera. Acts II and IV depend heavily on Calderón. The same elements also run through Part I. The first part of "Outside the City Gate" is a small processional masque; the Gretchen tragedy and the "Walpurgis Night" are both structured as operettas, the "Walpurgis Night's Dream" as a masque. The presence of these forms once again signals the true generic loyalties of the text.

Indeed, Goethe revives in *Faust* not only the various examples of nonillusionist drama but its central self-consciousness as well. *Faust* is a veritable Chinese box of plays within plays. The process begins with the double framing of the action by the two prologues. The bet between God and Mephistopheles in the "Prologue in Heaven" makes God a concerned spectator of the entire subsequent action to the death of Faust; thus the play is, in effect, played before God, just as it is in Calderón's *Great Theater of the World (El gran teatro del mundo)*, the epitome of the seventeenth-century world as a stage tradition.[15] But even this play is a play within the play, because the "Prelude in the Theater" shows us the director, poet, and clown discussing the play they are about to perform, namely, *Faust*. The Easter chorus in "Night" comes from the Easter sequence, the earliest form of religious drama, being performed in the neighboring church; "Auerbach's Tavern" consists of a series of vaudeville acts; the apes in "Witch's Kitchen" set up a mock court around Mephistopheles, then bring him a mock world; the climactic "Walpurgis Night" issues in the performance of the "Dream," to give only a few examples. I will argue that the Gretchen sequence, too, functions as a play within the play, for which we see Faust donning his costume of youthfulness in "Witch's Kitchen." Because the play-within-the-play motif, as indeed the whole world-theater tradition, is a revival in *Faust*, it does not, of course, have the same significance as it did in Shakespeare or Calderón. If in the seventeenth-century drama the motif can still serve as a relatively unproblematic metaphor for life, in

---

[15]"World as stage" was a widespread cliché in the seventeenth century. A major history of the period, for instance, was called *Theatrum mundi*. Cf. Shakespeare: "All the world's a stage" (*As You Like It*, II, vii) and "Life's but a walking shadow, a poor player" (*Macbeth*, V, v), and the motto of the Globe Theater, "Totus mundus agit histrionem." It underlies the popularity of the play-within-a-play motif in the period, from *Hamlet* to Corneille's *Theatrical Illusion* to Calderón's *Great Theater of the World*. On the history of the motif, see Curtius, 138–44.

the secularized eighteenth century, with its modern awareness of the arbitrary nature of all signs, it becomes rather a metaphor for art. And so it functions in Goethe, so that his use of the world-theater tradition is not only self-conscious revival of an already self-conscious mode but meditation on the mode itself and on the proper nature of drama. The nature and content of this meditation forms a central theme of my reading. At the most general level it leads to a consideration of allegory in the text.[16] I will argue, indeed, that the conclusion of the play focuses on the nature of tragedy, for when Goethe allows Faust to be blinded just before his death, this allusion to *Oedipus the King* returns us to the realm of Aristotle's *Poetics*, for which *Oedipus* was the model text. To juxtapose the paradigmatic tragic moment in the Western and particularly the Aristotelian tradition with the baroque opera of salvation that immediately follows is to invite reflection on the nature of tragedy in a context much broader than neo-Aristotelianism, that of world theater.

The Structure of *Faust*

I use *structure* here as a category of content. My concern is with the fundamental conceptual skeleton of the play, the underlying patterns of thought and organization. This discussion involves three issues: the surface level of content (the Faust legend), the underlying "dialectic" or organizing structure of the play, and the very possibility that one can talk about such an organizing structure in a work that was written in fits and starts over sixty years.

Everyone knows that Goethe diverged from the Faust tradition by saving his hero at the end. But few readers have consistently kept in mind the implications of that fact as they read the rest of the play.[17] I have tried to keep the relation of Goethe's version to the Faust legend and to Christopher Marlowe's tragedy of character in mind throughout my reading. As a result, I argue that Goethe consistently subverts

---

[16]Heinz Schlaffer, in *"Faust zweiter Teil": Die Allegorie des 19. Jahrhunderts* (Stuttgart: Metzler, 1981), has reestablished the question of allegory as a significant issue in the play.

[17]The major exception in this regard is Harold Jantz, *The Form of "Faust": The Work of Art and Its Intrinsic Structures* (Baltimore: Johns Hopkins University Press, 1978).

the basic Christian framework on which the Faust legend, a product of Protestant Reformation polemics, rests—a conclusion that conforms to what we know about Goethe's hostility to organized Protestant orthodoxy. Thus I will argue that the fundamental opposition of the play is not between good and evil or right and wrong (as it is, say, in Marlowe's *Dr. Faustus*) and thus that the organizing mode of discourse in the play is not ethical.

Rather, I consider the fundamental concerns of the play to be epistemological and aesthetic. The organizing structure that I will be concerned with is the European romantic "dialectic of consciousness." Let me hasten to explain that by *dialectic* I do not mean the specifically Hegelian or Marxist dialectic, according to which an opposition is sublimated or sublated (*aufgehoben*) in some unique but reconciling third term. I use the word in the more basic sense of a pattern of argument that proceeds by constituting oppositions and then relating them in essentially any way other than choosing one over the other. Resolution may involve combination, mediated combination into some categorically or ontologically different term, sublimation into a "higher" term, or sublimation into a higher opposition. Goethe's term for this last process, the one he tended to favor, was *Polarität und Steigerung* (polarity and enhancement); his image for it was the spiral. It is not an uncommon approach among Goethe scholars to look for such an underlying structure in his work.[18] What is less common in my approach is the consistency with which it is applied and its identification as a pattern typical of the period, not one unique to Goethe.

It is the double content of Goethe's dialectic that makes it paradigmatically romantic. On the one hand, the dialectic of *Faust* is based on the typically romantic opposition of subject versus object, the concern with the abyss between knower and object of knowledge. Some form of this opposition consistently underlies the thematics of identity so important to the period as a whole and to Goethe's play in particular. Equally important for Goethe and his contemporaries, however, was the revival of the Renaissance Neoplatonist dialectic of spirit (or mind) and world (or nature), in which the resolving third term was Nature (nature informed and organized by divine spirit).[19] The dialectic of

[18]Perhaps the most striking example in English is Peter Salm, *The Poem as Plant: A Biological View of Goethe's "Faust"* (Cleveland: Press of Case Western Reserve University, 1971).

[19]For a clear exposition in English of the historical circumstances related to this revival (the *Spinozastreit*) and its implications, see Thomas McFarland, *Coleridge and*

identity and the dialectic of nature reinforce one another and merge together by the late 1790s. While the first is concerned with the individual mind, the other is concerned with the mind of the universe. These two dialectics are repeatedly intertwined in *Faust*. The opposition appears not only in concepts but also in shifting pairs of characters, images, settings, behavior patterns, even sexual distinctions. (The play is full of hermaphrodites.) Ideas, characters, and motifs also shift their positions or value in the dialectic—from resolving term to opposing term, for example, and vice versa. The content of the pattern thus shifts constantly while the underlying structure remains the same. The almost infinite modulations of Goethe's dialectic are the analogic backbone that connects the vast range of issues addressed by the drama.

It is easy to drop phrases about *Faust* like "the vast range of issues addressed by the drama"; it is harder actually to address the entire range such a phrase evokes. Let me attempt to disarm criticism by saying that I have not intended to address all the issues raised by this drama; only a commentary can do that. I have tried rather to focus on those issues through which I could relate Goethe's text most clearly to the larger European tradition. Given the past focus of *Faust* scholarship, on the one hand, and the current climate in German studies, on the other, readers are most likely to miss a concern with ethics and with politics. I hope that my reading may offer a structure to organize observations about these topics in the text, but finally, I appeal to the good sense of my readers that no interpretation can be total and that this one does not pretend to be.

---

the Pantheist Tradition (Oxford: Clarendon Press, 1969), 53–106. The traditions of Renaissance Neoplatonism to some extent continued and to some extent were revived in the eighteenth century in a variety of popular interests—Protestant mysticism, alchemy (both Newton and Goethe took serious interest in it), the rituals of Freemasonry. These phenomena are surveyed in detail by Rolf Christian Zimmermann in *Das Weltbild des jungen Goethe: Studien zur hermetischen Tradition des deutschen 18. Jahrhunderts*, 1 (Munich: Fink, 1969). M. H. Abrams provides a concise description of how Neoplatonist thought structures manifest themselves in the occult tradition in *Natural Supernaturalism: Tradition and Revolution in Romantic Literature* (New York: Norton, 1968), 157–63. Harold Jantz calls attention to the Neoplatonist strain in Goethe's thought in *Goethe's Faust as a Renaissance Man: Parallels and Prototypes* (Princeton: Princeton University Press, 1951). Pietro Citati also touches on Neoplatonist aspects of *Faust* in *Goethe*, trans. R. Rosenthal (New York: Dial Press, 1974), esp. 233–34, 417. This often brilliant reading of the play, of which I was not aware until I had completed this book, is compatible with my reading, though presented from an entirely different stance, and merits the attention of both specialist and nonspecialist.

As I mentioned earlier, there is still no consensus that *Faust* can be read as a unified work. Although Stuart Atkins' unified reading of both parts of the play is widely recognized as one of the major books on the play, it has not definitively changed the pattern of books on *Faust*. The problem is that Goethe worked on the play from the early 1770s (the so-called *Urfaust*) until 1832, when he made his final revisions on the second part. At least some of the apparent contradictions, as well as the considerable stylistic and conceptual variation in the play, seem attributable simply to the long period of composition. Nevertheless, the following facts justify making the common-sense, heuristic assumption that the play is a single coherent text: (1) Goethe never published the *Urfaust;* we know it only from an admirer's copy of the manuscript, which came to light in the late nineteenth century; (2) Goethe first published scenes from *Faust* in 1790 with the explicit subtitle "fragment"; (3) more than half of what was published in 1808 as *Faust, Part I* was written between 1797 and 1801. I see the fundamental formal and conceptual structure in the play outlined in the prologues (written 1798–99); in effect, then, I read *Faust I* as a text of about 1800. Whatever the *Urfaust* may have meant in the 1770s, the current text of *Faust* places it in a context that *may* reinterpret it to what Goethe made it signify in the late 1790s. Since Goethe himself gave his imprimatur only to this state of the text, placing heavy emphasis on the material dating from the late 1790s is surely legitimate. On this basis, apparent inconsistencies between different historical levels of the text will be assumed to have thematic significance, not to be artifacts of careless or arbitrary compilation.

Reading the two parts of the play as a continuous text may seem more problematic, since Part II was written largely from 1825 to 1831 and since it had not been clear to anyone, Goethe included, that the second part of the play would ever be written. It was in fact a common practice around 1800 to publish the first part of a novel that was to be completed (but never was) by a second part of cosmic scope, such as Novalis' *Heinrich von Ofterdingen*. Nevertheless, the two parts of *Faust* are connected by numerous explicit allusions. Furthermore, Goethe's first drafts for the opening of the Helen episode (Act III) and for the death of Faust (the scenes "Midnight" through "Entombment" in Act V) date from 1800, when he was working on Part I. This fact suggests that what Goethe finally wrote had been conceived in essence twenty-five years before. It is also worth pointing out, with

28

Stuart Atkins, that Goethe was over fifty when he was finishing Part I and writing these initial drafts of Part II.[20] Goethe scholars delight in portraying the poet as a chameleon; nevertheless, it seems reasonable to expect substantial continuity in work produced after the age of fifty, especially in a writer who once characterized all his work as "fragments of a great confession."[21]

Thus it seems reasonable to regard *Faust II* as an extended reflection on Part I, as an elaboration, an unfolding and interpretation of what was implicit in Part I. Indeed, it would be more accurate to say that I have read Part I always looking ahead to Part II, have tried to offer the reading of Part I that is implied by Part II. Such an approach offers access to a complexity and richness in Part I that would otherwise remain invisible. At the same time it does somewhat narrow the focus of the reading of Part II, where I lay little emphasis on Goethe's response to the changing social conditions in the late decades of his life. I have deliberately accepted this narrowing of focus in the interests of coherence, the quality that has seemed to me most lacking in previous readings of *Faust*.

Faust's Place in the Tradition

No full response to Goethe's play can exclude a substantial moment of bewilderment. It is scarcely the function of an interpretation to make a text more bewildering than it already is; nevertheless, it is important to do justice to this aspect of it. No one has ever denied that Part II is extremely bizarre, but Part I, because of its highly polished exterior and reasonable familiarity to modern audiences, seems today less astonishing on first reading than it actually is. I have thus tried to open doors, to uncover complexities and problems in the text, by reading it in relation to a variety of other texts, Goethe's "sources." I argue that a single spirit governs Goethe's constant allusion to or dependence on earlier texts, namely, his desire to situate German literature in the European tradition rather than to establish an individual national tradition. But at the same time, Goethe's prolific imag-

---

[20]Atkins, *Goethe's "Faust,"* 2.
[21]In his autobiography, *Dichtung und Wahrheit* [Poetry and truth], pt. II, chap. 7; *Gesamtausgabe*, 8 (Stuttgart: Cotta, 1959), 336.

ination manifests this cosmopolitan spirit in intricate and ever-varied relationships to his large assemblage of literary forebears, relationships that are of considerable interest in themselves.

My real concern is not where ideas, motifs, or figures come from but what is implied by their use in the context of *Faust;* nevertheless, I use the term *source* for these texts because I do argue that these allusions are deliberately exploited. For essentially all of them *Faust* scholars have identified positive evidence that Goethe was interested in or at least knew the text apparently alluded to.[22] Fortunately the range of his documented reading was so broad, and his canniness in absorbing contemporary trends was so extraordinary, that in only a few cases have I gone beyond what can be positively documented and never beyond what could be documented to have been in the air. It is important to recognize the reality of the allusions in *Faust,* whether intentional or subconscious, because their very density and range constitutes an important strand of cultural-historical argument about the place of Germany in the European tradition.

From the great flowering of German literature in the twelfth century until the eighteenth century, no writer in German is thought of today as a great European writer or was even especially influential outside Germany in his own day. German critics and writers alike consistently looked abroad for inspiration in the seventeenth century and the first half of the eighteenth, most frequently to France. The only viable indigenous dramatic tradition in Germany in the early eighteenth century was the puppet theater, through which Goethe first became acquainted with the Faust legend and which was the only form in which he knew Christopher Marlowe's *Dr. Faustus* until 1818. Until the end of the eighteenth century there was no estab-

[22]Identifying sources for *Faust* has constituted no insubstantial portion of scholarly endeavor on the text, and I have gratefully used the results of a century's work. Although *Faust* specialists will recognize a few texts I have added to the canon, I realize that I have missed many allusions in this very dense text, and I could not discuss all those that I and other scholars have recognized within the confines of this reading. The two I am most aware of excluding are the Bible and Dante. E. M. Wilkinson has argued, in "Goethe's *Faust:* Tragedy in the Diachronic Mode," *Publications of the English Goethe Society,* n.s. 42 (1971–72): 116–74, that *Faust* is the first of the great modern works that try to keep the European tradition alive by constantly recalling it and that it may be related legitimately to any text or issue that can be "slotted in" smoothly, regardless even of whether Goethe can possibly have known the text or the issue. This can be a useful way of teaching *Faust* but one whose effectiveness depends on not invoking that "regardless" too frequently.

lished stage in Germany, and the various attempts to establish national theaters encountered considerable hostility. The earliest major attempt to establish a dramatic (as opposed to operatic) theater for Germany, by J. C. Gottsched, involved the establishment of a "German" repertoire consisting of translations and imitations of French and, occasionally, English neoclassical plays.

In the second half of the century German works of European stature began to appear—the Theocritean *Idylls* (1756) in rhythmic prose of Salomon Gessner, Friedrich Gottlieb Klopstock's Miltonic epic *The Messiah* (1748–1773), and finally, Goethe's *Sorrows of Young Werther* (1774). It is important that all of these works try to establish forms independent of the neoclassical canon and of France. German critics pursued various alternatives to the neoclassicist (essentially a Roman-French) tradition—the Greeks, the ancient Hebrews, and the "indigenous" (i.e., western and northern) cultural ancestors, such as Milton, Ossian, and above all Shakespeare. At the same time specifically German themes were sought. One, for example, is the defeat of the Romans at the Teutoburger Wald in A.D. 9, which prevented the Roman conquest of Germany; but the most important was the Faust theme, advanced by Gotthold Ephraim Lessing in 1759 as the quintessentially German theme.

Werther established Goethe as Germany's greatest literary genius. When it became known that he was at work on a *Faust*, German intellectuals immediately recognized that here was the masterpiece of the renascent national literature. This judgment persisted, as it has ever since, with the publication of the fragment in 1790 and of Part I in 1808. The expectations placed on this text by the nation even as it was being written in effect forced it to be a program for the new national literature, a statement, finally, about Germany and the German tradition. My argument is, once again, that the constant allusions to the larger European tradition, taken together with the consistent subversion of the values of the Faust legend, represent a concern to integrate Germany into a broad tradition and *not* to establish a separate national literature.[23] To many people the idea that *Faust*, the

---

[23]Goethe's programmatic concern with *Weltliteratur* (world literature) is a well-established topic in the scholarship and has been surveyed thoroughly in the standard work of Fritz Strich, *Goethe and World Literature*, trans. C. A. M. Sym (Port Washington, N.Y.: Kennikat Press, 1972). *Faust*, however, has not traditionally been read so thoroughly in the context of that concern as I will read it here.

embodiment of the German tradition, argues against a German tradition will appear renegade. The play was certainly not read this way in Germany in the nineteenth century, but then the play read by the German nineteenth century was not really the text I am discussing, the play taken as a whole. Thus I would argue that Goethe's play has had little real effect on the public conception of Faust except to popularize the figure. It is hard to imagine any writer who has had more impact yet less real influence than Goethe. The pessimism of this conclusion underscores the need to improve our understanding of *Faust*.

2

The Nature of the Play:
The Prologues

F_{aust} begins with three prologues—a poem, "Dedication" ("Zueignung"), and two dramatic scenes, "Prelude in the Theater" ("Vorspiel
auf dem Theater") and "Prologue in Heaven" ("Prolog im Himmel").[1]
Although preliminary poems or playlets were still the norm in the
theater of Goethe's day, three may seem like too much of a good
thing. Producers have evidently thought so, for the "Prologue in
Heaven," which has at least some relationship to the plot of the play,
was not performed with Part I until 1856; the others only later and still
only occasionally. Nevertheless, these prologues serve an important
function: they define both the nature and the terms of the drama.
Readers can ignore them only at the risk of seriously misunderstanding the central issues of *Faust*. In themselves and in their relationships to one another they are complex texts. In order to present
these relationships as clearly as possible, I will postpone discussion of
"Dedication" until after the "Prelude in the Theater."

The "Prelude in the Theater" defines the play to come, through a
conversation among the director, dramatic poet, and merry person. It

[1]All quotations from *Faust* are my own translations. I have attempted to be as literal
and precise as possible, but not tried to render either meter or rhyme. English-
speaking readers will find essentially all of the details of imagery I discuss accurately
rendered in the translation of Walter Arndt (*Faust*, Norton Critical Edition, trans.
Walter Arndt, ed. Cyrus Hamlin [New York: Norton, 1976]). A clearer translation,
which, however, often interprets details discussed here rather than rendering them
directly, may be found in *Faust I & II*, ed. and trans. Stuart Atkins (Boston: Suhr-
kamp/Insel, 1984).

is easy to see their different positions and how they relate to the play. What has been less easy to see is how they relate the play to a larger context; that is the aspect we will focus on here. The name "merry person" may seem somewhat puzzling, but the German term, *lustige Person*, was used in the eighteenth century to designate the *Hanswurst*, the harlequin or clown whom the Enlightenment had banished from the German stage. His very presence here is telling. Although the merry person is the only traditional figure in the scene, it is surely significant that the other two are not individuals but types, defined by their functions. The director's sole concern is to please the audience in order to fill his theater; the poet's, to write masterpieces for all eternity. And although the merry person prevails upon the poet not to walk out on them, none of the three substantially changes his position or attitude as a result of the discussion. Thus the characters do not, properly speaking (or speaking in Aristotelian terms), interact; rather, they present themselves to the audience in the manner of nonillusionist drama. The central function of the "Prelude" also places it in this tradition. As a self-reflexive play about the nature of drama, it reminds us that it is itself a drama. It also insists that the reader remain aware that the entire drama to come is a drama, an illusion to which he must not surrender himself.[2]

With the rest of *Faust* transformed by this prologue into a play within the play, we are very close to the realm of Calderón's *Great Theater of the World*. Indeed the director's final speech is generally recognized as a call for world theater:

> So pace out on the narrow boards
> The whole circle of creation,
> And walk with cautious speed
> From heaven through the world to hell.
> [ll. 239–42]

In juxtaposition to the "Prologue in Heaven," the "Prelude" seems even closer to Calderón. The stage direction near the end of the "Prologue," "Heaven closes" (after l. 349), shows that the action is on

---

[2]For the sake of brevity I will refer only to "the reader"; "spectator" is always to be understood as well. I intend no aspersions as to the theatricality or even stageability of *Faust*.

a baroque multiple stage with machines, and in fact repeats a stage direction from *The Great Theater of the World.*[3] The sequence from theater in the "Prelude" to the entire cosmos in the "Prologue" exactly replicates the phrase *theatrum mundi,* theater of the world.

Let us now consider what the figures themselves have to say about their play and how they say it. The director wants entertaining spectacle, regardless of its literary significance; he wants to please the crowd, to offer as much variety as possible in order to entertain a mindless and distracted audience. Appropriately, then, he invokes in his last speech the most elaborate and spectacular techniques of the illusionist stage:

> So spare me on this day
> Neither prospects nor machines.
> Use the great and small lights of heaven,
> Stars you may waste in profusion;
> Of water, fire, rocky cliffs,
> Of beasts and birds there is no lack.
> [ll. 233–38]

And immediately after, he makes the call for the cosmological world theater cited above. It is also the director who suggests that the audience comes with the same expectations as to a masquerade (l. 117). The director thus advocates the extreme version of nonillusionist drama, the mentality of the late seventeenth-century operatic extravaganzas that prompted the reforms of Metastasio.

There are, however, hints of the more serious aspects of nonillusionist poetics as well. The director repeatedly asserts that the audience wants to be amazed, to wonder (ll. 42, 92); we must remember here the importance of wonder in engendering illumination by the truth in Neoplatonist poetics, which underlies much of the world-theater tradition as it was practiced in the seventeenth century. The director also argues, somewhat ruefully, against Aristotelian unity of plot. First of all, he says, there should be lots of action (l. 89), then later that the play should be fragmented:

---

[3]I am not arguing direct influence here; there is no evidence that Goethe had any direct experience of this Calderón play. I use it simply as a paradigmatic example of a tradition Goethe clearly did have in mind.

> If you stage a play, then just stage it in pieces!
> With such a ragout you must succeed;
> . . .
> What good does it do to present a whole,
> The public will pick it apart for you anyhow.
>
> [ll. 99–103]

If the director speaks for the nonillusionist tradition, the poet articulates the purified aesthetics of the Enlightenment tradition. He is concerned with the purity and autonomy of art, with a world of eternal ideals, where the noisy demands of the hoi polloi cannot touch him. The sublimity of his purpose and diction is strongly reminiscent of the most serious German poetry written around the turn of the nineteenth century, particularly that of Friedrich Schiller and Friedrich Hölderlin. Above all, the mixture of noble rhetoric with the need for peace, harmony, and the simplicity of childhood corresponds exactly to the classicist ideal of Johann Joachim Winckelmann that so captured the imagination of the eighteenth century—"noble simplicity and calm grandeur."[4] A less serious hint that we are to hear the eighteenth century speaking in the poet is his lofty politicizing rhetoric.

> Begone and seek a different slave!
> Do you think the poet should wantonly trifle away his highest right,
> The right of man, conferred on him by Nature,
> For your sake?
>
> [ll. 134–37]

The rights of man, conferred by nature, evoke the highest political ideals of the period—although the age was probably not agreed that writing sublime poetry was foremost among those rights.

The utter antipathy of the poet to the director has nothing to do with personality, then. Two attitudes toward the nature of poetry, two poetics, are confronted, and we have already seen that Goethe confronts the two elsewhere in historical terms. Here the clown mediates between them. It is important to analyze on what terms he apparently

---

[4]The phrase comes from Winckelmann's influential essay *Gedanken über die Nachahmung der griechischen Werke in der Malerei und Bildhauerkunst* (Thoughts on the imitation of Greek works in painting and sculpture), which was published in 1755. Goethe's collection of materials on Winckelmann ("Winckelmann," 1805) attests to his awareness of Winckelmann's contribution.

succeeds, for these will define the terms in which Goethe proposed to reintegrate the nonillusionist tradition into the serious drama of the post-Enlightenment period.[5]

His solution is basically additive: the play should not so much combine as simply include what both have to offer, "Reason, understanding, sentiment, and passion" (l. 87), to become serious play. In the late-eighteenth-century context reason (*Vernunft*) and understanding (*Verstand*), passion (*Leidenschaft*) and sentiment (*Empfindung*) are almost opposites, reason and passion being sublime, understanding and sentiment being more mundane qualities. The clown frames these with his own contributions, fantasy (*Phantasie*, l. 86) and foolery (*Narrheit*, l. 88). The same tendency is reflected in the extremely paratactic language of the clown's second speech, which has as many as three main clauses in a single line. The play should combine realism with fantasy, variety with clarity, error with truth, play with revelation.

Clearly the clown's solution looks more like nonillusionist drama than like Aristotelian tragedy. *Faust* is not to be a reformed or purified spectacular drama; rather the serious elements are to appear more fancifully, more playfully than they would in Aristotelian tragedy. Play will supersede serious realism. In his last speech the poet talks about "Delight in fictions" (l. 193), echoing the clown's pleasure in illusion at line 181. Goethe is attempting nothing less than the recovery of the original significance of the illusionist stage, that delight in the power of man to manipulate the cosmos, a delight to which, since Goethe, we apply the adjective *Faustian*.

But the "Prelude in the Theater" not only defines the dramatic mode of *Faust;* it also defines the fundamental problem in the play. For the time being this problem may be identified as the dialectic of the real and ideal, and it is embodied again in the conflict between the director and the poet. Let us examine their positions once more, this time with emphasis on their attitudes toward the world rather than toward poetics.

The director, as we have seen, is utterly pragmatic. He is concerned with the real problems of the concrete present—what his audience expects, where it comes from and is going to. He thinks not

---

[5]The prologues date from the late 1790s, before Goethe became acquainted with Calderón. This fact would associate the director more closely with less serious forms of nonillusionist drama, especially opera.

in abstractions but in images: the audience is soft wood to be split (l. 111), a non-Aristotelian drama is a stew (l. 100). Only seeing is believing.

> They come to look, they want most of all to see.
> If there is a lot to look at
> So that the mob can stare amazed
> . . .
> Then you are a much-loved man.
>
> [ll. 90–94]

The audience is to be manipulated with tools (l. 110) or with machinery. As was probably typical of the opera director of the late seventeenth century, he regards the poet's main contribution as constructing a sequence of happenings rather than writing important or beautiful poetry. Meaning, beauty, ideals are irrelevant categories for him. He thus speaks for a world of unrelated, meaningless concretions, the everyday "real" world.

The world of the poet is completely opposite. He flees noisy reality to a transcendent, timeless realm of ideas and ideals. His vocabulary is religious, sublime, abstract. The favored sense is not vision but hearing, for the poet is interested above all in harmony (especially ll. 140–49). His ideal world cannot exist in proximity to the discordant real world, which makes his mind or spirit (*Geist,* l. 60) flee. Thus the poet speaks for the realm of the "ideal," the transcendent realm of mind or spirit.

Once again, the clown mediates, and once again, additively. In his first speech he opts unambiguously for the present of the director, as opposed to the eternity of the poet; in his second, for the real world.

> Just reach into the fullness of human life!
> . . .
> And wherever you grasp it, it's interesting.
>
> [ll. 167–69]

But at the same time, this "real" world is also significant; it also has a little light, a "spark of truth" (ll. 170–71). Plays are like love affairs, he says, in a not coincidental comparison; at first things seem random, but suddenly you realize something significant has happened (ll. 160–65). The play becomes a source of "revelation" (l. 175). Transcendence is to be perceived in reality, or reality becomes significant through the admixture of mind. While the director sees and the poet hears, the clown does both (ll. 175, 179). He also totalizes perception by using verbs like *feel* (l. 161). Finally, he transforms this synthesis of the earlier modes of perception in the image of drinking.

> Thus is the best drink brewed
> To refresh and edify the multitude.
> [ll. 172–73 and cf. ll. 176–77]

The image has strong religious overtones—as the word *revelation* reminds us (l. 175)—not only as the communion but also as a common image among mystics for intuitive perception of divine illumination.

With regard to poetics, it was the poet who moved toward the clown's position and adopted his language; this time it is the director, who picks up the drinking image and joins the clown's calls for deeds (l. 215). The solution to this conflict, the synthesis, is the same as for the other: in the illusion of the world-theater, in *Faust*, is to be found reality made significant, transcendence made perceivable through reality.

The structure of this conflict between real and ideal has been identified both here and in the introduction as a dialectic, yet also as additive. Strictly speaking, Goethe's pattern is not a true dialectic because the third term, the synthesis, is not dependably of a different category from the terms of the basic opposition, nor does the third term truly sublimate—that is, redefine—the terms of the initial opposition. In this respect, Goethe's basic thought structure is unique among those of the major German romantics. It shares the basic structure of opposition and resolution, but the resolution is not consistently a sublimation. Here Goethe's unique ambivalence appears in the fact that the same third term, the clown, resolves two different superimposed oppositions—between spectacular and Aristotelian drama and between real and ideal—with the same solution, serious play. In the case of the opposition between dramatic modes, the category "drama" remains constant; for the second opposition, the category shifts from abstraction (real/ideal) to action (play). In this respect too, then, the "Prelude in the Theater" sets the pattern for the bewildering fluidity of the dialectic in *Faust*.

The form and language of the "Prelude" thus identify both the poetics and the basic philosophical issue, an epistemological one, of *Faust*. As we have seen and shall shortly see again in the "Prologue in Heaven," the fact that the poetic and philosophical issues are super-imposed prepares for the use of poetry as an epistemological tool, as the way to relate the real and the ideal. In the meantime, the struc-tures we were able to identify can be used to interpret the first pro-logue, the poem "Dedication." It is all too easy to read this poem biographically as a description of the poet's feelings on returning to work on *Faust* after a long pause. The situation as the poem reports it, however, does not exactly correspond to what we know about the circumstances under which it was written. Goethe wrote it in 1797 when he resumed work on *Faust*. His earliest work on the play dates from the early 1770s, but after he moved to Weimar in 1775 and entered the government there, he seems to have stopped work on it. What the poem ignores, however, is that he had worked on the play in Italy in the late 1780s and had even published most of his manuscript of it in 1790. So there is not really the gap of almost a generation as the speaker of the poem claims. This being the case, the speaker's insis-tence on his distance from the material must have some other func-tion. Here our reading of the "Prelude" can help us to see how this distance relates to the aesthetic and philosophical structures being defined for the play.

In its form "Dedication" reveals its implicit concern with the non-illusionist drama. It is written in *ottava rima*, a highly formal stanza that Goethe otherwise used for allegorical poetry.[6] Thus the choice immediately suggests that here, too, allegory will prevail over realism. More important, *ottava rima* is the meter of Renaissance epic; except in seventeenth-century Spain, where various epic meters were con-sistently used in the drama, and in German romantic imitations of Spanish drama, it is not a dramatic meter. Thus the meter immediate-ly locates the play in the nonillusionist tradition. The references to legend (l. 11) and cantos (l. 17) emphasize this quasi-epic aspect, which is again typical of non-Aristotelian drama. And indeed, the figures in the first stanza approach the meditative poet as "wavering apparitions" (l. 1) in a procession wafted about with enchantment. First love, friendship, grief are evoked in the second stanza as if they were allegories passing before the eyes of the speaker and, in the case

---

[6]E.g., another "Zueignung" (Dedication) and "Die Geheimnisse" (The Mysteries).

of grief at least, describing themselves. The poet has cast the act of memory into the form of a processional masque.

From the vantage point of the "Prelude in the Theater" it becomes clear that the same stances are represented here in embryonic form. Stanza two evokes the vocabulary to be used by the merry person, especially in his last two speeches. "Life's labyrinthine and erratic course" (l. 14) corresponds to "To flit toward a self-appointed goal / In gracefully erratic way" (ll. 208–9). Happiness and grief, love and youth (the speaker remembers his own youth in this stanza) are precisely the components of the real world that the clown advocates as subject matter. And in both cases these elements coalesce into a fiction, a story—legend (l. 11), romance (*Roman*, l. 165; the first meaning of this word is "novel"). Finally, the only occurrences in these scenes of the word for image, *Bild*, are in the first line of this stanza and in the second speech of the clown (l. 170). The third stanza similarly anticipates the vocabulary of the director, with its repetition of words for crowd (ll. 19, 21), the reference to applause (l. 22), and the emphasis on scattering and confusion. The longing, the stillness, the spirituality, the references to music, the melancholy—all associate the final stanza with the stance of the poet. Here the speaker makes the transition from real world to imaginary world; similarly the poet will learn to find reality tolerable by transforming it into illusion.

The perceptive reader will immediately object that the tone of "Dedication" is completely different, despite the parallels to the "Prelude." That is true. Not only is the tone different, but the dialectic is different as well; the progression here is from recovery to loss to more complete recovery through the acceptance of loss (suggested by the tears of l. 29) and the acceptance of illusion.[7] If we were to compare it to the dialectic of real–ideal–illusion in the "Prelude," the sequence of figures embodying it there was director–poet–clown; but here it is embodied in the sequence clown–director–poet. The neat correspondences between the two prologues would seem to be all jumbled up.

But this jumbling is precisely the point. On the one hand, problems are solved in different ways by the same series of figures; on the other

---

[7]The elegiac tone and the theme of loss adumbrate the problem of history and historicity; however, this theme does not become central until late in Part II, so that all discussion of it will be postponed until then.

hand, the same problem is seen practically and humorously—in the tone of the director—in the "Prelude," but seriously—in the tone of the poet—in "Dedication," whose *ottava rima* continues into the first speech of the poet in the "Prelude." Let the reader stand warned that *Faust* is not schematic; the dialectic can shift, the same material can be seen comically or seriously. The combination of these two prologues is a warning not just that *Faust* is illusion and not to be mistaken for reality but above all that the world *Faust* attempts to make sense of, and hence *Faust* itself, is protean, that any single view of it taken alone is inadequate, that the reader must maintain the same distance from the play as its author, that he must understand it in terms of the relationship among its parts and not accept any individual part unconditionally.

The "Prologue in Heaven" is central to the application of this lesson, for it provides a reference point outside the drama proper to which scenes within the drama can be compared. Let us consider, first, what kind of play it is. It is, in itself, the ultimate illusion. The cosmos is embodied in the three archangels, creatures that hard-line Aristotelians of the German eighteenth century insisted could not appear in literature; and God appears in the form of an elderly gentleman, even though the archangels themselves insist that he is ineffable (l. 268). What for Calderón would be representation of the highest—God and archangels on stage—functions here as allegory for something higher yet, in effect, the Neoplatonic One (of which the Old Testament demiurge is an emanation), the Absolute.

The archangels' stanzas also make clear that we are in the realm of ultimate illusion, for the nature they describe comprises the totality of the cosmos. Raphael describes the harmony of the spheres and thus heaven. Gabriel describes the earth and its oceans. Michael describes the violence of this world—storms, thunder, and lightning. The presence of fire suggests we might think of this aspect as the equivalent of hell, so that the world described is indeed the traditional total cosmos. In his final lines Mephistopheles punningly resumes this totality with the sequence of references to God, man and devil.

> It's awfully nice of a great lord
> To speak so humanely even with the devil.
> [ll. 352–53]

Since the archangels' description follows directly upon the end of the "Prelude," it appears as the immediate response to the director's call to walk "From heaven through the world to hell" (l. 242). The "Prologue" is precisely the world theater demanded by the "Prelude," the highest fiction of the merry person.

Just what does this illusion consist of? The world is described in eternal motion; there is often violent conflict among its elements, the traditional quartet of earth, air, fire, and water; like its creator it is ineffable. Yet the viewpoint of the archangels makes this chaos appear orderly; the apparently random violence of the elements is subsumed in the repetitive circulation of the heavenly spheres. Furthermore, the heartening effect of the sight of the sun upon the angels, the fact that it is heard as well as seen (which repeats the synthesis achieved by the clown), and the fact that it is ineffable according to the same formula by which God is called ineffable in their unison stanza—all suggest that the sun is established here as a symbol, a visible sign, of the Absolute. Thus the archangels describe not a meaningless material world but a world informed with spirit; their vision orders and gives higher significance to the natural world. We are dealing here with what was identified in Chapter 1 as the Neoplatonic dialectic of spirit or mind and nature. The resolving term of that structure is, here and in the rest of *Faust*, Nature with a capital *N*, that is, nature or the material world informed with spirit so that it manifests the otherwise inaccessible, indeed unperceivable, Absolute.

Thus the two major versions of the romantic dialectic come together in this speech for the first but by no means last time in *Faust*. As the ultimate illusion of the clown—that is, as the art of world theater—it resolves the polarity of real and ideal. As Nature, it resolves the polarity of world and spirit. In a paradox typical for many romantics, the vision of the archangels is recognized to be both Nature and art, and Nature and art are seen to be equivalent, if not identical, modes of perceiving the Absolute. Against this background, then, a highly artificial God and devil, both of whom express themselves in terms of nature imagery, confront one another over the issue of Faust.

I suggested above that the "Prologue" is the kind of fiction called for by the merry person. Certainly the mixed tone of the dialogue between God and Mephistopheles would seem to correspond to the mixture he advocates. But an even more important aspect of the mixture of comic and serious in this scene is the parody of the opening of the Book of Job. With some variations in the balance, the comic and the serious will mingle in the play wherever Goethe draws on well-known and—today, at least—less well-known sources.

The basic structure of the dialogue between God and Mephistopheles is borrowed from the first two chapters of Job, where Satan challenges God's faith in Job's integrity and receives permission to torment him. The difference in tone, however, is striking: both the level of diction and the relative chattiness of Goethe's characters make his heaven a much more human, "real" place. Both God and Mephistopheles continue the celebration of nature begun by the archangels, expressing themselves through nature imagery (e.g., ll. 287–92, 310–11, 322, 345–47). The first two chapters of Job, by contrast, are utterly devoid of any references to nature. Goethe's modernity would thus seem to lie in his emphasis on nature over the divine order, and Job would appear to be only a convenient device.[8]

The situation is not, however, that simple, for Job contains the finest and most extended celebrations of nature in the entire Old Testament. Job finally repents not because God reveals His own cosmic greatness but because He reveals to Job the larger context in which he must see his problems; and this larger context is not the astronomical cosmos but Nature, a world full of animals catalogued in loving detail. The ultimate revelation of God's greatness is not Himself crowned in glory in the sky (the scene of the first two chapters and of the "Prologue") but the crocodile (*New English Bible*; older translations read "behemoth" and "leviathan"), the most powerful creature in nature. In Job as in *Faust*, Nature is the supreme realm, not heaven.

Goethe is not simply borrowing and modernizing Job. Instead, the emphasis on nature in the "Prologue" uncovers a profound affinity to the biblical source; Goethe continues and interprets a tradition. His own work gains significance by the corroboration of the biblical text; at the same time, Job is given fresh relevance, so to speak, to the concerns of the romantic generation in this pantheistic reading. It is especially appropriate that this first and most basic book in our culture should stand first in the long series of "parodied" texts in *Faust*.

---

[8]This position is represented by, for example, G. Wilson Knight, *The Christian Renaissance* (London: Methuen, 1962), 105–16.

Job also helps to illuminate the moral question in the "Prologue." Because God and Mephistopheles are more "natural" than their equivalents in Job, they seem to have lost their stature as basic powers or forces that move the universe. Rather, they appear more as attitudes toward the nature of man. In the biblical account God gives Satan the power to touch Job; in *Faust* he gives Mephistopheles permission only to tempt him. Over and over again in the play we will see Mephistopheles excuse himself with the limitation or even total lack of power. God and Mephistopheles have much more in common with the poet and clown of the "Prelude" than with their counterparts in Job. Indeed, God characterizes Mephistopheles as the rogue (l. 339) among devils. He is, in some ways, the counterpart of the merry person.

This equivalence, even if it is only partial, raises important moral questions. Clearly, to the extent that the equivalence is there, Mephistopheles cannot be an evil principle.[9] Nor does God see him as such, for he says that Mephistopheles' function is to keep man active so that God can reward him:

> A man's energy can go slack all too easily,
> He's always ready for peace and quiet;
> That's why I like to give him this companion,
> Who pricks and pokes and has to work as devil.
>
> [ll. 340–43]

There can, then, be no real bet between God and Mephistopheles, at least not from God's point of view. God has already told Mephistopheles, "Man ever errs, so long as he strives" (l. 317). He really means it, and Goethe really means it.[10] Erring had already been part of the clown's synthesis in the "Prelude."

> To flit toward a self-appointed goal
> In gracefully erratic way;
> That, old boys, is your duty
>
> [ll. 208–10]

[9]Interestingly enough, modern biblical scholarship now also sees the meaning of *Satan* in this book simply as a legal term meaning adversary or accuser, not as the proper name of the devil or as a principle of evil (*New English Bible*, Oxford Study ed., ed. Samuel Sandmel [New York: Oxford University Press, 1976], 529).

[10]A thorough discussion of Goethe's theory of error may be found in Paul Requadt, *Goethes "Faust I": Leitmotivik und Architektur* (Munich: Fink, 1972), 45–58.

Indeed, "Dedication," too, had spoken of "Life's labyrinthine and erratic course" (l. 14). Proper behavior is to strive constantly; the proper response to the discovery that one's striving has been false or in the wrong direction is not to repent in sackcloth and ashes but to set off afresh in a new and, it is hoped, better direction. Indeed, it is the rule for this striving to be mistaken; it is the condition of being human. The categories of sin, guilt, and repentance are conspicuously absent from Goethe's version of Job, as they are from *Faust* as a whole. The play is essentially amoral.

Faust is not the only character of Goethe's for whom the trammels of conventional morality seem not to exist. He created a whole group of characters whose names, like Faust, mean happy or fortunate. There is Faustina, for example, the poet's mistress in the "Roman Elegies," the cycle of love poems, published in 1795, that appalled most of Goethe's contemporaries by its frank treatment of a successful love affair. The important point here is the connection of the name to a situation outside the bounds of conventional morality. In *Wilhelm Meister's Apprenticeship* (1795–96) and *Wilhelm Meister's Travels* (1829) there is a child named Felix (Latin for happy, fortunate) who has a way of luckily escaping from life-threatening situations brought on by his own greediness. In the *Travels,* for example, he cuts his hand while peeling an apple given him by a woman several years his senior who ought to know better. This oblique reference to the Fall is the closest either novel comes to any explicit moralizing. There is also in the *Travels* a kind of "Dear Abby" figure named Makarie (Greek for blessed). It is widely assumed that she will solve everyone's personal problems, but actually either the problems solve themselves or they remain unsolved. Makarie also leads a strange double existence, for in spirit, we are told—as seriously as we are told anything in this novel—she is journeying out of the solar system, eventually to leave it behind forever. She is thus the most extreme of such creations, who are all "fortunate" because Goethe excuses them from concern with their fellows; they are permitted to develop their own bents without interference, to pursue their own paths and leave the rest of the world behind.

This position must be distinguished from what could easily be misconstrued as the immorality of the "Faustian quest." Goethe's Faust is not a Nietzschean superman determined to realize his own will even at the cost of alliance with the powers of darkness. The "Prologue" makes it impossible to talk about an evil principle in the play. The kind of striving God has in mind is striving for some higher good.

> A good man in his dark urge
> Is ever conscious of the proper course.
> [ll. 328–29]

Nevertheless, the amorality of the position is staggering. The reader must be aware that *Faust* does not represent Goethe's first or last word on morality. What English-speaking readers in particular tend to leave out of account is that Goethe had another lifelong literary project that spanned almost as much of his career as *Faust*, namely, the two novels about Wilhelm Meister. With regard to morality, at least, these novels constitute a *réplique* to *Faust*. The "Faustian" Felix and Makarie are minor characters. The central figure is the good-natured Wilhelm Meister himself, who, like Faust, strives, but whose striving is always defined by his relationships to the world around. Indeed, Wilhelm finally becomes a surgeon, for his entire concern is to help the people around him. (Faust, by contrast, has renounced medicine before the play begins.) Thus the Wilhelm Meister novels explore the demands society imposes on the individual, *Faust* those that individuals impose on themselves. Only the two taken together can be the basis for a judgment of Goethe's ultimate moral stance.

It is very tempting, now, to think that there are three prologues because there is one for each point of view represented in the "Prelude." "Dedication" articulates the serious idealism of the poet, the "Prelude" the professional staginess of the director, and the "Prologue" the clown's synthesis of serious play. Whether we actually make this association or not, its possibility reiterates once again the way in which all three define our expectations about *Faust*. The discussions of both dramatic form and morality make it impossible to understand the term *tragedy* in Goethe's subtitle in the Aristotelian sense. Ultimately we must consider how the play defines tragedy for itself.

3

What Faust Wants: "Night"
and "Outside the City Gate"

Although we have by no means yet penetrated into the ultimate play within the play, with "Night" we have finally arrived at the story of Faust proper. Once again, then, it becomes necessary to explore the terms of this new level of the drama and its relationship to the issues defined by the prologues. The sets for these first two scenes define their basic problem: Faust wants to escape from imprisonment in his "high-vaulted, narrow Gothic study" out into nature. And here the full symbolism of each word in the description of the first set is operative. Confined physically, intellectually, and historically, Faust seems to long for the transcendence symbolized by the strong verticals of the Gothic set. Yet the two scenes show Faust longing to move outward into nature, not upward. It turns out, then, that we will need to consider *what* Faust wants but will need to devote even more attention to *how* Faust wants. The two scenes proceed through a series of five emotional climaxes, connected with one another by consistent patterns of action and by verbal echoes, each of which defines or redefines the modality of Faust's quest. Each of these emotional high points is marked by a passage in which Faust's ecstasy at the thought of final escape from his prison overflows in especially rich and sublime rhetoric. They are: (1) the address to the moon (ll. 386–97); (2) the description of the sign of the macrocosm (ll. 430–53); (3) the invocation of the earth spirit (ll. 460–81); then, after Wagner's interruption, (4) the suicide speech (ll. 690–736); and finally (5) the description of the sunset in "Outside the City Gate" (ll. 1070–99). Taken together they allow us to reinterpret Faust's initial visionary stance as an epistemological mode dependent on the mediation of both nature and art. These issues have already been addressed in the prologues. Here Goethe shows how they are implicit in the Faust theme from the very beginning.

It would be well to consider the genre of the scene briefly before we begin this analysis. The play suddenly looks, for the first time, Shakespearean. Readers familiar with Marlowe's *Dr. Faustus* will recognize the opening monologue, which Goethe adapted not directly from Marlowe, whom he did not read until 1818, but from the debased puppet versions of Marlowe's play still performed at German fairs in Goethe's childhood. But this similarity does not last long, for Elizabethan monologues end after some reasonable number of lines, but Faust's is interminable. When an interlocutor finally appears—and the earth spirit may remind one at first of the witches in *Macbeth*—he refuses to engage in dialogue: the play refuses to enter into Aristotelian action. This mode is known as monodrama, and it had musical accompaniment and an operatic conclusion, like the final Easter chorus in "Night."[1] We are back in familiar territory. "Outside the City Gate" begins with a procession of typical figures each of whom has one speech, like the figures in a masque. The songs and dances on stage also place the scene in the realm of vaudeville and operetta, the realm of the director. The unified, psychologizing rhetoric with which "Night" begins may mislead us into thinking that the poet of the "Prelude" has taken over, but instead, we have the additive synthesis promised by the clown.

The opening monologue of "Night" already identifies what Faust wants. He begins by cataloguing the deficiencies of his situation: he lacks knowledge, he lacks strong feelings (fear and joy), he lacks the ability to help others, he lacks money or any other connection to the outside world. Nevertheless, what he seeks in magic is not power or wealth, like, say, Marlowe's Faustus, or knowledge in general, like his

---

[1]Pointed out by Stuart Atkins in *Goethe's "Faust": A Literary Analysis* (Cambridge: Harvard University Press, 1964), 26. Atkins provides, section by section, a thorough formal description of the structures and verse forms of the play, to which the reader is here referred once and for all. I will discuss them only where the implications are particularly illuminating for my argument. Atkins provides the most thorough and most important close reading of the play in any language. It is an analysis with which mine will converge and diverge too often to document.

pedantic assistant Wagner, or even secret, forbidden knowledge. Rather he seeks direct vision of nature.

> In order to *perceive* what holds
> The world together within the very center,
> To *see* the energy and germ of all enactment
> And do no more word mongering.
>
> [ll. 382–85; emphasis mine]

Faust seeks direct perception of the cosmos without the mediation of words; both in its immediacy and in its object, this is a form of gnosis on the typical Neoplatonic model. Faust stands in the place of the archangels in the "Prologue"; what he really wants to know and to see is what they identify as ineffable, what I called the Absolute. And here, as in the "Prologue," that Absolute is embodied not in the King of Heaven but in the world with its forces of life; the powers of spirit (l. 378) are to reveal the innermost workings of the real world (ll. 382–84).

Let us explore the nature of the gnosis by examining more carefully what Faust looks at in each of the climaxes and his reaction to what he sees. The objects are, in succession, the moon, the sign of the macrocosm, the sign of the earth spirit, the vial of poison, the sun. These disparate objects are all perceived in terms of light imagery and described in language that recalls the description of the moon in the first passage. The language of this passage will be echoed so many times in the play that I cite it here in full.[2]

> Oh, would that you looked, bright moonshine,
> For the last time upon my suffering,
> You who so many midnights
> I watched for at this desk:
> Then over books and papers,
> Melancholy friend, did you appear!
> Ah, would that I could walk on mountain heights
> In your dear light,

[2]The speech to the macrocosm echoes the bathing reference (ll. 445–46); that to the earth spirit refers to the moon (l. 469); the weaving of the earth spirit repeats the weaving motion of the drifting spirits in the moon speech. The mood and language of the moon speech recur in the suicide speech with "Like moonlight wafting round us in the woods at night" (l. 689), and again in the sunset speech with "I'd see in eternal evening rays" (l. 1076).

Hover with spirits around mountain caves,
Weave on the meadows in your twilight,
Rid of the fume of knowledge,
Bathe myself whole in your dew.
[ll. 386–97]

Faust's reaction to the sign of the macrocosm is "It's becoming so bright!" (l. 439), while the earth spirit appears in fire and scarlet lightning. Similarly, it is the moonlight brightness (ll. 688–89) of the crystal vial that first attracts his attention to the poison, and the thought of suicide immediately modulates into the idea of a new day and sunlight. The sunset speech is introduced with a call to gaze at the evening light. Each time Faust catches sight of something, a light goes on. The imagery thus implies that he reaches new levels of insight. Finally, the pivotal term in the pact Faust will make with Mephistopheles puns on words for vision. The pact is that Faust will die when he stops striving, that is, if he ever says to the moment, "Tarry a while!" (l. 1700). The German word for moment is *Augenblick*, literally "the glance of an eye." Faust's striving is above all a striving to see, to perceive. This formulation is both more precise and more typically romantic than the cliché that Faust seeks total knowledge or, in the even worse formulation, forbidden knowledge. The emphasis on light and the random character of Faust's looking—the fact that he responds to what he happens to catch sight of—indicate that Faust really seeks a perception that transcends systematic knowledge.

The movement to higher knowledge is often associated with a mystical rebirth, and the motif occurs with each of the individual climaxes. Faust will bathe himself back to wholeness in the dew (moon speech) or the dawn (macrocosm)—note the overtones of the rite of baptism here. Each experience, especially that of the earth spirit, gives Faust a new surge of energy and vigor. Even the suicide turns out to be a rebirth, as Faust cries out:

Out to the open sea am I directed,
The mirror-flood shines at my feet,
A new day lures on to new shores.
[ll. 699–701]

Death is no longer "ebbing" but suddenly a "new day," and the act of suicide is a toast to the morning. Immediately afterward the Easter hymn resounds, affirming the importance of the motif of rebirth. The sun, as Faust describes it in the speech to the sunset, constantly renews the day and the world, offering him eternal rebirth into the eternal light of the knowledge of God or the Absolute.

The final aspect of Faust's visionary gnosis is the tendency to synthesize the various perceptive modes defined by the "Prelude" and the associated importance of drinking imagery. The first impulse in the moon speech, as in all of the climaxes, is visual; but then Faust's desire to bathe in the dew recalls the use of drinking imagery in the "Prelude" to express the totality of perception. The fact that Faust wants to fly out the window here, to cross the boundary between inner and outer, also indicates the concern for a new state of consciousness.[3] Faust's first response to the sign of the macrocosm exactly repeats the summation of perceptive modes in the "Prelude." First Faust feels a surge of new life, rather as it was described by the clown, while the bathing imagery again suggests a connection to the drinking imagery. Then Faust sees a show (*Schauspiel*, l. 454), repeating the stance of the director. Finally, in his ecstatic vision (ll. 447–53), he also hears the harmony of the heavenly spheres and suddenly sounds like the poet. As the vision fades he returns explicitly to the problematics of the "Prelude." Vision is not enough, he needs to *drink* directly from the breasts of Nature (ll. 454–58). As soon as Faust sees the sign of the earth spirit, his language is flooded with forms of the word *feel*, and he feels as if he had been drinking. Where the language about the macrocosm suggests order, understanding, happiness, light, harmony—in short, heaven—that about the earth spirit is concerned with power, feeling, terror, darkness, flame—the fallen earth.[4] In the two signs, rational and irrational perceptive modes—understanding and intuition—are contrasted, repeating in reverse the opposition between the harmonious Enlightenment idealism of the poet and the

---

[3] A classic discussion of this kind of window symbolism in the romantic period is to be found in Richard Alewyn, "Ein Wort über Eichendorff," in *Eichendorff Heute*, ed. Paul Stöcklein (Munich: Bayerischer Schulbuch Verlag, 1960), 15–17.

[4] Good work has been done in English on the oppositions represented by the two signs. The most thorough and convincing thematic analysis is that of Eudo C. Mason, *Goethe's "Faust": Its Genesis and Purport* (Berkeley: University of California Press, 1967). Two recent and very stimulating essays on the semiotic implications of the opposition are by Neil M. Flax, "The Presence of the Sign in Goethe's *Faust*," *PMLA* 98 (1983): 183–203, and an as yet unpublished essay by Cyrus Hamlin, "Image and Intertext: Rembrandt and Goethe's *Faust*."

intuitive common-sense realism of the director. In the suicide speech, Faust almost drinks on stage, and clearly to do so signifies for him the leap into the beyond, into knowledge of the transcendent Absolute. By the time he makes his speech to the sunset he has finally drunk on stage with the peasants. Now drinking, in all senses, becomes possible: "I hasten on to drink [the sun's] eternal light," he says (l. 1086). And now that he can envision more clearly what it would be like to achieve this totalizing perception (for the speech still, like all the earlier climaxes, expresses only a wish), the language tends to synthesis in almost every line of the speech—the hills aflame, the valleys calmed (l. 1078); silver brooks and golden rivers (l. 1079); mountains and sea (ll. 1081–82); sinking and awakening (ll. 1084–85); day and night (l. 1087); sky and sea (l. 1088). Faust's view readily encompasses all the elements—the fiery sun, the air, the earth, the sea. The move from tension and longing to synthesis, temporary though it is, thus repeats and elaborates the structure and imagery of the "Prelude." Like the poet, Faust initially seeks a visionary truth beyond the reach of human science, but by the end of "Outside the City Gate" he, like the poet again, seems to have accepted the compromise of the clown.

This tempering of Faust's visionary urge is brought about by the opposite pole of the dialectic of the prologues, the real world, here invoked as nature. Thus while Faust yearns to perceive a truth that transcends human sciences and systems, he constantly seeks to achieve it by immersing himself in nature, by flying *out* his window, not up toward heaven. To understand what it means here that Faust uses nature as a medium of transcendence, we need to explore what nature is and how Faust's perception of it and relation to it changes in each of the five climaxes.

Behind the spirits dancing over the meadows in Faust's speech to the moon we can recognize the Paracelsan conception of nature as a spirit realm, a stepping stone to knowledge of something higher. The same is clearly the case for the sign of the macrocosm, which is nothing other than a diagram of the organization of the cosmos in terms of the four elements, the arrangement of the planets, and the relationship of human, natural, and divine spheres. In his sign of the macrocosm, Robert Fludd, a well-known disciple of Paracelsus, places the the world of human arts, symbolized by special hieroglyphics and by an ape holding a mirror, at the center. This sphere of the earth, comprised of the elements earth and water, is surrounded by the

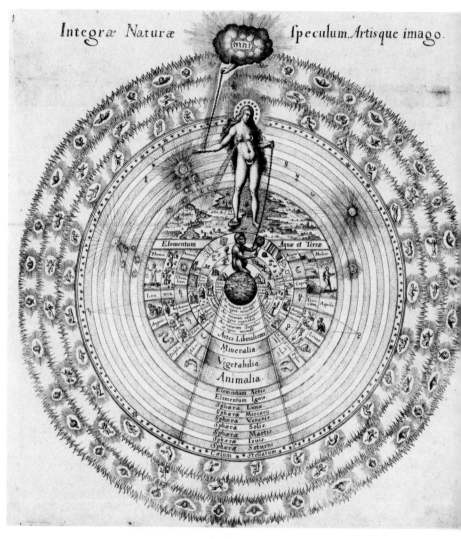

Robert Fludd included this sign of the macrocosm in his *Utriusque cosmi . . . historia* published in 1617. Courtesy of The Huntington Library, San Marino, California.

planets and the fixed stars in the air, and by the triple sphere of fire, one part for each of the orders of angels. This is the sphere of God, symbolized by a cloud inscribed with the Tetragrammaton, the holy name of God. Nature stands on the earth, crossing the spheres of the air so that her head reaches into the divine realm of fire. Her right hand is connected to the divine cloud by a chain, her left to the ape by another. The sign diagrams the Neoplatonic dialectic of spirit and nature (or world), with Nature as the mediating term. Goethe's text recreates the important aspects of the diagram. The ecstatic climax of the speech (ll. 447–53) emphasizes the aspects of totality and interconnectedness. The sign shows everything interwoven (l. 447); forces rise and descend, passing golden ewers to one another; the harmony pervading heaven and earth (ll. 452–53) recalls not only the hymn of the archangels in the prologue but also the ancient music of the spheres. The diagram's orderliness appears in the calming effect of the sign; the containment of the concentric spheres and of the paths of the planets reappears in the way joy runs along the pathways of the nerves and blood vessels and fills the heart (ll. 433–36) and in the way Nature surrounds Faust (l. 438). (The point is that everything is enclosed.) This is Nature as sign.

We saw earlier how the signs of the macrocosm and the earth spirit embody an important opposition. Yet this opposition is anything but absolute. Imagery of weaving, the basic reciprocal motion of nature, connects the two. The earth spirit weaving the living garb of the Godhead at the loom of time is essentially similar to the up-and-down interchange of the golden ewers in the vision of the macrocosm as the creative force of Nature. It is also the same as the weaving dance of the sprites drifting over the twilit meadows in the speech to the moon. Faust identifies the sign of the macrocosm as "creative Nature" (l. 441); similarly the earth spirit creates that nature in which divinity is clothed or embodied, the mediating Nature of the "Prologue in Heaven." The difference between the macrocosm and the earth spirit is only the difference between Raphael's view of the harmony of the spheres and Michael's view of the stormy earth; they are opposite ends of a continuum. All three of the climactic passages in this scene really present different views of the same phenomenon—creative Nature, *natura naturans*.

This view of nature seems to be in accord with Faust's visionary approach. The situation is not, however, entirely so simple; very early nature takes on an importance in itself that goes beyond its apparent function as a stepping-stone into transcendence. The unmistakable language of eighteenth-century sentimentality at the beginning of the sequence—the moon is the "melancholy friend" of midnight vigils—gives an air of contemporary reality to nature and thus a status quite different from the way it appears in the signs or even later in the first speech. Nature is not only something that can be allegorized and diagrammed; it is also something real: it is accessible to the sensibility as well as the mind. As a result, the moonlight passage subtly undermines the occultist world view embodied in the sign of the macrocosm. And in Goethe's re-creation of the diagram we may note the importance of Nature. Faust sees the sign as a revelation not so much of cosmic order as of creative Nature. Even in the final climax, although he talks about heavenly powers (1. 449), what interests him is the connecting link between heaven and earth; as this vision fades he cries out for "boundless Nature" (1. 455). The shift in emphasis implied by the concrete reality of nature in the play is to be found also in the echo from Jacob's dream in Genesis 28. Although the image of Jacob's ladder is common in discussions of the macrocosm in occult and mystic texts, Goethe is unlikely to have overlooked the context of so famous a passage. Jacob, fleeing from Esau to Laban, has a vision in sleep first of the angels going up and down the ladder, then of God standing above him and promising him all the land about for his multitudinous descendants. The revelation is not of transcendent grace but of a special connection to God *in the world.* Jacob is promised not heaven but the earth. The emphasis is shifted away from the transcendent spirit, for which Nature is a mediator, to the mediating term itself. Faust himself, let me hasten to say, will not clearly articulate this shift until the beginning of Part II, but we will see it sooner and in more obvious terms when Gretchen takes the place of the naked woman in the macrocosm diagram. This is romantic rather than occultist Neoplatonism.

The opposition between macrocosm and earth spirit thus also embodies the opposition between nature as sign of transcendence and as real world. The two signs contrast not only modes of perception, as we saw above, but also different directions of striving—upward to the infinite, downward to limited reality. These figures thus link the concerns of the "Prelude" with the two souls of which Faust speaks later in "Outside the City Gate."

One clasps, in love's fierce desire,
The world with clinging organs;
The other rises powerfully from the dust
To the realms of lofty forebears.

[ll. 1114–17]

This is perhaps the most familiar of all the formulations of Faust's problem, for it is the problem of Plato's soul-charioteer in the *Phaedrus* (sec. 26), with his horses pulling in opposite directions.[5] Now the opposition between Faust's natural and transcendental drives is explicit.

After the earth spirit scene the focus of striving shifts openly from gnosis to mediated knowledge of the Absolute through activity in the world. We are dealing here not so much with an evolution in Faust's attitude as with Goethe's elaboration and reinterpretation of the significance of the original *Faust* of the 1770s, for the material up through Wagner's interruption belongs to the earliest parts of the play, while the rest of the scene and "Outside the City Gate" date from around 1800. The "two souls" passage is typical of the way the later material schematizes issues implicit in the earlier text and at the same time reinterprets them by changing the emphasis from modes of perception to spheres of activity. The same is true of the suicide speech. On the surface Faust continues his desperate attempt to transcend the human realm. The act of drinking here signifies an act of transcendent perception, a leap into the beyond. And yet the beyond Faust pictures, with its seashores and sunrises, looks suspiciously like the real nature just outside his cell, not some transcendent "other" world. At the same time the language of erring or straying (l. 667), striving (ll. 697, 716), activity (ll. 705, 712), and the cosmic imagery locate the passage in the framework of the "Prologue in Heaven." The director is also recalled in the emphasis on deed, while Faust's sentimental reveries inspired by the Easter chorus remind us of the poet after he has been touched by the clown. We saw an implicit emphasis on Nature over the transcendent Absolute in Faust's three previous escape attempts; now the focus on Nature is explicit. Faust's place is in the world, not above it; this is the message of the Easter chorus.

[5]For a general discussion of the range of Goethe's use of this image, see L. A. Willoughby, "The Image of the Horse and Charioteer in Goethe's Poetry," *Publications of the English Goethe Society* n.s. 15 (1946): 47–70.

In this context we can now argue that the function of most of "Outside the City Gate" is to provide a new, more "real," more superficial view of what nature is. First a brief masque defines the elements of the human world, centered apparently on love and war. The combination may seem clichéd at first; nevertheless, love and war are the activities that fill all the rest of the play. Love is really a specific name for Nature, as it turns out; war, for striving. In their multiple transformations and redefinitions the concepts will become profound; as "the eternal feminine" and historicity they will be the themes that sum up the ultimate concerns of the play. But at the moment, they appear as deliberately superficial social phenomena, against which Faust articulates his newly awakened enthusiasm for concrete nature (ll. 903–40), as opposed to his earlier poetic vision of it in the moon speech. Yet society and nature are not opposites. Both are newly awakened (like Faust) from the confining sleep of winter; indeed, Faust deliberately conflates the two worlds (ll. 914–15) when he substitutes people for flowers. The Easter symbolism is thus translated, as it were, from the mystical transcendent context into a more natural, more concrete context of spring and human society.

As nature takes on more independent importance, Faust's relationship to it relaxes. At first he had sought total immersion in nature: in the moon speech he wanted to become completely one with it; there and in the macrocosm speech he wanted to bathe in it. In the transition to the earth spirit Faust switches from bathing to drinking; in the suicide speech he finally does not drink but listens to the Easter chorus instead. This interruption decisively shifts the focus of Faust's striving and thus clarifies a structure that up until now has been only implicit. At the first sound of the chorus Faust puts down his glass; he gives up the attempt to ascend directly to higher spheres (cf. ll. 702–5). In the sunset speech, drinking ceases to be problematic. In the wake of the Easter experience Faust is able to participate in a symbolic drinking ceremony with the peasants and then to accept drinking as a metaphor. When Faust talks about drinking in the sunlight (l. 1086), what he is really doing is *looking* at nature, the mode he rejected so violently with the sign of the macrocosm. In his new mode of relating to nature in the sunset speech Faust is no longer closed off from it, but he is also not immersed in it. Instead, from his vantage point on the hilltop, he desires to be both in it and out of it; he participates yet maintains an overview. Although part of this looking is still only a wish, he is actually standing on a hill looking out. While Faust himself may not find this climax more satisfying, it does signify a real difference to the reader.

At the same time, the direction of Faust's striving has changed. Up until the sunset speech his attempts to escape were all appeals to heaven or calls for a spirit to descend, that is, all vertical motions. In the "Prologue in Heaven" Mephistopheles had compared man to a grasshopper; the image is exactly appropriate to Faust's repeated unsuccessful leaps into the infinite. The characteristic motion of Nature in this play, by contrast, is circular: the archangels described a cosmos in constant rotation. If Nature moves in circles and man moves in erratic straight lines, it is no wonder the two cannot meet. But here, for the first time, in his longing to follow the sun as it circles the earth, Faust assimilates himself to the circular motion of Nature.

This assimilation radically alters the nature of the experience Faust seeks. To circle the earth is not to immerse oneself in nature, as he longed to do earlier; on the psychological level this means that his desired relationship to Nature would be less passive and intuitive. At the same time, in following the path of the sun around the earth, he would never leave the earth completely behind. Thus he has apparently renounced the contact with the supernatural that he had sought so eagerly. Faust's initial desire to achieve transcendence through immersion in nature was fundamentally paradoxical, as all dialectical movements are. But now we can see how the resolution of that paradox is achieved through the double renunciation of transcendence *and* total immersion in nature. A new nature and a new attitude toward it have replaced the original ones: Faust has now defined his proper sphere as the middle one between the earth and the Absolute, the realm of Nature. Of course, this middle sphere is also in truth unattainable for Faust, as he immediately realizes. Once again, he must call upon a spirit to descend to him. But this time when he calls upon spirits to descend from the middle realm, he is, as we will see shortly, successful. In the pact with Mephistopheles, finally, this middle realm will be once more redefined as the concrete, everyday world and Faust will at last accept this definition.

Until now we have focused on the mediacy of Nature in its most literal sense, on its being a middle realm or one that comprehends oppositions. But the "Prelude" has already defined a figurative level of mediation, namely, play. Even in the Neoplatonist dialectic Nature has a representative function: it manifests the spiritual order that can be imposed on the chaos of the world. In the terms of the dialectic of real and ideal, mediation takes place in the realm of art or play. In this context, the most important aspect of the sunset speech is the establishment of a symbol for the Absolute. Earlier Faust sought supernatural experience; now he is willing to drink in the sunlight. The sun comfortably represents the power that earlier was evoked with supposedly powerful magical signs. There is no difficulty substituting the formulation "goddess" (l. 1084) for the image at one point, because this is a mythological god with a small g, one that is already recognized to be an image. The willingness to accept symbols is the logical conclusion of a development in these two scenes, in which little dramas or "plays" gradually displace what should be direct manifestations of transcendence.

This development can be traced through our series of climaxes. Faust rejects the moon vision because he thinks that it is only a subjective illusion, because it is a wish rather than a reality. The sign of the macrocosm is not an illusion in that sense—the sign is really there—so that Faust must mean something different when he complains that it is only show (*Schauspiel*, l. 454). Partly, it turns out he means it literally. The sign is *too* visual; the emphasis is all on what he sees; the feelings it arouses in him initially remain confined to particular channels and paths, the experience is not the total communion he seeks. But the reference to show is also symptomatic; Faust has no use for plays or shows, as his conversation with Wagner reveals. He is a literalist, unable to appreciate how illusion points beyond itself to higher truths. For the same reason, of course, immersion in nature does not provide him the transcendent experience he seeks; he is unable to "read" Nature as a manifestation of the Absolute. Faust must learn something, then, about how to read.

The function of the earth spirit scene in this context appears problematic at first. It seems likely that Goethe based the earth spirit scene on the famous etching by Rembrandt of the scholar in his study, sometimes identified as Faust, for Goethe used a copy of it as the frontispiece to the first publication of scenes from *Faust* in 1790.[6] Its use tells us definitely that by 1790 he intended his reader to juxtapose

---

[6]Hamlin surveys the evidence for Goethe's use of Rembrandt, as well as its intertextual ramifications in detail, in "Image and Intertext."

The scholar in this Rembrandt etching is often identified as Faust. The etching dates from 1652. Courtesy of Spencer Museum of Art, Gift of Senator August W. Lauterbach.

his and Rembrandt's treatments of the motif. The similarities are both striking and obvious; of more interest for our purposes is one major difference. What appears to Rembrandt's scholar is a luminous sign, at whose center are the immediately recognizable initials of Jesus, INRI. Rembrandt's scholar "reads" a verbal sign, he does not mistake' the sign for the Godhead itself, and thus need not turn away. When Goethe's Faust conjures the earth spirit (the figure is apparently Goethe's own invention) he looks at, presumably, some similar verbal sign in his book; what appears before him, however, is a form. Faust is overwhelmed by this form, as if it *were* the Godhead and turns away. Goethe appears to have modified Rembrandt's conception so as to move away from reading.

Yet Goethe's revisions of the passage suggest quite the opposite. In the version of the seventies the spirit appears "in repulsive form"; this phrase is deleted in the 1790 version. Much later, in 1819, Goethe specifically indicated that the spirit was *not* to appear repulsive and that in staging the scene he would project a giant head modeled on the Zeus of Otricoli in the Vatican Museum.[7] The substitution of the classical head for the repulsive figure shows that the shift from revelation to image is indeed significant. In confronting a famous and recognizable object of classical art Faust cannot be perceiving any great natural force directly; he sees only a picture. Like the God of the "Prologue in Heaven," the earth spirit is an *image* of an incomprehensible power, not the power itself; like the vision of the Rembrandt etching, the earth spirit is also a sign, this time pictorial rather than verbal. By taking the sign for the power it represents and turning away Faust fails to read the sign. It is for this reason that the spirit says Faust cannot "comprehend" him—"You resemble the spirit you comprehend / Not me!" (ll. 512–13). After the earth spirit disappears Faust calls out in his continued incomprehension, "I, the image of the Godhead! / And not even like you!" (ll. 516–17). Faust has yet to learn the true significance of images. He cannot understand that likeness is different from identity, but without this understanding no reading is possible.

The reference to the Zeus of Otricoli adds another dimension as well. If the earth spirit is represented by a head of Zeus surrounded

---

[7] In a letter to Graf Brühl, June 2, 1819 (*Weimarer Ausgabe*, pt. 4, vol. 31, 162–64). Brühl had raised the possibility of modeling the head on Goethe's own features, a suggestion to which the poet did not actively object.

This head of Zeus, found at Otricoli, has been attributed to Bryaxis, a Greek
sculptor of the fourth century B.C. Courtesy of the Vatican Museum.

63

by flames, Faust, unable to confront him, plays the part of Semele, mother of Dionysus, who was burned up when Zeus appeared to her in his glory as King of Heaven. Faust, however, turns away in time. The scene thus reenacts a well-known classical myth about the impossibility of direct contact with the transcendent realm, with the ironic difference that art is seen to be a safer mode of contact with the supernatural, for it is possible to turn away in time. Previously Faust's longing for transcendence was redirected toward nature. Now art—both objects of art and reenactment (i.e., drama)—becomes the implicit mode of relating to the transcendent Absolute. Furthermore, because a Germanic source (Rembrandt) is displaced by a classical myth, this passage also foreshadows the tradition into which Goethe intends to set *Faust* and, by implication, the new German literature.

In his blindness Faust denies the validity of this relationship to transcendence in his conversation with Wagner. The structure here evokes the double plotting of Elizabethan tragedy, with the pedantic Wagner serving as a comic parallel to Faust, and reminds us anew how self-consciously theatrical Goethe's play is, with its origins in puppet versions of Elizabethan drama. There is therefore a special irony in the way Faust repeatedly and vehemently rejects drama, especially puppet drama (e.g., ll. 581–85), for he thereby unwittingly denies his own existence. And then, finally, the scene is juxtaposed to Faust's inability to comprehend the "image" of the earth spirit. Faust's negative use of theater imagery thus justifies this reading of the earth spirit passage as a mediated rather than direct confrontation with the spirit of Nature.

If this seems too subtle a reading of the text of the 1770s, the Easter chorus, added in the late nineties, shows Goethe elaborating this aspect of the original version. The Easter chorus, we have said, shows Faust his place is in the world. At first it seems inconsistent that Goethe uses the direct revelation of the angels to convince Faust of the inaccessibility of the Absolute. But in fact there is no inconsistency because there is no direct revelation and there are no angels. The voices come not from above but from a nearby church, where the Easter sequence is being performed. This is the "Quem quaeritis" sequence, the oldest play in Western Europe, in which Christ's followers come to seek his body in the grave, only to be told by the angels that he is risen. The vehicle of Faust's reawakened sense of life is a play. Revelation and epiphany do not occur directly in *Faust* but only through the medium of art. Although Faust is aware that he is responding to a play, nevertheless he talks as if he had received some direct manifestation of divine grace, for he describes the singing as celestial (l. 763), as coming from the beyond (ll. 767–68). But only when he becomes fully aware of the nature of his access to the Absolute will he gain more control over it. The first glimmer of any such awareness is the increased importance of metaphor and symbol in his speech to the sunset. Not until Part II will Faust's understanding of this issue be sufficiently clear that it will give him much control over what happens in the play. It is the reader who should have learned most in this scene, not Faust.

This acceptance of nature and natural symbolism must condition our understanding of the function of magic in the play, a topic to be discussed at greater length below. For the time being, we should at least register not only that Faust criticizes his father's alchemical activities but that he scarcely even takes them seriously; he regards them as "crotchety" (grillenhaft, l. 1037). Goethe evidently shares this point of view. When Faust longs for some spirit to reconcile his conflicting urges without actually expecting a figure to appear, Wagner absurdly understands his statement literally and thus in this context magically, for he thinks Faust is conjuring the winds. Magic will be valid in this play only in a symbolizing context.

In a typical Goethean irony Faust's metaphorical conjuration of some reconciling spirit is the only effective conjuration he practices in all of Part I. Having realized that he has not yet achieved the kind of synthesis projected in the sunset speech, Faust reanalyzes his problem into the conflict of two souls—one that longs for earth, one that longs for transcendence. Shortly after Faust calls for some spirit that hovers between heaven and earth (again using the word for weaving [l. 1119] and thus tying the wish to all the earlier ones), a black poodle appears. It accompanies Faust home and turns out to be Mephistopheles. With neither his own nor the audience's awareness, Faust has successfully conjured the devil. But conjuring is a creative act, for it forces the transcendent to take on perceivable form. Faust's one successful creative act, then, is unconscious. Most of Part II will be devoted to achieving conscious control over the creative act. It is the simultaneous acceptance and control of imagination that is at the heart of *Faust*. Now the play can finally begin.

4

What Mephistopheles Offers:
The Pact Scenes

At long last the devil appears. This is what we have all been waiting for; this is what the Faust story is really about. Strangely enough, Goethe did not write the pact scenes until 1800, long after he had conceived the outlines of his Faust drama and after he had written the prologues. We can understand his hesitation when we see the kind of devil he finally created and consider the kind of sources he was working with. His new conception of the devil and of the Faust problem in turn will determine a new structure for the traditional pact with the devil.

That Faust should set about translating the Bible while the devil hides behind his stove is a tour de force as bizarre as his unwitting conjuration of the devil. Faust is attempting to translate the beginning of John: "In the beginning was the Word, and the Word was with God; and the Word was God." The word at which he stumbles is—appropriately—*Word*. Has not Faust's problem all along been a problem of the Word, the incommensurability of human discourse and the divine One? To pursue Faust's alternative translations for *logos*—word (l. 1224), sense (l. 1229), power (l. 1233), deed (l. 1237)—is to resume the various stages defined by the series of climaxes in "Night." Faust rejects "wordmongering" (l. 385) in his initial rejection of the various branches of university learning. "Sense," dictated, we are told, by the spirit, corresponds to the visionary stage of the macrocosm, to be succeeded by "power," precisely the quality that distinguishes the earth spirit from the macrocosm. "Deed," finally, is the stage of the suicide speech, where Faust looks forward to new spheres of activity. The Bible translation functions, therefore, as a capsule summary of how the thirst for transcendent knowledge has modulated into a search for significant activity in the real world. This, we are reminded, is to be what Faust gets from his pact with the devil.

Let us consider, then, what Goethe's devil really is. The poodle that later turns out to be Mephistopheles first appears after Faust invokes some middle term to reconcile the conflict between his two souls (ll. 1118–21). The call is for a spirit not from hell but from the golden middle realm that joins the world and heaven, the realm of Nature as we have defined it. Indeed, these hovering spirits are the same as the spirits Faust sought to join in his speech to the moon; here, too, the German text uses the word for weave. Faust "conjures" yet again the spirit of nature, *natura naturans*. There is an old tradition that the devil as *spiritus familiaris* took the form of a dog; Goethe draws on that tradition here but also naturalizes it by turning him into a hippopotamus and elephant, instead of the supernatural forms he dons in the Faust book. It is appropriate that Mephistopheles finally settles on the human form of wandering scholar rather than friar as in the Faust book. He remains consistently in the realm of the natural and real and avoids the supernatural and religious. Faust assumes that the creature behind his stove is some kind of Paracelsan nature spirit and first tries to exorcise him in terms of the four elements. It does not work, it is true, but when Mephistopheles lulls him to sleep later in the same scene, his spirits, too, sing of air, earth, fire (implied in wine), and water. Their song celebrates nature, with nothing infernal about it. Goethe's devil is a nature spirit.

The original meaning of *Satan* seems to have been opponent, and Mephistopheles at first seems to introduce himself as a genuine opponent. He defines himself only in terms of what he is not—as part of the force that desires evil but does good (l. 1335–36), the spirit that denies (l. 1338), "part of the dark which bore itself the light" (l. 1350). Indeed, he not only assumes the existence of what he wants to destroy but actually celebrates it. His speeches constitute a paean to the process of eternal rebirth in nature. Night bears the light (l. 1350); light makes things beautiful (l. 1355); life is indestructible (ll. 1362–71); life constantly renews itself (ll. 1372–76). Mephistopheles appears from the other world only to tell Faust what he had already been shown in "Night," that his proper sphere of action is the real world of eternally self-renewing nature. He does not really negate the creation; he affirms it.

Once he is recognized to be a part of Nature, we can also see the sense in which Mephistopheles is truly an opponent. As the opponent of light he is the opponent of transcendence; he is the "world" pole in our Neoplatonic dialectic of world and mind, the realist in our real-ideal dichotomy. He is opposed, of course, to the idealist Faust, whose language, as we have already seen, most closely approaches the sublime rhetoric of the poet. The behavior of the two at the signing of the pact is especially telling in this respect. The idealist Faust thinks his promise—his intentions (that is, ideas)—should be sufficient warranty for his actions, but Mephistopheles insists upon the concrete foundation of a written document. Faust accuses Mephisto not only of hocus-pocus but also of pedantry, Wagner's vice; but Wagner is a pedant precisely because he cannot *transcend* the literal level.[1] In his relationship to the word as well as to Nature, Mephistopheles represents the principle of the real.

We may ask, of course, whether Mephistopheles is not pretending to be a nature spirit in order to lure Faust to his damnation. The evidence suggests that this is not the case, indeed, that if any deception is practiced, it is rather upon Mephistopheles himself. The only special power Goethe grants Mephisto is control of nature spirits, the elements, and animals. Even the magic cloak on which the two ultimately depart is not really magic; it floats perfectly naturally on the hot air generated by Mephisto's control of the elements. In the Faust chapbook and Marlowe's *Dr. Faustus*, Mephistopheles is only a go-between between Faust and Lucifer, behind whose plots looms an elaborate and well-staffed hell; Goethe's Mephistopheles stands alone. Scholars have tried to escape the implications of Mephisto's obvious unsuitability to represent the hellish powers by arguing that he is only a minor devil and that the Satan of the unused portions of the Walpurgis Night scene is the true representative of evil in the drama. There are two answers to this argument. The first is that Goethe in fact decided to exclude the Satan passages. The second is that the Satan of these unused passages is no more terrifying or super-

---

[1]This problem is analyzed in detail under the rubric "spirit versus letter" and connected to other parts of the play and the context of Goethe's work by Paul Requadt, *Goethes "Faust I": Leitmotivik und Architektur* (Munich: Fink, 1972), 163–71.

natural than Mephistopheles is. The Satan scene was to consist of presentations and awards presided over by a master of ceremonies—that is, it was to be satire of court ceremonial. And indeed, the one presentation that Goethe executed is straightforward political satire. Like Mephistopheles in the student scene, Satan advocates gold and sex, but—as we will see in the student scene—here, too, these are specific examples of a more general connection with nature. The chorus says of Satan: "He shows you the trail / Of eternal life / Of most profound nature."[2] The message differs very little from that of the angels in the Easter chorus. Most important of all are the ways in which Mephisto's presentation of himself is undercut by what has come before. If the sun is a valid symbol of the Absolute, Mephisto's fire is not his private element, as he claims (ll. 1377–78), but simply a part of the force that always achieves the good. And in the "Prologue in Heaven" God had said the same thing in effect when he assigned the devil the role of keeping man from being too lazy (ll. 340–43). If God and the devil agree, then Mephisto deludes himself to think that he is anything but a part of the eternally self-renewing natural order. The reader at least should spare himself the delusion that Mephistopheles represents or has access to any independent principle of evil.[3]

Mephistopheles states explicitly at the beginning of the second study scene that he has come to offer Faust the experience of life (l. 1543). Faust, who has reverted temporarily to his earlier desperation, rejects the whole idea of life and claims to have been tricked by the Easter chorus. Curiously enough, Mephistopheles' spirit chorus repeats the message of the Easter chorus: Faust should begin a new life on earth (ll. 1617–26). Faust hears the message right away; he enters into the pact because the world beyond this real one is indifferent to him. He continues, "From *this* earth my joys spring forth, / And *this* sun shines upon my sorrows" (ll. 1663–64; emphasis mine). By betting

[2]*Gesamtausgabe der Werke und Schriften in zweiundzwanzig Bänden*, 5 (Stuttgart: Cotta, n.d.), 612 (translation mine).

[3]The cosmology of the influential mystic Jakob Böhme (1575–1624), which Goethe certainly knew, would at first appear to apply to this scene. Böhme sees the evil principle, whose element is the dark fire, as part of God, whose element is light. His system is thus fundamentally Manichean: the universe is governed by the tension between the good and evil principles. However, the subordination of the devil to God in *Faust*, as well as the equal participation of God and the angels in what would normally be "fallen" nature, precludes a Böhmist reading.

Mephistopheles that nothing on earth can satisfy his infinite striving, Faust transforms the old pact into a wager that will focus his activity in the real world for the rest of his life. At the end of the scene Mephistopheles whisks Faust off on the magic carpet he had wished for in the two souls speech. He takes him not on an odyssey through the cosmos but into genre scenes of low life and the simple world of Gretchen. This is the world described by the clown in the "Prelude" as the proper place to synthesize the demands of the realist director and idealist poet. Mephistopheles, the rogue, as God had called him, plays the part of the merry person here as well. He is not only joker and tease but also mediator between the conflicting demands of Faust's realist and idealist souls in the real world.[4]

Mephisto's similarity to the clown—indeed, the two have been played by the same actor—defines the nature of his mediation. Mediation between real and ideal will take place in the real world, but through the means of play. The liar—the devil is the "prince of lies"—by definition plays roles.[5] We have already seen Mephistopheles appear in different forms; indeed, can he be said to have any true form of his own? In "Witch's Kitchen" we will shortly see that

---

[4]Cf. the assertion above that Mephistopheles is associated with the realist pole of the real–ideal dichotomy. It was already the case in the "Prelude" that the director and clown were closer to one another than to the poet. Thus the easy transition between—indeed deliberate confusion of—the two positions need not surprise us here. Faust clearly has adopted the idealist position of the poet, which needs to be corrected by a large dose of realism, whether from an opposing realist or a mediator. In a variant to the pact scene Mephistopheles reverts to the director's eating imagery: "Such a ragout of truth and lies, / That is the cuisine that appeals to me most" (*Gesamtausgabe*, 5:607; translation mine). One wonders if the lines were not dropped because Goethe wanted Mephisto to sound less like the realist-director and more like the mediator-clown, who used drinking imagery. Atkins (*Goethe's "Faust": A Literary Analysis* [Cambridge: Harvard University Press, 1964], 49–50) points out that Mephisto's shift to the plural form of *you* in his speech which begins at l. 1785 suddenly makes him sound like the clown; this is just the point at which he starts to talk about acting.

[5]Compare here Mephisto's self-analysis (spoken, we remember, by Goethe) in "The Masque of 1818":

> They say I am an evil spirit,
> But don't believe it! Indeed I am no worse
> Than many who praise themselves to the skies.
> Deception, they say, is a terrible vice,
> But we all live by deception

He proceeds, then, to point out how much the audience appreciates the deception of the actors in the masque, thus explicitly redefining his role from that of evil spirit to actor (*Gesamtausgabe*, 3 [Stuttgart: Cotta, 1959], 1345; translation mine).

even his allies do not always recognize him because his form changes with the times. At the end of this scene Mephistopheles dons yet another role, that of Faust, to converse with the student, and this discussion will summarize the central issues of Faust's development. Like the crucial moments in that development in "Night," the summary will once again be in the form of a play. We begin to understand the significance and importance of play. Reality is essentially formless; it can only be communicated when given shape as art.[6]

Goethe's treatment of the pact thus thoroughly transforms the Faust tradition, and this transformation is worth exploring. The important elements of this tradition for our purposes are the Faust chapbook, first published in 1587 but reprinted into the eighteenth century; the Faust puppet play; and Christopher Marlowe's *Tragical History of Dr. Faustus* (1588).[7] The Faust chapbook found its way to England immediately, probably through English actors touring in Germany; Marlowe's play is clearly based on it. His play was in turn brought back by English actors to Germany, where it eventually degenerated into the puppet plays Goethe saw as a child in Frankfurt. Although Goethe thus did not, strictly speaking, use Marlowe's play as a source, it is nevertheless illuminating to compare the two treatments of the theme in order to distinguish more clearly the uniqueness of Goethe's approach to the material.

The chapbook attacks the typical Renaissance scientist-magus with a collection of legends and anecdotes about an apparently real Dr.

---

[6]In this respect Goethe is very close to Schiller's formulation and interpretation of the real-ideal dialectic. In Schiller's *Über die ästhetische Erziehung des Menschen in einer Reihe von Briefen*, available in English as *On the Aesthetic Education of Man*, trans. Reginald Snell (New York: Ungar, 1965), the real pole is seen as pure content (*Stoff*), the ideal as pure form (*Form*); their synthesis is play (*Spiel*), understood in both English meanings. Although Goethe is normally considered not to have shared Schiller's propensity for philosophical abstraction, I have documented elsewhere his affinity for the thought structures of the *Aesthetic Letters* in the late 1790s ("Schiller und die Ironie von *Hermann und Dorothea*," *Goethezeit: Studien zur Erkenntnis und Rezeption Goethes und seiner Zeitgenossen. Festschrift für Stuart Atkins*, ed. Gerhart Hoffmeister [Bern: Francke, 1981], 203–16).

[7]Both the chapbook and the puppet play exist in many versions. Selections from both are available in English translation in the apparatus of the Norton Critical Edition of *Faust*, trans. Walter Arndt, ed. Cyrus Hamlin (New York: Norton, 1976), 382–89. A modernized version of the original English translation of the Faust book, *The Historie of the Damnable Life and Deserved Death of Doctor John Faustus* (1592), ed. William Rose (London: Routledge, 1925), was reprinted by University of Notre Dame Press in 1963.

Faust, who seems to have lived from around 1480 to 1540. The hostile Protestant author offers Faust as an egregious example of the talented man gone wrong. To begin with, Faust gave up theology to become a physician. Goethe, however, was intensely interested in the controversial physician-magician of the Renaissance, Paracelsus, almost an exact contemporary of the historical Dr. Faust. Indeed, a number of the stories about Paracelsus seem to have attached themselves to the figure of Faust. Thus the prominently placed information that Faust was a physician suggests both that Goethe correctly understood the Faust book as an attack on what Paracelsus stood for and that he did not share the chapbook's hostility toward its hero.

What did Paracelsus stand for? He is famous as the first physician to use chemical remedies; this use, however, was based not on modern scientific principles but rather on an elaborate system of analogies between microcosm and macrocosm, the pansophic Neoplatonic world view so widespread in the Renaissance and, as we have seen, so prevalent in the early parts of *Faust*.[8] What makes him especially interesting in this context, and especially suspect to the Reformation, is his positive attitude toward nature. Knowledge of God, for Paracelsus, depends upon knowledge of nature.[9] Indeed, it was typical in the eighteenth century to associate interest in Paracelsus with interest in the real world. Samuel Johnson, for example, says of Pope, "When he entered into the living world . . . he was less attentive to dead masters: he studied in the academy of Paracelsus, and made the universe his favorite volume. He gathered his notions fresh from reality."[10] It is not hard to see why Paracelsus would have been attractive for Goethe or how the primacy of nature could be so readily associated with the Faust material.

The Faust chapbook, by contrast, demonstrates all the hostility of the religious establishments of the age to magic and related endeav-

---

[8]On specific connections between Paracelsus and the main currents of Renaissance Neoplatonism, see D. P. Walker, *Spiritual and Demonic Magic from Ficino to Campanella* (London: Warburg Institute, 1958; repr. Nendeln, Liechtenstein: Kraus, 1969), 96–106.

[9]Theophrastus von Hohenheim genannt Paracelsus, *Liber de nymphis, sylphis, pygmaeis et salamandris et de caeteris spiritibus*, ed. Robert Blaser, Altdeutsche Übungstexte, vol. 16 (Bern: Francke, 1960), Prologus, passim; Tractatus III and Tractatus IV, passim.

[10]Johnson, "Life of Pope," in *Rasselas, Poems and Selected Prose*, ed. B. H. Bronson (New York: Holt, Rinehart & Winston, 1971), 475.

ors, such as "modern" science and theater. Magic threatened the churches as a rival orthodoxy; even magicians who claimed to work only with natural means threatened the orthodox establishments by their supposed ability to perform naturally what Christianity had arrogated to itself as miracles.[11] The Faustus of the Faust book does, it is true, want "to know the secrets of heaven and earth," but in his negotiations with Mephostophiles (*sic*) this position is gradually distorted until the pact itself indicates that Faustus wishes to be given his "desires."[12] A brief survey of the table of contents reveals the true range of those desires. The first fifteen to twenty chapters (depending on the edition) deal with Faust's fall and theological questions; the next twelve or so chapters are basically "scientific" in focus as Mephostophiles shows Faust the cosmos. These two parts could properly be said to show Faust thirsting for knowledge, but by far the greater bulk of the book, approximately sixty more chapters, is devoted to comic anecdotes and coarse pranks. Faust's dreadful end is described at some length in the final eight chapters. The Job reference at the opening of the chapbook shows Goethe's distance from it especially clearly.[13] Faustus' parents were as careful for his spiritual welfare, we are told, as Job was for that of his children; Job stands as a model of piety, a man whose sole interest is to please God. As we have already seen, Goethe's Job is no longer the man who reveres God above all, but the man who learns to revere God because of the way He manifests himself in nature. Goethe makes the Book of Job a representative of the Paracelsan viewpoint that the chapbook attacks.[14]

The differences between Goethe's and Marlowe's treatments are also important to bear in mind. Marlowe's Faustus is interested above all in power. There is nothing in Goethe, for example, to compare to the end of Faustus' first monologue:

[11]See D. P. Walker, *Spiritual and Demonic Magic*, 83.

[12]For the convenience of the English-speaking reader I will cite the excerpts from the Faust book in the Norton Critical Edition. These are from the beginning of chaps. 2 and 6, pp. 382, 386.

[13]Unfortunately the first chapter is not included in the Norton Critical Edition. The reference is not in the earliest version of the chapbook, which was the basis of the 1592 English translation, and thus is also not in the Rose edition.

[14]The Faust of the puppet play has even less in common with Goethe's figure. His first formulation of his goal is to discover the philosopher's stone, that elusive arcanum of the alchemists, which was to convert base metals into gold. It quickly becomes evident that his true concern is wealth.

> [Magical things] are those that *Faustus* most desires.
> O what a world of profite and delight,
> Of power, of honour, and omnipotence,
> Is promised to the Studious Artizan?
> All things that move betweene the quiet Poles
> Shall be at my command: Emperors and Kings,
> Are but obey'd in their severall Provinces:
> Nor can they raise the winde or rend the cloudes:
> But his dominion that exceeds in this,
> Stretcheth as farre as doth the mind of man:
> A sound Magitian is a Demi-god.[15]

The knowledge he seeks remains until the end of the play knowledge from books: magicians bring him books; Mephistopheles brings him a book; in the very last line of the play Faustus offers to burn his books to escape damnation. Although Faustus' rhetoric often suggests a striving that goes beyond book knowledge, worldly power, and wealth, he never in fact passes beyond these limits. The most telling parallel in this respect is the imagery of eating and drinking. In Goethe it is a metaphor for a kind of total, transcendent perception, and Faust is always thirsty, but in Marlowe it is just the reverse. The prologue already tells us Faustus overeats,

> And glutted now with learnings golden gifts,
> He surfets upon cursed Necromancie.[16]

Shortly after, Faustus repeats this image and even proposes to send spirits around the world to fetch him exotic foods; at the end Faustus dies of a "surfet of deadly sin."[17] Marlowe's *Faustus* thus points up the striking absence of language of power and sin in Goethe.

All three versions of the legend we have discussed handle the pact in essentially the same way. Conjuring the devil requires great effort. Circles and figures are drawn, blasphemous incantations recited, the devil repeatedly invoked. He appears at first with sound and fury in various terrifying forms. There are extensive negotiations—conditions, counter conditions, goings and comings to Lucifer, bribes, de-

[15]*The Tragedie of Doctor Faustus*, in *The Complete Works of Christopher Marlowe*, ed. Fredson Bowers, 2 (Cambridge: Cambridge University Press, 1973), ll. 79–89.
[16]Ibid., ll. 24–25.
[17]Ibid., l. 1833.

bates between good and bad angels. Faust finally signs the pact in blood; the moment is heightened by the miraculous appearance of the words *homo fuge* (flee, man) on his arm as he draws the blood. These circumstances effectively define our "normal" expectations about pacts with the devil. By contrast, Goethe's treatment seems quite tame. Faust translates the Bible instead of blaspheming; when Mephistopheles appears Faust tries to exorcise him rather than conjure him; Mephistopheles takes the form, not of dragons and fiery monsters, but of quite real, if somewhat ludicrous, animals—poodle, hippopotamus, elephant. The pact is indeed signed in blood, but the scene is more comic than dramatic, since Faust treats the whole ceremony as a pedantic absurdity. It is crucial for the reader to appreciate the unique aspects and not to mistake Goethe's pact for an ordinary pact with the devil.

Goethe's transformations update the story into eighteenth-century terms. It was typical in this century devoted to theodicies (theories to justify the presence of evil in God's perfect universe) to deny the existence of a principle of evil. Goethe's devil is—in good eighteenth-century tradition—a charming rogue, inclined to steal the show. When Goethe coached the actor Karl von La Roche as Mephistopheles, he insisted that the devil appear as an elegant, worldly baron, not as a grimacing monster.[18] Goethe even toyed with the idea of saving Mephistopheles as well as Faust.[19] Had he done so, he would not have been the first. As the doctrine of eternal torment came under first covert, then open attack in the eighteenth century, religious extremists in both England and Germany asserted in all seriousness that Satan would ultimately be saved.[20] Klopstock, the great German

---

[18]The nineteenth century had little sympathy for this view of the devil. La Roche's interpretation came to be rejected as too tame, and doubts were quickly raised as to whether he really had Goethe's authority for it. The controversy is surveyed and analyzed in Harold Jantz, *The Form of "Faust": The Work of Art and Its Intrinsic Structures* (Baltimore: John Hopkins University Press, 1978), 3–13.

[19]It is hard to know just how seriously to take this suggestion, made in conversation in 1816 (in H. G. Gräf, *Goethe über seine Dichtungen*, II, 2 [Darmstadt: Wissenschaftliche Buchgesellschaft, 1968], 225). It comes up because Goethe is piqued that Madame de Staël thought Mephistopheles insufficiently devilish in the "Prologue"; so he casts around here for ways to irritate his audiences for the next 150 years. Jantz discusses the implications of this intention taken seriously in *Form of "Faust,"* 21–29.

[20]See D. P. Walker, *The Decline of Hell: Seventeenth Century Discussions of Eternal Torment* (Chicago: University of Chicago Press, 1964), 225, 228, 240. Walker marshals substantial evidence that the leading thinkers of the period—the Cambridge

exploiter of Milton, had indeed created a flurry by redeeming his devil, Abbadona, in *The Messiah*. Against this background Milton's Satan and the worldly devil of Alain-René Lesage's popular novel *The Devil on Two Sticks* (*Le Diable boiteux*, 1726) become significant forerunners of Goethe's Mephistopheles.

Goethe seems to have been among the first to recognize that Milton's devil is more sympathetic than his angels. Interestingly enough, he sees this fact as a "triumph of nature" in *Paradise Lost*, which he reread in 1799 when he was working on this part of *Faust*.[21] It is not difficult to find Milton asserting the same congruity of religious and natural order that is implied in Goethe (e.g., "God and Nature bid the same" [VI, 176]; "that were to extend / His sentence beyond dust and Nature's Law" [X, 804–5]), or celebrating the protean richness of the creation in the mood of the "Prologue in Heaven." And in fact, in its dignity, cosmography, and cast, the "Prologue" is thoroughly Miltonic. The Faustian problem of the limitation of knowledge is an important theme, for example, in the exchanges between Adam and the archangel Raphael, who adjures Adam to confine his desire of knowledge "within bounds" (VII, 111–30). Like Faust, Adam ultimately turns to the real world: at the end of the poem Adam and Eve, fallen, literally descend from Paradise into the world. It is easy to read Milton's Fall, with Goethe, as the necessary and appropriate lot of humanity and to see the devil, therefore, as a necessary part of the natural order.

Another important precedent for Goethe's worldly devil is the lame Asmodée of *The Devil on Two Sticks*. The novel seems to have appealed greatly to Goethe, who refers to it at various times from the 1780s till late in his life as if all his readers would know it.[22] The hero

---

Platonists, Locke, Newton, Burnet, Malebranche, Leibnitz, Shaftesbury—did not believe in the doctrine of eternal torment in Hell. Goethe was well informed not only in general contemporary theology, as the holdings of his library show, but also most likely in the more aberrant extremist Protestant sects through his pietist connections in Frankfurt (he spent the year 1770 studying alchemy with a pietist mystic).

[21]See Goethe to Schiller, July 31, 1799: "Indeed the strange, unique case—that as an unsuccessful revolutionary he manages better with the devil than with the angels—has a great influence on the outline and construction of the poem. . . . Therefore the work will always be unique and, as I said, whatever it may lack as art, Nature will triumph so much the more" (*Briefwechsel mit Friedrich Schiller*, ed. Karl Schmidt, *Gedenkausgabe*, 20 [Zurich: Artemis, 1964], 734; translation mine).

[22]The references may be found in English in Eric A. Blackall, *Goethe and the Novel* (Ithaca: Cornell University Press, 1976), 84–86. Blackall assesses the importance of this novel and hints at its relevance to *Faust*.

of this novel accidentally rescues Asmodée, the devil of lust, otherwise known as Cupid, from a magician. In reward Asmodée takes the hero on his cloak to the top of a high tower, removes the roofs of the houses, shows him the private life of the city, and eventually finds him a wife. Lesage's devil is the same kind of mediator as Goethe's. He offers his "master" the real world, and he is even less devilish than Mephistopheles. Lesage turns innumerable jokes on the limitations of his powers and indeed shows Asmodée to be essentially natural rather than supernatural when he explains that the only difference between the devil and nature is that the devil acts more rapidly (chap. 4). Magic is openly acknowledged to be a shortcut to enable Lesage to present his satire more efficiently. We will see shortly that Goethe adopts this technique, too, just as he clearly adopted the idea of a "natural" devil.

Satan and Asmodée are interesting not only because they are "natural" devils but also because they are classicists. As we remember, Germans who rebelled against the hegemony of French neoclassicism in the later eighteenth century turned to the Faust legend because it was thoroughly Germanic. How curious, then, that Goethe makes Mephistopheles speak in classical allusions. The view of creation implied by his description of himself,

> I am a part of the part that in the beginning was all,
> A part of the darkness, which bore itself the light,
> The proud light that now contests with Mother Night
> Her ancient rank, her realm
>
> [ll. 1349–52]

is basically classical. In the Bible, God disperses the primal darkness by creating light, but in Hesiod the primal Chaos gives birth to Night, who in turn gives birth to Day. Both the tendency to mythologizing personification in the speech and the absence of a demiurge, a creating divinity, enhance the classicizing effect. Furthermore, Mephistopheles' ideas on the nature of light, that it streams out from bodies, is suspiciously like Plato's theory of color.[23] Mephistopheles also refers to Greek mythology quite unselfconsciously in line 1636, where the vulture gnawing at Faust's life derives, of course, from the Pro-

---

[23]See Goethe's own documentation of Plato's theory in his collections of materials for the historical parts of his *Theory of Color*. See *Gesamtausgabe*, 21:489–90, 22:498, 503.

metheus myth. Scholars have also long recognized that the spirit song describes a classical landscape, which one might ordinarily assume to be unfamiliar to a northern devil. Goethe has displaced this devil into a classical context; the result is the anomaly that *Faust* is the masterpiece of German "classicism."[24] Naturalness becomes, in effect, determined by proximity to the classical position; thus revision of the Faust tradition and solution of the romantic conflict between real and ideal are part of Goethe's effort to integrate German culture into a larger tradition.

Lesage's novel is peppered with classical allusions; they are, however, consistently frivolous and subordinate, as, for example, when Asmodée, leaping into a burning house to save a damsel in distress, is given up to the fate of Empedocles by the spectators (chap. 11). Typically for this novel, the humor of the reference depends on the gulf between Empedocles' sublime intentions (he leaped into Mount Aetna in order to become one with nature) and the more practical ones of Asmodée. Although Goethe sometimes uses classical references in this way in his prose, he does not do so in *Faust*. Instead, as we have just seen with Mephistopheles, he built them into the serious purport of the play.

In its profundity Goethe's classicism is closer to Milton's, although Goethe does not share Milton's moral self-consciousness. This connection to Milton must be understood, however, in the context of contemporary German discussions of classicism. In 1779 Klopstock, the greatest German imitator of Milton and the acknowledged leader of German letters, attacked Milton for his classicism.[25] English being a Teutonic language, Klopstock reasoned, Latinate vocabulary and syntax were inappropriate if not downright absurd. To be fair to Klopstock, he attacked Milton as part of a consistent campaign to free German culture from the trammels of French neoclassicism. Although Klopstock almost single-handedly established the hexameter as a via-

---

[24]German literary history traditionally splits the German romantic movement into groups, the classicists (Goethe and Schiller) and the romanticists (most of the rest). Goethe was not actually the first to mix classical elements with the Faust tradition. A Faust opera performed in Hamburg in 1738, for example, began and ended in the underworld realm of Pluto. It is difficult to know just how classically this ephemeral and subliterary underworld may have been portrayed; in any case Goethe was the first to raise the combination to lasting literary significance.

[25]In any essay on sublime style titled "Vom edlen Ausdrucke" (On noble diction).

ble German meter, nevertheless he justified it by its appropriateness to the unique genius of the German language and even asserted that German hexameters could be superior to Greek and Latin ones.[26] In both prose and verse he rejected even classical subjects for modern writers;[27] and in his own otherwise extremely Miltonic epic, *The Messiah*, he avoided classical references.

Although Goethe always professed the greatest respect for Klopstock, he rejected Klopstock's Teutonizing. The references to Klopstock both in the literary essays and in the autobiography usually somehow belittle the eccentricity or one-sidedness of the great predecessor, while pretending to praise him.[28] But Goethe also indicates that Klopstock's Teutonic mythology is much inferior for literary purposes to its classical counterpart.[29] His practice, of course, bears out this assertion. Furthermore, he allies himself with the criticisms of the classicist Johann Heinrich Voss, who considered Klopstock's hexameters to be very poor by classical standards.[30] Since Goethe repeatedly criticizes Klopstock for one-sidedness, his concern is evidently to connect German literature to the mainstream of the tradition; renewal is to take place not by avoiding the classical tradition but by embracing it.

Thus Milton is present in these scenes as the great Teutonic embracer of the classical tradition. Goethe's proximity to Milton's rather than Lesage's classicism is telling, for it locates that mainstream in England and not in France, the bastion of neoclassicism. In this re-

[26]In "Von der Nachahmung des griechischen Silbenmasses im Deutschen" (On the imitation of Greek meters in German), in *Ausgewählte Werke*, ed. Karl August Schleiden (Darmstadt: Wissenschaftliche Buchgesellschaft, 1962), 1049–50.

[27]In "Eine Beurteilung der Winckelmannischen Gedanken über die Nachahmung der griechischen Werke in den schönen Künsten" (An evaluation of Winckelmann's ideas on the imitation of Greek works in the fine arts), and in the poem "Der Hügel und der Hain" (The hill and the grove).

[28]See especially the general assessment of Klopstock in *Dichtung und Wahrheit*, pt. II, bk. 10; *Gesamtausgabe*, 8: 468–70. Extended discussion of Goethe's ambivalence toward Klopstock under the aspect of "anxiety of influence" may be found in two essays by Meredith Lee, "Goethe, Klopstock, and the Problem of Literary Influence: A Reading of the Darmstadt Poems," in *Johann Wolfgang Goethe: One Hundred and Fifty Years of Continuing Vitality* (Lubbock: Texas Tech Press, 1984), 95–113, and "A Question of Influence: Goethe, Klopstock, and 'Wanderers Sturmlied,'" *German Quarterly* 55 (1982): 13–28.

[29]*Dichtung und Wahrheit*, pt. III, bk. 12; *Gesamtausgabe*, 8:628.

[30]*Kampagne in Frankreich* (Campaign in France), continuation of the autobiography; *Gesamtausgabe*, 10: 465.

spect Goethe is a little closer to Klopstock, who recognized England as Germany's closest cultural relative among the major powers. The presence of Milton here signals the importance of the English tradition as the model according to which Germany was to link itself to the European tradition, and thus provides a context for the extensive concern with Shakespeare in the rest of the drama.

It is in light of all this that we must consider Faust's pact with Mephistopheles. In earlier treatments of the Faust legend, Mephistopheles promises Faust twenty-four years of service in return for his soul. Goethe's Faust, however, enters into a bet with Mephistopheles, not a pact. Mephistopheles is to have his soul if, and only if, he can make Faust cease to strive, if he can make him say to the passing moment, "Tarry a while! thou art so fair!" (l. 1700). Theoretically, Faust could live forever under the terms of this bet; in fact Goethe does let him live to a high old age. Should Faust ever say the forbidden phrase, then, he says, "The clock may stop, the hand may fall, / Let time be over then for me!" (ll. 1705–6). The essence of this wager is time to live.

The implications of the shift from pact to wager are extraordinary in terms of the morality of the drama. Faust becomes Mephistopheles' property only when he ceases to strive. His ultimate salvation has nothing to do, then, with what he does during his life, so long as he does something; indeed, in the "Prologue" God had already said, "Man ever errs so long as he strives" (l. 317). Mephistopheles' obligation in this bet is to provide Faust the wherewithal to try to satisfy his appetites—in theological terms, to tempt him. Faust's responsibility is not to avoid sin; it is to accept the temptations of the devil as fast as he can. To win the bet Faust must fall over and over again; to be delivered from temptation would be to lose his soul to Mephistopheles! To err is not simply human, it is the necessary condition of humanity and of salvation; concern with reparation, repentance, or grace is conspicuously absent.

The essence of this bet is not salvation but time. Clearly time is not conceived as preparation for eternity in this play. What is it, then? We can get some sense of it from what Faust expects from the time the bet offers him:

> Let us plunge into the rush of time,
> Into the whirl of events!
> There may pain and pleasure,

> Success and disappointment
> Follow one another as they may;
> Man is active only when he does not rest.
>
> [ll. 1754–59]

And shortly after:

> To frenzy I dedicate myself, to agonizing enjoyment,
> To loving hate, refreshing vexation.
>
> [ll. 1766–67]

In these terms, to enter into time is to enter into change, as the language swings back and forth between the extremes of joy and pain, success and failure. Faust also sees this as a human realm; he describes violent feelings. Ultimately, he says, "And what is allotted to all humanity / I will enjoy in my innermost self" (ll. 1770–71). Temporality means for him the changing fortunes of human life, the lot of man. It is also important to remember that nature has been constantly seen in the play in terms of motion, in the cosmic turning of the spheres in the "Prologue," the weaving of the spirits, or the rising and setting of the sun. Nature and temporality are inseparable. When Faust finally leaves his study to enter the world with Mephistopheles, they go first to Auerbach's Tavern, a setting precisely located in history. To enter the world is to enter the temporal flux.

While it may seem obvious that to live in the world and to live in time are identical, it was not obvious to Faust in "Night," when as a human subject to time he sought to transcend the world. It was also not obvious to Rousseau, from whom Goethe appropriated the crucial gesture of wishing time to stand still. In the famous fifth promenade in *The Reveries of a Solitary Wanderer*, published in 1777, there appears in italics: *"Je voudrois que cet instant durât toujours."*[31] The citation defines Goethe's attitude toward Rousseau and, because of Rousseau's seminal position, to the romantic view of the place of man in the world. Let us examine it more carefully.

The sentence falls as Rousseau laments man's subjection to the temporal flux:

Everything on earth is in continuous flux: nothing preserves a constant fixed form, and our affections toward external things necessarily pass and

[31]Jean-Jacques Rousseau, *Les Rêveries du promeneur solitaire*, in *Oeuvres complètes*, 1 (Paris: Gallimard, 1959), 1046.

change with them. . . . there is nothing solid to which the heart can attach itself. Also, there is scarcely a pleasure here below which does not pass; as for enduring happiness, I doubt that it can be known. In our most vivid joys there is scarcely an instant at which our hearts could truly say: *Would that this moment might last forever*; and how can one call that transient state happy which still leaves our hearts disturbed and empty, which makes us regret something beforehand or still desire something afterwards.[32]

The desperation of this passage is Faust's. The focus on human emotions is the same and the message is the same: nothing on earth can give satisfaction. What is different, however, is the solution. In a dialectical shift Faust enters into the temporal flux, he embraces what makes him desperate. Rousseau's fifth promenade offers quite a different solution: "a state in which the soul finds a base solid enough to rest completely . . . where time does not exist for it, where the present lasts eternally without any measure of duration and without a single trace of succession, with no other sentiment, either of privation or of joy, of pleasure or of pain, of desire or of fear, but only of our existence to itself."[33] This, for Rousseau, is the state of true happiness, and it is to be achieved lying on your back listening to the waves lap against your drifting boat. Rousseau successfully transcends time here and the limitations of the real world, just what Faust had sought at the beginning of the play. He does this, however, by letting his boat drift masterless, by ceasing to strive.

Goethe has reversed the value of the phrase from Rousseau: the terms of Faust's bet constitute serious and committed criticism.[34] As late as 1826 Goethe continues to see the Rousseau of the *Reveries* as a neurotic at the mercy of every whim of his too active imagination and compares him with his own Tasso (who goes mad) and Werther (who commits suicide).[35] Despite its apparent immorality in traditional

[32]Ibid.; translation mine.

[33]Ibid.; translation mine.

[34]I have no intention of making Goethe sound like Irving Babbitt (*Rousseau and Romanticism* [Boston: Houghton Mifflin, 1919]), although I think Babbitt in fact fails to see the degree to which Goethe distanced himself from Rousseau. Goethe's relationship to Rousseau is very rich and complex and a thorough analysis of it remains to be written. It has been surveyed in English by Carl Hammer, *Goethe and Rousseau* (Lexington: University Press of Kentucky, 1973); some parallels to *Faust* are summarized on pp. 77–80.

[35]In a review in *Über Kunst und Altertum* of the French translation of his works, *Gesamtausgabe*, 15: 560–76. The reference to the *Reveries* is on p. 568.

Christian terms, Faust's bet nevertheless expresses an ethical commitment of special significance to the romantic movement, a commitment to control of the imagination. This must not be mistaken for an outright rejection of imagination. Faust, like the earlier heroes Tasso and Werther, is interesting for Goethe precisely because of his powerful imagination; indeed Goethe identifies an overactive imagination as his own personal problem in the passage just referred to. This is a version of the epistemological problem of the romantics, the problem of relating real and ideal, or object and subject. Thus the formulation of the bet constitutes, above and beyond criticism of Rousseau, Goethe's position on the central romantic problem of consciousness: access to the ideal—the Absolute—must be through the real, the temporal world, and the temporal world is only accessible to the disciplined consciousness. At the same time that Goethe rejects the ethical grounding of the Protestant tradition he restores a more sophisticated and cosmopolitan ethics through his classicizing and his critique of Rousseau.

The interlude with the student constitutes a comic coda to the pact, for the student is a little Faust, and Mephisto offers him the same "temptations." The student scene belongs to the *Urfaust*, while most of the rest of the pact scene was written around 1800. Since the Wagner interruption in "Night" has already established the pattern of parodistic reflection of Faust by lesser characters, it seems safe to assume that this was the original function of the student scene as well. Thus, strictly speaking, we should see the student scene as the kernel from which the rest of the scene was elaborated. Like Faust, the student is oppressed by the university buildings and longs for nature (ll. 1881–87); Mephistopheles ironically uses the language of nature that we saw in "Night"—imagery of breasts and weaving—for the university. The whole epistemological problem is parodied in the student's muddled concern for the connection between word and concept (ll. 1990–2000). But when Mephisto finally speaks in his own tone, he sends the student back into the real world; the student should study medicine and learn to seize the *moment*, he says, because that leads to life and love. He is also about to lead Faust to life and love, and everything in the play has identified that as the best thing that could possibly happen to Faust. When Mephistopheles plays himself he serves God best. Thus it is consummate irony on Goethe's part when the devil writes in the student's album, "Eritis sicut Deus, scientes bonum et malum." These are the words of the

serpent tempting Eve: "Ye shall be as gods, knowing good and evil."
The drama has shown us that to follow Mephisto's advice, to fall into
temptation, is indeed the path to salvation; by explicitly connecting
Mephisto to the biblical tempter Goethe emphasizes the impossibility
of a Fall in *Faust*. The drama has now subverted the essence of the
Faust tradition.

5

Mephisto's World: "Auerbach's Tavern" and "Witch's Kitchen"

Faust and Mephistopheles have now flown off on a magic cloak out into the world—or have they? At first glance Mephistopheles' world is scarcely the sun-drenched nature Faust longed for in his sunset monologue; it is a dark tavern—German taverns were traditionally in cellars—and the stuffy witch's kitchen. Earlier Faust tried to escape such enclosures. We seem to have fallen from the metaphysical level of the earlier scenes into the old Faust pattern with its emphasis on magic and tasteless nonsense. The play seems to regress, or at best to stand still, rather than go forward. This last concern may be dismissed immediately as an artifact of Aristotelian prejudices. If the play is episodic rather than a tight structure of rising and falling action, then we must interpret the significance of the episodes. It is necessary to understand, then, the real function of the magical hocus-pocus, how the earlier concerns of the play are continued, and the significance of the various "nonsensical" performances that fill these scenes.

In "Outside the City Gate" and the pact scenes, the magical elements were consistently burlesqued or, if absolutely necessary to the Faust story (like the conjuring of Mephistopheles), naturalized. Faust regarded his father's alchemical efforts as crotchety; Mephistopheles' various animal incarnations were more circus-like than terrifying; the actual signing of the pact appeared as ridiculous hocus-pocus. Here, too, the magical elements appear as low-humor triviality and hocus-pocus, which Faust rejects out of hand; even the besotted denizens of the tavern see Mephisto as a prankster who performs parlor tricks (l.

2267) and even Mephisto calls the witch's preparation hocus-pocus (l. 2538).

This does not mean, however, that magic is simply comic relief or a humorous arabesque dictated by the Faust legend. Faust's requests for a natural alternative to the witch's elixir of youth identify the new function of magic in the play. According to Mephistopheles, the alternative is to live the circumscribed life of the poor peasant who tills, harvests, and fertilizes his own field, a beast among beasts (ll. 2353–61). Faust, who wants to experience everything, has neither time nor patience to lead such a limited life, of course; so once again he turns to Mephisto's magic. Thus magic is a shortcut to provide Faust the time promised him by the wager. In effect, it is not really Faust's shortcut so much as it is Goethe's. Faust could potentially live forever under the terms of the bet, but Goethe's audience cannot watch forever. Magic—flying carpets, seven-league boots, potions, mirrors or whatever—functions as a poetic shorthand to enable the play to cover a broad range of human experience as compactly as possible. It is another kind of "show" and must always be understood symbolically.

If we ask what the magical elements "symbolize" in these two scenes, we will see how the scenes continue the concerns of the beginning of the play. In both scenes the hocus-pocus centers on the act of drinking. In "Auerbach's Tavern" one might first assume that Goethe plays with the age-old cliché that drinking is the German national sport.[1] But until now drinking in the play has signified the most direct, most total perception of the Absolute and has been associated with Faust's redefinitions of his striving. And so it is here, as well. For the students in the tavern, drinking is a physical pleasure; it releases in them not the flights of ecstatic rhetoric that it does in Faust but the extraordinary refrain

> We feel quite cannibalistically fine,
> Just like five hundred swine!
> [ll. 2293–94][2]

---

[1]For documentation of this cliché for the sixteenth century, see H. W. Janson, *Apes and Ape Lore in the Middle Ages and the Renaissance* (London: Warburg Institute, 1952), 247. In Lesage's *Devil on Two Sticks* Germans consistently appear as drunkards.

[2]The English-speaking reader must be aware that animal imagery is much more negative in German than in English; to call someone a pig verges on obscenity.

It gives them utmost fullness of experience, though not quite the same experience Faust seeks. Small wonder Faust is utterly bored. Nevertheless the motif defines Mephisto's world as exactly opposite to the prison of transcendent longing in which Faust started, for the tavern is a place where one can drink freely.

The drinking motif in "Witch's Kitchen" functions the same way. There Faust is to drink the witch's potion in order to be rejuvenated, to shed thirty years (l. 2342). Mephistopheles, it is true, sees the potion less as an elixir of youth than as an aphrodisiac:

> You'll soon see, with this draught inside you,
> A Helen in every woman.
>
> [ll. 2603–4]

But Mephistopheles always sees creation, like everything else, only in concrete terms. The broader implications cannot be overlooked. While this tactic does indeed suit Mephisto's strategy to ensnare Faust in worldly pleasures, the gesture of rejuvenation and rebirth was intimately associated with the act of drinking in the Easter passage of "Night"; furthermore, it extends back to the poet's desire for rejuvenation in the "Prelude" as the precondition for creativity and to the same desire of the playwright in "Dedication." There can be, then, nothing evil or devilish about Faust's acceptance of the potion. Everything that has come before tells us that the act of drinking is shorthand for the act of memory, the gathering of the self that initiates the connection to transcendence, to the act of creation.

The other magical element in this scene, the mirror, is also part of this larger structure. Faust has caught sight of a beautiful woman in a mirror and is inspired by it, just as in "Night" he reacted to a series of visual stimuli. This parallel already suggests that the image of the woman yet again embodies the goal of Faust's striving, and the language of the passage confirms it. Faust perceives the figure immediately as transcendent, "a celestial image" (l. 2429), and, as in the sunset monologue, wishes for wings to fly up to her. At the same time, however, he is willing, almost eager, to believe that the woman pictured might actually exist in the world (l. 2440). Mephistopheles, principle of reality that he is, assures him that of course she exists. We have moved another step away from the pure transcendent yearning of the poet in the "Prelude" and one closer to the synthesis of the clown, which consisted, we remember, of a love story in the real world. When, in the abrupt scene shift after "Witch's Kitchen," Faust turns from the image in the mirror to the living Gretchen, the synthesis of the clown will have been achieved.

Thus the image takes its place in the series macrocosm, earth spirit, sun. Like these other elements, it, too, is a sign, an image. Our earlier insight about the role of Mephistopheles and of magic necessarily precludes, I think, any possibility that this image is demonic or false and therefore a less valid image of the Absolute than the earlier ones. If we look ahead, the last lines of Part II—"The eternal feminine / Draws us upward" (ll. 12110–11)—would also seem to preclude a demonic reading of the image in the mirror. The pose, too—the figure reclines (l. 2438)—is that of a Renaissance Venus, a figure that celebrates the beauty, not the evil, inherent in the world.

The centrality of this image and the importance of interpreting its value correctly suggests that we should explore the content and significance of imaging in both these scenes as thoroughly as possible. Even a brief survey indicates that images (including, as earlier, dramatic imitations) are very important. "Auerbach's Tavern" actually consists of a series of vaudeville acts. First the students tune up like a barbershop quartet, then people take turns performing odd love songs, then Mephistopheles performs his magic act, which, once again, is referred to as hocus-pocus. Finally, Mephistopheles punishes the drinkers by turning them, in effect, into performers in a miniature play. They themselves think that they are in a vineyard, but Mephistopheles, Faust, and we see them play-acting. It is all, as Siebel recognizes at the end, lies and illusion (l. 2333); the drinkers are no better "readers" than Faust was in "Night." "Witch's Kitchen," too, is full of elements that suggest image and play. The combination of mirror and ape appears in Renaissance imitation emblems and thus suggests imitation here. Furthermore, since the Middle Ages apes have been popular street performers and are even addressed here as puppets (l. 2390). The apes present a little show for Mephistopheles, during which they roll out an imitation world. Then they draw Mephistopheles into their show as an imitation king. Mephisto even jokingly—or perhaps not so jokingly—calls them poets (l. 2464). His indecent exchange with the witch brings in the Mephistophelean view of creation, sex; we may also remember that a kitchen is a locus of yet another kind of creation. Music, too, is generated by the humming

The reclining nude was a common Renaissance symbol of beauty. This example, *Venus with Lute Player*, was painted by Titian ca. 1565–70. Courtesy of The Metropolitan Museum of Art, Munsey Fund, 1936.

vessels as the witch prepares to give Faust the potion. We may connect it, on the one hand, with the musical performances in "Auerbach's Tavern" but also, on the other hand, with the humming music of the spheres at the beginning of the "Prologue in Heaven." The various images and plays in these scenes, then, grow directly out of the more general creative power of nature.

Let us consider now the content of these images and plays. It was not hard to identify the image in the mirror as another version of the mediated Absolute, but it is not obvious that the same could be said for the rest. Indeed, the apes seem to offer the opposite, the world understood under the aspect of mutability. Their world is one that rises, falls, and constantly changes. Evidently we are to think here of the wheel of Fortune, for the ape's previous speech is about gambling (ll. 2394–99). But the ball of the apes is more than just the wheel of Fortune; it is the Christian fallen world, for the apes warn that it is hollow, that it is made of clay and will break. This is the *vanitas* or *memento mori* topos. The connection of apes to it is traditional.[3] And yet this world is still something more. Continuous motion and change have been defined in *Faust* as positive categories, characteristic of creative Nature. The ball rings like glass and thus also participates in the music of the spheres, and it gleams brightly—that is, it shares in the light that has joined all of the earlier manifestations of the Absolute. The imitation world of the apes, then, is the fallen, "real" world, yet with a spark of the divine spirit that points to something higher.

The apes, too, at first appear as entirely negative figures. Since the early Middle Ages apes have been associated in northern European culture with worldliness, with willful imprisonment in the pleasures of the body to the detriment of the soul.[4] At different times in this period they appear as types of the devil himself, of Adam, of human sinfulness, weakness, or folly. The thirteenth-century mystic Mechthilde of Magdeburg talks of the soul casting off "the ape of worldliness."[5] Luther himself considered the ape an animal of the devil, and it was often associated in art with other diabolical animals, such as owls and goats.[6] The sins with which apes were particularly associated are all

[3]See Janson, *Apes and Ape Lore*, 214–16.

[4]The discussion follows Janson, *Apes and Ape Lore*, here. There is also a very brief excursus on ape imagery in Ernst Robert Curtius, *European Literature and the Latin Middle Ages*, trans. Willard R. Trask (New York: Pantheon, 1953), 538–40.

[5]Cited by Janson, *Apes and Ape Lore*, 51.

[6]Janson cites Luther on apes, ibid., 131.

relevant to *Faust*. As the imitator of man the ape was the type of the man who sins by striving to be like God (think of Faust and the earth spirit). Apes were also associated with carnal lust (think of the Gretchen tragedy), with drunkenness (think of "Auerbach's Tavern"), and with avarice (gold will become a central motif in *Faust*). In sixteenth-century theories of the four temperaments, apes were particularly associated with drunken sanguinity, which was usually represented in its sober state by the courtier.[7] It is not by chance, then, that the apes in *Faust* set up a mock court around Mephistopheles, who himself appears as courtier. In the eighteenth and even into the nineteenth centuries the figures seen crowned atop or scrambling up and sliding down the wheel of Fortune in the Tarot deck, a great repository of traditional iconography, often appear as apes.[8]

But once, again, there is a significant ambiguity. The Renaissance, in the wake of Boccaccio's *De genealogia deorum gentilium*, reversed the value of the ape as imitator.[9] *Ars simia naturae* (art is the ape of nature) became the slogan of the defenders of the value of the visual arts; to imitate nature was to imitate God and was, therefore, the highest activity one could engage in. This idea is associated, of course, with Platonic theories of art as well as with the general Renaissance tendency to embrace the world. The Enlightenment once again reversed the value of the motto, because it set imitation of classic forms above imitation of nature; thus the motto appears in Winckelmann in an attack on naturalism. The one realm in which the ape remained a positive figure for nature was the occult sciences, especially alchemy. In Fludd's diagram of the macrocosm an ape symbolized the lower, human world, this pattern occurs repeatedly in Fludd, who was, we remember, a follower of Paracelsus. The apes in *Faust* are engaged in a most serious form of imitation, for they perform a play.

Two famous sixteenth-century German treatments of apes that Goethe is likely to have known admit of this ambivalence indirectly.

---

[7] See ibid., 250.

[8] The Tarot deck does not seem to have acquired any occult significance until it was "interpreted" by Antoine Court de Gebelin in the late 1780s. Until then it was—especially in the eighteenth century—a popular game deck that, like many others, happened to use widespread traditional iconographic motifs. See Michael Dummet, *The Game of Tarot: From Ferrara to Salt Lake City* (London: Duckworth, 1980), 96–101 and 102–63. For a wide selection of illustrations of eighteenth- and nineteenth-century Tarot decks, see Stuart R. Kaplan, *The Encyclopedia of Tarot* (New York: U.S. Games Systems, 1978).

[9] See Janson, *Apes and Ape Lore*, 290–304.

The first is an anecdote about the origin of apes by Hans Sachs, after whom the verse form of Faust's opening monologue is modeled. In this story, which found its way into Grimm's *Fairy Tales* in Goethe's day, Christ rejuvenates an elderly beggar in a smith's forge. The next day the smith attempts to do the same for his mother-in-law; two pregnant women who see the horrid results of his failure give birth to apes.[10] The second is an early and popular engraving, *The Madonna with the Monkey*, by Albrecht Dürer. A fettered monkey crouches at the feet of the Madonna, while the Christ child in her lap feeds a small bird (common image of the soul), which has alighted on his finger. "Witch's Kitchen" shows that Goethe was able to read out of these two works—regardless of what Sachs and Dürer originally intended—a connection between apes and rejuvenation. Within the context of both works the apes represent the impossibility of redemption for those given to the pleasures of the world; to the extent that they lurk behind the conception of "Witch's Kitchen," Goethe has once again subverted the traditional Christian moral by placing Faust's rejuvenation in the world of the apes.

Even the apparent nonsense of the witch contains a spark of the higher world of spirit. Her ritual is to be perceived first as nonsense, since both Faust and Mephistopheles describe it as such. Nevertheless, Mephisto's commentary reveals interesting parallels to Faust's quest in "Night." The witch's arithmetic sounds at first like parody of an especially mad *Naturphilosoph*, as romantic non-Newtonian scientists were called, but Mephistopheles turns it into satire of theological verbal juggling and thus of the "wordmongering" Faust had rejected in his first monologue. Similarly, he describes the drink as a penetrating power (l. 2595); this power, combined with the flame that makes Faust first draw back, is the distinguishing quality of the earth spirit, now suitably controlled through metaphorical processes so that Faust need not turn away. In this context the witch's second speech,

> The high power
> Of science,
> Hidden from the whole world!

---

[10]"Der Affen Ursprung," *Sämtliche Fabeln und Schwänke*, ed. E. Goetze, II, Neudrucke deutscher Literaturwerke des XVI. und XVII. Jahrhunderts, 126–34 (Halle: Niemeyer, 1894), 304–8. It appears in Jacob and Wilhelm Grimm's *Kinder- und Hausmärchen* as "Das junggeglühte Männlein" (The old man made young again).

And whoever does not think,
To him it is given,
He possesses it without effort.
[ll. 2567–72]

describes the kind of intuitive, visionary knowledge (possession without thought) represented by Faust's encounter with the sign of the
macrocosm. Once again, as in the Bible translation passage, the main
stages of the epistemological development in the play are resumed,
this time not by Faust but by Mephistopheles and the witch. In
Mephisto's world the principles of striving for the Absolute still
obtain.

What justifies taking these two scenes seriously rather than seeing
them as grotesque parodies that illustrate Mephisto's real attitude
toward Faust's striving? There are various kinds of responses to this
question. The first is that everything we have learned so far about the
genre of *Faust* prohibits the psychologizing implied by asking about
the *attitude* of Mephistopheles. The devil is a cosmic force, a reality
principle, in this play, not a personality. A second kind of response
would be to ask what possible function devilish parody of Faust's
striving could have, either for Mephistopheles or for Goethe. Faust
displays no interest at all in Mephisto's antics. If Goethe intended the
parodies to show that Mephistopheles does not understand the true
nature of Faust's striving, that would surely have been belaboring the
obvious. The final response would be to pursue the logic of the ironies
in the scene. As we have seen, the apes articulate the traditional
Christian warning against the vanity of the world. If the apes and
witches are creatures of the devil, their message is automatically
wrong and we must understand that Goethe means the reverse. Then
the scene must be understood as an affirmation of the world, even at
its most confusing. If, however, we accept Mephistopheles as a reality
principle, then his creatures are metaphors for a confusing world that
looks meaningless and dangerous but that nevertheless has sparks of
something higher. The real irony of "Witch's Kitchen" is that, no
matter what value we attach to its denizens, the scene still forces us to
accept and affirm the confusion of the real world.

Thus these two scenes embody the real world; the real world is
chaotic, it generates anxiety, but it is not evil. It does, however, need
to be infused with significance. This infusion takes place, as it has
repeatedly up until now, by an act of creative imagination. Faust's

impassioned reaction to the vision in the mirror makes it into an image of the transcendent Absolute. Faust's love for Gretchen—also the projection of his own powerful subjectivity—will temporarily give his life the focus and meaning it had lacked; she will be his ideal in the broadest sense of the word.[11] If "Auerbach's Tavern" and "Witch's Kitchen" embody the "real" pole of the real-ideal dichotomy, why, one might reasonably ask, are they so stagey, so insistent on the importance of performance and image? The most obvious answer is the issue we have just explored from a different point of view: staginess—or artificiality—permits the infusion of significance, of Mind, into the chaos of reality. Imaginative creation (re-creation) of reality is an act of control; chaos is ordered under the aspect of some higher meaning. In this case the "meaning" is the revelation of the place of the real world in the larger structure of real and ideal through the various ways in which it is connected to the ideal—the Faustian images and structures, and the positive view of the apes, for example.

Beyond this, however, the staginess of these scenes, like that of the "Prelude in the Theater" and the "Prologue in Heaven," indicates that these scenes, too, constitute yet another prologue, this time to the so-called Gretchen tragedy. Faust's seduction of Gretchen constitutes, together with most of "Night," the *Urfaust*, the earliest level of the play. It is the most direct, most accessible, and most realistic segment of *Faust*. It is the part of the play readers are most likely to read as a study in human psychology, and thus it is the part of the play most in need of a prologue to prevent readers from succumbing to the dramatic illusion. In "Witch's Kitchen" Faust is rejuvenated to prepare him for the role he is to play in the Gretchen tragedy. He dons his costume (youth), in effect, just like the figures in Calderón's *Great Theater of the World*, while Mephistopheles and the witch appropriately play the role of Calderón's World. Thus the Gretchen tragedy constitutes yet another level of play within the play in *Faust*, and the

---

[11]Apes also appear in conjunction with the real–ideal dichotomy in Goethe's novel *Die Wahlverwandtschaften* (Elective affinities), 1809. There the heroine Ottilie becomes an ever more remote and inaccessible ideal for the characters around her. By starving herself to death, she retreats into a world of pure spirit and rejects the claims of physical reality. She is contrasted with her foster sister Luciane, who is interested only in the superficialities of social existence and whose favorite animal is the ape. Like Mephistopheles' witch, Luciane is not evil, only one-sided and mindless—or rather, Mindless. Both represent the real world, the worldly side of our familiar Neoplatonic dichotomy of world and mind (spirit).

staginess of its prologues warns yet again that it must be understood as artificial, shaped reality, not as ordinary nature.

Goethe's witch-prologue with its bubbling cauldron is not the first in European literature, and this fact raises important questions. The witch derives, of course, from Shakespeare's witches in *Macbeth*, who function as prologues to the play and later, as conjurors of apparitions, as prologues to the main events of the dénouement. Up until now I have avoided the subject of Shakespeare. His dramaturgy antedates Enlightenment neo-Aristotelianism but, unlike that of Calderón, was compatible enough with it that in England at least he could maintain his stature through the Enlightenment; he was defended by the argument that he was an original genius and intuitively followed the spirit of the Aristotelian rules. Goethe was in the forefront of the movement that established Shakespeare in Germany as *the* great dramatist, but not because he saw him as a natural Aristotelian.[12] On the contrary, he saw and admired Shakespeare as a poet and not as a dramatist for the stage.[13] For him Shakespeare is the great "epitomizer" of nature, and his details and sets are all significant, not naturalistic.[14] Most important of all, Shakespeare both stimulates and requires the participation of the reader's imagination in reacting to his plays.[15] This participation is more than an act of interpretation; the reader actually

[12]In his earliest Shakespeare essay, "Shakespeare Day Speech" (1771), he says Shakespeare freed him from the imprisonment of the Aristotelian unities (*Gesamtausgabe der Werke und Schriften in zweiundzwanzig Bänden*, 15 [Stuttgart: Cotta, n.d.], 29). The terms of this passage, strongly reminiscent of Faust's address to the moon in "Night," suggest that neoclassical dramatic form is one of the many restrictions of superficial knowledge rejected there. Although the tone of Goethe's reaction to Shakespeare calmed considerably with passing years, his basic assessment of him never changed. The later essay "Shakespeare ad Infinitum," published in 1815 and again in 1826, studiously avoids the issue of the rules; but in its insistence that stage performance limits the effect of the plays it implicitly criticizes the contemporary illusionist stage, which cannot adequately accommodate a Shakespeare. I will cite this essay henceforth in English from *Goethe's Literary Essays*, ed. J. E. Spingarn (New York: Ungar, 1964), 174–189.

[13]"Shakespeare ad Infinitum," 185.

[14]Ibid., 186–87.

[15]E.g., "But Shakespeare speaks always to our inner sense. Through this, the picture-world of imagination becomes animated, and a complete effect results, of which we can give no reckoning. Precisely here lies the ground for the illusion that everything is taking place before our eyes" ("Shakespeare ad Infinitum," 175). Or "We pass with him from place to place; our power of imagination provides all the episodes which he omits. We even feel grateful to him for arousing our imagination in so profitable a way" (ibid., 185–86).

shares in the creative act. To the extent that he can do this, he thus is able to participate in solving the problem that confronts Faust. We can begin to see, at least, the extraordinary goals implied by the allusion to Shakespeare here. It will remain to be seen in detail, with the Shakespeare allusions in the Gretchen tragedy and later, whether Goethe succeeds in such an assimilation of Shakespeare as a resolving imaginative force. In the meantime the allusion to his image-making witches indicates the extent and direction of his ambitions.

6

Faust's World:
The Gretchen Tragedy

We have approached each new section of the play with the sense that we have finally arrived at the "real" *Faust*. Nowhere is this sense stronger than in the story of Gretchen, Goethe's most famous addition to the Faust legend.[1] Here we find the oldest core of the play, the most coherent sequence of scenes, realism, accurate psychology, a delicate grasp of social issues—in short, the culmination of the eighteenth-century love tradition and the great tragic love story of the nineteenth century. How many readers have secretly wondered why Goethe disfigured this well-made play with all that philosophical baggage and esoteric grotesquerie? Or, perhaps, whatever made him add the seduction of the innocent girl to the Faust story? Not everyone may perceive the question in such extreme terms; nevertheless the central interpretive problem confronting us here must be: How does the Gretchen sequence relate to—much less further and develop—the issues in the rest of the play? In what sense is it the ultimate play within the play? This turns out to be a profitable question to raise, for it enables us to begin to penetrate the wealth of these scenes. Not only do they constitute a masterpiece of psychological portrayal in the

---

[1]The so-called Gretchen tragedy comprises all the scenes from "Street" through the end of Part I, excepting only the "Walpurgis Night." Although later revised, the scenes all date from the earliest level of the play in the 1770s. "Forest and Cavern" received substantial additions (only ll. 3342–69 appear in the *Urfaust*), and most of the text was recast from prose into verse before it appeared in Part I; otherwise the only major change was the addition of the final line, which announces Gretchen's salvation.

theater, but beyond this human element (which the reader can respond to without the aid of the critic), the sequence develops all the earlier issues with great sophistication and subtlety. Armed with the critical distance provided by the presence of "Witch's Kitchen" as a prologue, we can distinguish how the Gretchen tragedy develops the romantic dialectic, how it deals with the historical-cultural issues raised by the use of Shakespearean material in "Witch's Kitchen," and finally, what direction it implicitly proposes for the new literature.

Those familiar with the play will recognize that these are not the usual questions to ask about this part of the play, and they will lead to a reading that will be unfamiliar to *Faust* scholars. No part of the play has suffered so much from the practice of reading episodes in isolation and from reversion to unarticulated expectations and sentimental clichés. There is no difficulty in reading the Gretchen tragedy as a sentimental love tragedy. I am deliberately trying here to distance my readers from such a reading but at the same time to offer a larger context for such a reading, to show how the traditional ethical and social issues of this segment (the willful destruction of innocent purity, the aristocrat and the girl of the people) are the logical culmination of tendencies innate in the literary tradition in which I have located the play.

To ask how the Gretchen tragedy develops the central dialectic of the play is really to ask: What does Gretchen signify for Faust? I use the term *signify* deliberately here, for the question is not about her emotional, psychological, or human importance for Faust, but rather about her relationship to his goals, which we were able to formulate in highly abstract terms. The play defines this "significance" in a variety of ways—in the spaces in which it shows her, in the language of Faust's response to her, in her own function in the action, and finally, in the moral complexities of the final scene.

From the beginning of the play emotional and philosophic issues have been projected in spatial terms. The tension between the drive for transcendence and unity with nature appears in the incompatibility of linear striving with the circular motion of the heavens; Faust's narrow Gothic chamber embodies his sense of entrapment in the traditional intellectual structures. So well established is this pattern that it scarcely surprises us that Faust's first extended encounter with Gretchen, the scene that characterizes her most fully, takes place in her absence. For in "Evening" Mephisto not only smuggles Faust into Gretchen's room in her absence but indeed claims to be able to do so *only* in her absence. Clearly, then, we are to learn something from the nature of this space.

The room is, we are told, small and orderly. Limitation—in terms of class, religious viewpoint, perception—is the very essence of Gretchen. Such limitation was Faust's problem at the beginning of the play, he felt imprisoned; Gretchen's world, too, is a prison (l. 2694), but a prison transformed. What explains this strange reversal of values? Has Mephistopheles succeeded so quickly in making Faust renounce his striving? The answer lies in the other aspect of this space, its orderliness. Faust's cell was disordered, with books and apparatus of all sorts lying helter-skelter amid the dust. Gretchen's room, however, is neat and clean. The furniture, like the objects in Faust's study, is old, but it has the context of generations of family life to keep it alive and give it a particular place and a meaning. The context of order itself in the play is also illuminating. Order is the quality of divinity, of the Absolute, whether in the balanced interaction of the heavenly spheres in the "Prologue in Heaven," in the rising and descending ewers in the vision of the macrocosm, or in the eternal weaving of the earth spirit. The control of the imagination that Faust seems to be approaching is another aspect of this order. And indeed, Faust's ability to perceive Gretchen as a manifestation of the Absolute, that is, to focus his striving temporarily on a limited real goal, documents the control he has gained.

There can be no doubt that Faust perceives her as a manifestation of what he has sought all along. His long speech in her room recapitulates yet again the familiar sequence defined by the speech to the moon, the macrocosm, and the earth spirit. The beginning of the speech (ll. 2687–94) repeatedly echoes the speech to the moon— twilight shine answers to moonlight (*Dämmerschein, Mondenschein,* ll. 2687, 386) and to twilight (*Dämmer,* l. 395); weaving to weaving (*weben,* ll. 2688, 395); love-suffering to suffering (*Liebespein, Pein,* ll. 2689, 387); dew to dew (both *Tau,* ll. 2690, 397); the peace and order to the hovering in the lovely rays of the moon and to the idea of bathing. In Gretchen's room Faust finds what he sought from the moon. He also finds the macrocosm and the earth spirit: the spirit of plenitude and order, the thoughts of piety and heaven at lines 2700– 2708 recall the first, while Nature weaving images at line 2715 clearly recalls the second. And if Faust perceives Gretchen in exactly the terms he earlier used to define his longing, her song "The King in Thule" tells us that we, too, must understand her in the same terms. For this apparently artless folk ballad, written of course by Goethe, is organized around the act of drinking, the play's central image for achieving unity with the Absolute. In the ballad drinking is an act of communion with the dead mistress, an ultimate experience both literally and figuratively. Unlike the mistress in the ballad, Gretchen is not dead, and to achieve communion with her does not destroy the lover. And unlike the earlier versions of Faust's longing, Gretchen is not transcendent. She is real and she is alive; she is the embodiment of transcendence in the world, of the Absolute in nature, of the ideal in the real. Only in this way can we understand why she is introduced as absence, and only in this way can we understand why Faust shifts his attention so readily from the sublime concerns of the opening to the confinement of middle-class life.

Let us consider, now, her function in the action. At the end of "Witch's Kitchen" Mephisto had promised that Faust would soon find a Helen in every woman; Gretchen would appear to be the first woman to cross his path. It is hard to decide whether this is fortunate or unfortunate for Mephistopheles. On the one hand she serves Mephisto's traditional purpose in that Faust will sin by seducing her, perjuring himself, and murdering her relatives; yet on the other hand, she seems to counterbalance the influence of Mephistopheles by transmuting Faust's lust into love (ll. 2721–28). While Mephistopheles sings a song about a king who degraded himself by loving a flea, she sings one about a king who ennobled himself by loving a woman. Both songs deal with extreme loyalty in love, though in opposing tones and with opposite consequences for society. This pairing is telling. Gretchen is less the tool of Mephistopheles than an opposing pole. The two are like the good and bad angels in Marlowe's *Dr. Faustus* or like Faust's two souls.

Yet we must not lose sight, at this point, of our hard-won understanding of Mephisto's function. The two are not simply good and bad angels. If Gretchen is the ideal embodied in the real, she is impossible without a Mephistopheles to provide that element of reality; Mephistopheles' reality must exist before Gretchen's ideality can be perceived at all. Or, to change the terms slightly, God in the "Prologue" justifies the existence of the devil as a force to keep man from relaxing too much; his function is, so to speak, to prick from underneath.

Gretchen is clearly a force that attracts Faust upward (compare again the moon and the macrocosm), and in the last scene of Part II we will see Faust literally following Gretchen ever upward. Thus the two do not, like good and bad angels, pull Faust in opposite directions, but both in fact work together to keep Faust striving. Paradoxically, Gretchen and Mephisto serve identical functions.

Understanding Gretchen's function in these terms alleviates some of the difficulties in understanding Faust's assessment of his situation in "Forest and Cavern." There has been endless debate about the nature of the spirit to whom Faust addresses his great monologue. Yet the functional identity of Gretchen and Mephistopheles shows that it ultimately does not matter if it is a "good" spirit or a "bad" spirit, the earth spirit or some other spirit. The dialectic of the play ineluctably relates spirit to spirit and spirit to natural being. More important than the identity of the spirit is that the monologue, like Faust's monologue in Gretchen's room, reevokes the imagery of the speech to the moon, once again as a vision fulfilled. It combines it, however, with the imagery about memory from "Dedication," the first of the prologues. The fulfillment of Faust's longing is thus associated with memory; the transcendent knowledge Faust has sought is discovered here to be nothing other than self-knowledge, the secret wonders of his own breast (ll. 3233–34). But both "Dedication" and the poet in the "Prelude in the Theater" define this kind of self-knowledge as poetic inspiration. Faust is on the verge here of articulating the insight that the drama has already demonstrated: ultimate knowledge is achievable only through the mediated vision of play, through the disciplined imagination. In the tumultuous concluding monologue he backs off from this insight and completely immerses himself in his role as titanic seducer, but only to allow it to emerge all the more articulately at the beginning of Part II.

If Gretchen embodies what Faust previously identified with the moonlight and with the macrocosm, it is indeed an appropriate climax that she—like Mephistopheles at the end of the pact scene—should as her final act send Faust out of a prison. Nevertheless, the moral issues surrounding this dismissal are much more complex than they had been earlier. Gretchen is now guilty of the deaths of her mother, her brother, and her child; Faust shares the guilt for these three deaths and in addition has seduced Gretchen. Yet, Goethe assures us, heaven has forgiven the one, while the other goes scot-free. How

Goethe makes this happen once again shows how the Gretchen tragedy develops the main issues of the play.

Let us consider first what saves Gretchen. When Faust enters to
her in the dungeon she is insane, but when he calls her by name she
suddenly becomes lucid and her chains fall from her as if by magic.
The astonishing aspect here is what Gretchen does in her lucid moments. Her first and most intense concern is to embrace Faust and to
be embraced by him. To recognize Faust is to recover the first moments of their love (ll. 4475–78) and to be saved (l. 4474). All she
wants is to be kissed. Only when earthly love fails her does she turn to
divine love; only when Faust refuses to kiss her does she "repent."
Under the circumstances this repentance seems less than perfect;
nevertheless a voice from above still assures us she is saved. Either
human love or divine love can save Gretchen; rebirth into the world is
as good as translation into heaven. Love as the force that generates
new life is the crucial factor here, not whether that love is worldly or
transcendent. Gretchen is saved because she loves: this insight gives
us a new name to associate with her orderliness, with the manifestation of spirit in the world. The significance of Gretchen's act of love
will be interpreted and articulated fully in the final lines of the play;
"The eternal feminine / Draws us upward" (ll. 12110–11).

Faust, too, is evidently saved, but why? He appears to have abandoned Gretchen to her brutal fate, but a close look at the language of
the scene will show that he has in fact narrowly escaped damnation.
Gretchen, as we have seen, wants Faust to kiss her, while Faust wants
only to escape. The language used here is telling:

> FAUST: (*straining away*) Come with me, come with me!
> MARGARETE: Oh tarry!
> I so like to tarry where you tarry! (*caressing him*)
> [ll. 4479–80]

This is precisely the terminology of the pact: the desire to strive must
always overcome the desire to tarry, or Faust will be damned. Paradoxically enough, the forsaken Gretchen now voices the one real
temptation of Mephistopheles, the temptation to stop striving. In
seeking to relive the first moments of their love Gretchen seeks to
stop time, to achieve a permanence outside of the real world; she thus
surreptitiously offers Faust the opportunity to transcend the temporal

flux of the real world. However, Faust has learned the lessons of "Night" and "Forest and Cavern" too well to succumb. As a *memory* those moments preserve for Faust the accessibility of the ideal in the real world and can inspire him to future achievements, but they cannot be literally relived. "Let the past be past" (l. 4518), he cries, affirming that he can live only in a real world of time and change. Both Gretchen and Faust are saved here. The principle of love and the principle of striving work in parallel. And at bottom they are indeed similar, for love is the force that brings about birth and rebirth to enable an eternal new beginning. Once again, the final lines of the play will clearly articulate their relationship.

We are confronted here, even appalled, by the amorality of the play. As we have already seen in the "Prologue in Heaven" and in the pact scene, all action in the world necessarily entails a fall. "He who acts is always without conscience; no one has a conscience but the observer," as Goethe was to formulate the issue twenty years later.[2] The discrepancy between the pathos of these scenes, especially in the original version, in which Gretchen is not saved, and the inexorable logic of salvation imposed by the prologues has contributed no small part to scholars' refusal to read *Faust I* as a unity. But the very existence of the aphorism just quoted suggests the opposite. Part I emphatically dramatizes the tragic paradox that all attempts at realization of an ideal or of the self—that is, all attempts at creation— necessarily involve a destruction also. To turn Gretchen into the vessel of Faust's ideal vision, as he does, is necessarily to destroy her as an ordinary member of a real community. From the perspective of real individuals in a real world, the focus is on tragic loss; in Part II, Goethe will contextualize this loss in various larger frameworks— biological and historical evolution, artistic and practical creation—yet always the tragic discrepancy between what seems right in individual terms and what the order of existence demands will be present with greater or lesser insistence. As Faust recedes into a world of art in Part II, he appears less destructive; as he returns to creative efforts in the real world in the last two acts, he is no better than he is here. His less destructive counterpart, Wilhelm Meister, becomes, in the second

---

[2]*Maximen und Reflexionen* (Maxims and reflections), 241, from *Über Kunst und Altertum*, 5 (1824), 1; *Gesamtausgabe der Werke und Schriften in zweiundzwanzig Bänden*, 2 (Stuttgart: Cotta, 1950), 682; translation mine.

novel about him, nothing but a reader of various texts that the novel collects, an observer par excellence. That is, he retains a reasonable degree of moral purity by not acting. In this sense, *Faust* is, in good eighteenth-century tradition, a theodicy, an attempt to understand the presence of evil in the world.

"Witch's Kitchen" prepared us not only for some kind of extra-psychological significance in the Gretchen tragedy but also for the advent of Shakespeare in the play. And indeed, we can find Shakespeare in the superbly realistic psychology, in the blank verse of Faust's great monologue in "Forest and Cavern," and above all in the parallels between Gretchen and Ophelia. Madness, drowning, a melancholy lover associated with the university at Wittenberg, the murder of both parent and brother by the lover immediately connect the two figures. Goethe follows Shakespeare in the representation of madness. Like Ophelia, Gretchen sings snatches of old songs that illuminate the roots of her condition. He explicitly calls attention to the parallels by including Ophelia's Valentine's Day song, which provokes the duel that ends in the death of Gretchen's brother Valentine, who probably takes his name from the *Hamlet* connection.

The *Hamlet* parallels are so effective that it is all too easy to overlook how very un-Shakespearean the plotting of the Gretchen tragedy is. Ophelia's story is presented in tiny fragments throughout *Hamlet;* Gretchen's in basically one large chunk, interrupted only by the "Walpurgis Night," and there too a vision of her appears. As we shall see shortly, Goethe had thought long and hard about the plot of *Hamlet;* in any case he was much too good a reader and imitator to overlook such a fundamental aspect. We can only conclude that he did not intend the Gretchen tragedy as a splendid Shakespearean inset and climax to *Faust;* we can better understand the function of Shakespeare here if we consider the non-Shakespearean aspects of the play and understand their implications as well.

The structure and most of the motifs in the plot are typical of the eighteenth century. The intensity of plotting is not at all Shakespearean, but it is completely typical of serious eighteenth-century drama. The same is true of all the important motifs in the plot except for the infanticide. Indeed by the 1770s there was a well-established tradition of seduction dramas, which were extremely popular. We may take as our typical example Nicholas Rowe's *Fair Penitent* (1703), the play that established the popularity of the genre. Indeed, the term "gay Lothario" derives from the seducer in this play. At the beginning of the play Calista has already been seduced and abandoned. Despite her professed rage, Lothario easily rewoos her on the day of her marriage to the devoted, handsome, and virtuous choice of her father. The new husband kills Lothario, whose faction in return murders Calista's father, but not before she has promised him to take her own life to make good the tarnished honor of the family. This she does, over the corpse of the beloved seducer, while the husband vainly offers forgiveness and a new life.

There are fundamental similarities to the Gretchen tragedy here. Like Calista, Gretchen continues to love her seducer, even as she is condemned to death for the murder of their child. And this climatic profession of faith takes place in very similar settings, for *The Fair Penitent* ends in a black-draped hall of death, where Lothario's corpse is displayed on a bier surrounded by the traditional reminders of death—skull, bones, book, and lamp. Lothario is undeniably Faustian in his insatiability; in what was to become typically Goethean language he cries out early in the play, "I snatched the glorious golden opportunity" (I, i, 156). And like Faust, Lothario finds his ultimate justification in the "naturalness" of his behavior.

> But like the birds, great Nature's happy commoners,
> That haunt the woods, in meads, in flow'ry gardens,
> Rifle the sweets, and taste her choicest fruits,
> Yet scorn to ask the lordly owners leave.
> [II, ii, 124–27]

In the course of the century, the roles of seducer and hero will coalesce. Calista is very much the *grande dame*, which Gretchen correctly claims not to be; nevertheless the model for Gretchen's devoted domesticity is to be found in Lavinia, the other important woman in the play. These two roles also coalesce in the course of the century, so that Gretchen combines Calista's absolute love with Lavinia's humble devotion. Clearly, fundamental elements of the Gretchen tragedy derive from Rowe's popular play.

It is easy enough to trace the tradition that connects Rowe to Goethe, and thus to see the accumulation of additional significant aspects of Goethe's plot. George Lillo's *London Merchant* (1731) translates the seduction plot into prose and into a middle-class environment. It also, incidentally, reverses the terms, so that the young man is seduced. In *Clarissa* (1747) Samuel Richardson translates the plot again, this time into an epistolary novel, which, however, remains oriented toward the drama in its use of gesture, in its scenic technique, and in its structure of references to dramatic literature. Clarissa retains most of Calista's firmness of character but is at the same time not nearly so violent. Lavinia and Calista have already begun to coalesce. In 1755 the plot migrates to Germany as *Miss Sara Sampson* by Lessing. The title betrays its English origins; the play is deeply indebted to *Clarissa*, as well as to Rowe and Lillo, whose plots it joins (the hapless Sara is seduced by one Mellefont, who had been seduced previously by an older woman). Lessing was not the only German writer to exploit this tradition. In 1759 he (convincingly) accused Christoph Martin Wieland, the most eminent German writer of the day, of plagiarizing his *Johanna Gray* from the *Jane Gray* of Nicholas Rowe.[3]

Thus in the 1770s, when Goethe came to the seduction theme, the problem was not to adapt it to the German stage and the German middle class; it was rather to invigorate the German stage by giving the theme significance beyond its limited social milieu. He did so by infusing generous doses of Shakespeare into it. Just as Faust breaks through Protestant moral limitations, Goethe's use of insanity on the stage breaks through rationalist unwillingness to see madness; and the Shakespeare material raises the Gretchen tragedy to a level of almost mythological significance previously unattained in German drama. It is important to recognize that Shakespeare does not supplant Rowe in Goethe's novel treatment of the theme. The Gretchen tragedy is, in a sense, *Hamlet* rewritten from Ophelia's point of view, but it is also *Hamlet* translated into eighteenth-century terms, and those terms are provided by Rowe's essentially neoclassical form. Shakespeare functions here, not as an alternative to the tradition, but as a wild strain, so to speak, which has been grafted onto the domestic one to revitalize and enrich it.

The "Gretchen episode" in Goethe's autobiography enables us to assess the extent to which the Gretchen tragedy expresses Goethe's cultural-political views.[4] In this episode the adolescent poet falls in

---

[3]*Literaturbriefe*, 63–64, in *Lessings Sämtliche Schriften*, ed. Karl Lachmann and Franz Muncker, 8 (Stuttgart: Göschen, 1892), 166–78.

[4]*Dichtung und Wahrheit*, pt. I, bk. 5.

love with a virtuous, poor young woman identified simply as Gretchen. Whether this youthful intrigue is really a source for *Faust* is irrelevant; what is important is that Goethe plainly intended his readers to see the episode (written in 1811) in relation to *Faust*. The "love story" is narrated in pieces; interspersed among these pieces are descriptions of the election and coronation of Joseph II as Holy Roman emperor in 1765. By connecting this "source" for *Faust* to the celebration of German cultural unity, Goethe thus presents the Gretchen tragedy as a kind of paradigm of German culture. If this is so, then its blending of Shakespeare with eighteenth-century forms can only be taken as prescriptive. To become more "German," German literature should embrace, not break with, the European tradition.

But the Gretchen tragedy is in fact not the only text of the period to juxtapose Shakespeare and the contemporary tradition, and its place in the group of texts that do so has important implications. Rowe himself had prepared the first complete edition of Shakespeare subsequent to the folios (1709) and had compiled the life of Shakespeare that remained standard throughout the century. Indeed, Rowe may in some sense be said to have tamed Shakespeare for the eighteenth century in that he made him accessible to the neoclassical sensibility by dividing the plays into acts and scenes, indicating the locations of scenes, and listing the dramatis personae. The impact of Rowe on Goethe's assessment of Shakespeare can be seen in the fact that the four plays Rowe identifies as Shakespeare's greatest—*A Midsummer Night's Dream, Macbeth, Hamlet,* and *The Tempest*—are the four most important Shakespearean sources for *Faust*.[5] It is scarcely surprising, then, that Goethe should juxtapose the two writers.

It is even less surprising when we realize that Samuel Richardson, Henry Fielding, and Oliver Goldsmith had already done the same thing in *Clarissa, Tom Jones* (1749), and *The Vicar of Wakefield* (1766). I will discuss only *The Vicar of Wakefield* here as a specific example of how this juxtaposition tends to work, since it was one of a handful of works that Goethe considered crucial to his literary devel-

[5]Rowe, "Preface to Shakespeare," in *Eighteenth Century Essays on Shakespeare,* ed. D. Nichol Smith (Oxford: Clarendon Press, 1963), 13. This list contrasts with the list of plays that were most popular in the eighteenth century, which were, according to Louis Marder (*His Exits and His Entrances: The Story of Shakespeare's Reputation* [Philadelphia: Lippincott, 1963], 64), *Hamlet, Macbeth, Richard III, Romeo and Juliet, Othello,* and *King Lear.*

opment.[6] In Chapter 18 of *The Vicar of Wakefield* the vicar falls in with a company of players; together they mourn that only the Elizabethans are popular now and that no one will come to see Dryden or Otway. But, strangely enough, when the troupe then performs a play, it is Rowe's *Fair Penitent*, not an Elizabethan play or one by Dryden or Otway. The discrepancy is troubling until we realize that the germ of the plot and the source of the hero's name, Primrose, is a speech of Ophelia's in *Hamlet:*

> But, good my brother,
> Do not, as some ungracious pastors do,
> Show me the steep and thorny way to heaven,
> Whiles, like a puff'd and reckless libertine,
> Himself the primrose path of dalliance treads,
> And recks not his own rede.
>
> [I, iii, 46–51][7]

Evidently Goldsmith is involved in the same activity as Goethe, but here the Rowe reference is overt, while *Hamlet* is referred to so obliquely as to be dissipated into the real life of the novel. But consistently in these eighteenth-century comparisons Shakespeare is seen as superior to Rowe.

Goethe himself juxtaposes the two works in *Wilhelm Meister's Apprenticeship* (1796); this return justifies the juxtaposition in *Faust* retrospectively and at the same time points up its larger implications. *Wilhelm Meister* contains a famous interpretation of *Hamlet* in Book IV, where Wilhelm pushes for a production of *Hamlet* as part of his effort to transform the ailing German stage into a leader of European culture. The interpretation emphasizes Ophelia's unconscious sensuality and accompanies a performance of *Hamlet* in which the characters really all play themselves. Ophelia is played by an actress who has been seduced and abandoned by a handsome young nobleman named Lothario, a true "gay Lothario" (some six mistresses are mentioned),

---

[6]I have discussed these relationships more fully in "The Theatrical Mission of the *Lehrjahre*," in *Goethe's Narrative Fiction: The Irvine Goethe Symposium* (Berlin/New York: DeGruyter, 1983), 69–84.

[7]Argued by Ronald Paulson in "Life as Journey and as Theater: Two Eighteenth-Century Narrative Structures," *New Literary History* 8 (1976): 54–56. One wonders, indeed, if the heroine's name, Olivia, might not have been chosen for its similarity to Ophelia.

whose major problem in the novel is that he once casually slept with his fiancée's mother. Hamlet is played by the comparatively tame hero of the title, Wilhelm. Yet even Wilhelm has begun his career in the novel by seducing, then deserting a young actress; at the end he has become Lothario's best friend and prospective brother-in-law. As in *Faust* the seducers are the heroic figures; it is in the proper way of nature for women to succumb to them. That Goethe intends to confront Rowe and Shakespeare is emphasized by the fact that Lothario first appears in the immediate wake of the Shakespeare performance. On her deathbed the actress who played Ophelia sends Wilhelm— her play seducer—to carry her last words to Lothario—her real seducer.

The material in *Wilhelm Meister* not only validates our previous reading of the Gretchen tragedy but modifies Goldsmith's juxtaposition in an important way. In *The Vicar of Wakefield*, as we saw, the *Hamlet* reference was covert, while *The Fair Penitent* appeared as a play. Goethe reverses the status of the two in *Wilhelm Meister;* there the Rowe material is associated with the limitations of the contemporary social milieu while *Hamlet* has the favored status of an aesthetic ideal. Goethe is much more vigorous in his endorsement of Shakespeare as an aesthetic leader.

Let us consider now the implications of all this. Goethe has done more than conquer Shakespeare for the German tradition by integrating *Hamlet* successfully into *Faust*. As the juxtaposition of Rowe and Shakespeare in *The Vicar of Wakefield* shows, *Faust* evidently addresses itself to an issue "under discussion" (if one may use the term in this context) in England. He has not simply imported certain kinds of material into Germany but matter-of-factly joined the discussion as if he were an English writer. The effect is not only to adopt Shakespeare as a literary ancestor for German drama;[8] it is also to move German literature into the mainstream of literary discussion in the eighteenth century. In other words, by entering into the Shakespeare "discussion" as it was being conducted in the English novel, Goethe internationalizes it; had he used *Hamlet* without the juxtaposition to Rowe, the effect would have been to declare Shakespeare, in effect, a German or at least Germanic dramatist. This internationalism dis-

---

[8]Though this is no small or insignificant achievement. Within fifty years Shakespeare was to be established as *the* classic of the German stage.

tinguishes Goethe from most of his contemporaries and successors, who did indeed see Shakespeare as a German genius. Goethe's ideal for the future of German literature was that it become European literature, or rather, world literature (*Weltliteratur*), that is, that it transcend local and temporal limitations to speak to—indeed, to help generate—an international community.[9] The presence of this internationalism in the Gretchen tragedy shows that it belongs to the earliest stage of the play and was not grafted retroactively onto the work.

We have still exhausted only half of the program here, for there are generic concerns as well. The full significance of the *Hamlet–Fair Penitent* discussion emerges only when we consider what the opposition itself signified. *Hamlet* was the most performed and, we therefore conclude, the most popular Shakespeare play of the eighteenth century.[10] It is worth reflecting for a moment why this should be so. It is surely not because it is the most neoclassical of Shakespeare's plays; this dubious honor belongs rather to *Romeo and Juliet,* which has neither subplot nor double plot. And, in fact, *Romeo and Juliet* was the most popular of Shakespeare's plays until the middle of the century. The popularity of *Hamlet* coincides with the increasing hostility to the Aristotelian rules. Wilhelm's proposed stage version of *Hamlet* in the *Apprenticeship* shows Goethe's sensitivity to this issue. There Wilhelm proposes to emphasize the inner unity of the play by replacing all the extraneous details and subplots with a single new background plot that he himself would invent. In other words, he wants to transform *Hamlet* into a unified neoclassical tragedy.[11] Indeed,

---

[9]For an extensive discussion of this concept in Goethe, see Fritz Strich, *Goethe and World Literature,* trans. C. A. M. Sym (Port Washington, N.Y.: Kennikat Press, 1972). Evidently another important function of Goethe's concept of world literature—of tangential interest here—is to overcome the effects of what Harold Bloom has termed the anxiety of influence (*The Anxiety of Influence* [New York: Oxford, 1973]). In conversation with Eckermann (January 2, 1824) Goethe shows that he is well aware of the incapacitating anxiety a great writer can generate in his successors. His specific example is the enormous difficulty facing English dramatists after Shakespeare. Things were much easier for himself, Goethe continues, because he had no great predecessors in Germany; had he been born English he would have had a much harder task. Nothing is said here of Goethe's own use of Shakespeare, but it is hard to overlook the implication that the distance created by linguistic and national differences makes it possible to cope with the greatness of the ancestor. See Johann Peter Eckermann, *Gespräche mit Goethe in den letzten Jahren seines Lebens, Gedenkausgabe,* 24 (Zurich: Artemis, 1948), 543.

[10]Marder, *His Exits and Entrances,* 64.

[11]In fact, eighteenth-century stage versions of *Hamlet* in England do tend to cut the political background figures that Wilhelm cuts in his version, but I have not found any

Wilhelm specifically points out that the extraneous details are wrong in the play. We must by no means mistake Wilhelm's position for Goethe's, for Goethe treats his hero with considerable irony. The point here is thus that *Hamlet* does not fit the neoclassical mold; it is an appropriate punishment for Wilhelm's attempts to revise the play into such a mold that he finds himself in the midst of Rowe's genuinely neoclassical play in real life. Eventually Wilhelm is eased out of the theater company, which then starts producing operas. And in *Faust*, Goethe does the same thing, for his dramatic blend of Shakespeare and Rowe is closest in nature to the eighteenth-century ballad opera (*Schauspiel mit Gesang* or *Singspiel*), that is, sentimental-comic play with inserted songs, and closest especially to the founding example of the genre in England, *The Beggar's Opera* by John Gay (1728).

On the face of it this assertion may seem quite astonishing; however, the widespread, if vague, recognition that *Faust* is operatic should give pause for thought, as should the fact that *Faust* inspired so many settings of songs and scenes, as well as whole operas. And finally, Goethe's serious interest in precisely this form of opera was much greater than is generally known. Indeed, at one time, Goethe contemplated devoting himself seriously to libretto writing in order to purify the genre. The 1770s saw not only the first version of the Gretchen tragedy but four *Singspiele* as well; two more were written in the early eighties. The performance of Mozart's *Abduction from the Seraglio* in Weimar in 1785 convinced Goethe that the genre was alive and well without his help, and thenceforth, as director, he saw to it that Mozart was performed regularly on the Weimar stage.

If we look at the Gretchen sequence in the context of these early libretti, it is immediately clear that it has much more in common with them than with Goethe's famous tragedy of that decade, *Götz von Berlichingen*. Like the libretti, the Gretchen tragedy is small and plays in a limited range of mainly domestic settings. The prison setting, similar though it is to the hall of death at the end of *The Fair Penitent*, nevertheless is a favorite setting for the ends of Goethe's libretti. In three of them the final turn to a happy end takes place in a prison or underground vault; in a fourth it takes place in an isolated

---

that actually add the new background plot Wilhelm suggests. However, Nahum Tate's version of *King Lear*, which was the standard stage version into the nineteenth century, added a successful love relation between Edgar and Cordelia to unify the play and to motivate Cordelia's fateful silence in the first scene.

hermit's hut, which is clearly the equivalent. The prison remains a favorite set in nineteenth-century opera, which evolved out of so-called comic opera, the French version of ballad opera or *Singspiel*. Like these operas—really operettas—the Gretchen tragedy has a great many inserted songs; the scene in Martha's garden in which the contrasting pairs Faust-Gretchen, Mephisto-Martha alternately cross the stage is in fact as complex an ensemble number as is to be found in Goethe and might well be staged as a kind of dance. The reader must not be misled by either the simplicity of the songs or by the fact that some appear to be folk songs or traditional prayers. This not only characterizes Goethe's own libretti but constitutes an important part of the popularity of *The Beggar's Opera*, whose songs were all set to traditional or currently popular melodies. The use of Mephisto and Martha as a comic contrast to the sentimental main couple appears also in Goethe's libretti, although the most famous pair of this sort is surely Papageno and Papagena in Mozart's *Magic Flute* (1791). The language, too, is at least continuous with the language of opera, Goethe's included, especially that of the comic figures. But even at its most serious, in Faust's great final speech in "Forest and Cavern" (written in the seventies), the play inclines to the language of opera. Faust's image of himself as a destructive mountain stream can be found in one of the best known of the highly conventionalized serious operas of the century, *Dido Forsaken* (1724) of Pietro Metastasio:

> I'm not unlike the humour-laden stream
> Which made torrential by the melting ice
> Drags with it headlong and without a curb
> The woods, the flocks, the herdsmen and their homes.
> And if it sees it is restrained by dykes
> It scorns its bed, its margins overflows
> And with disdainful rage unfettered roams.[12]

Although I have no intention of claiming that the Gretchen tragedy is itself a *Singspiel*, clearly it utilizes, indeed exploits, the idiom of the genre.

The most obvious difference is of course that the Gretchen tragedy lacks the typical, often arbitrary, happy end, in which Faust and

---

[12]Pietro Metastasio, *Dido Forsaken*, trans. Joseph G. Fucilla (Florence: Valmartina, 1952), II, xiii (p. 49).

Gretchen would leave the prison hand in hand to take up a life of virtuous bliss.[13] And yet, as we have seen, it is hardly clear that the Gretchen tragedy ends "tragically." In fact, when the voice from above calls out that Gretchen is saved, what appeared to be tragedy is arbitrarily wrenched into a happy end, not quite the expected one, to be sure, but nevertheless a happier one. The specific source for this sudden wrench from tragic to comic conclusion is *The Beggar's Opera*, parent of the operatic tradition we have been discussing.[14] At the end of *The Beggar's Opera*, Macheath departs for the scaffold in a parody of a famous, highly tragic, scene in Thomas Otway's *Venice Preserv'd*. Here the opera is interrupted by the Beggar (author of the opera) and the Player from its prologue. The Player objects that the Beggar has written a tragedy, not an opera; in response the compliant Beggar has Macheath reprieved so that the opera can end happily.

Are we to understand Goethe's arbitrary wrench out of the tragic mode as a deliberate reference to Gay? I believe that we are, for Goethe's "Prelude in the Theater" clearly owes something to the very similar prologue in *The Beggar's Opera*.[15] Indeed, *The Beggar's Opera* established the popularity of this kind of prologue in English comedy. If this is truly the case, the "voice from above" is no longer to be understood only as a voice from heaven but also as the voice of an outsider to the illusion of the play. Is it perhaps the voice of the poet

---

[13]That Goethe was aware of just how arbitrary this happy end was is shown clearly by *Die Fischerin* (The fisherman's girl), 1781. In this libretto the heroine pretends to have drowned; when it is discovered she has not, her wedding to her presumably well-loved fiancé is set for the following day, to the great job of all except herself. Here the play ends. This sudden shadow suggests that simple happy ends are only for the mob.

[14]*The Beggar's Opera* was well known in Germany. Schiller, for example, claimed to have had it in mind when he wrote *The Robbers* (1781). See *Schillers Werke: Nationalausgabe*, 42 (Weimar: Böhlaus Nachfolger, 1967), 282.

[15]*Faust* commentaries identify the source of the "Prelude" as the *Shakuntala* of the Indian playwright Kalidasa, whom Goethe is known to have read and admired. Kalidasa's play does, it is true, begin with a prelude between the director and the actress; there is, however, no discussion of the genre of the play, as there is in Gay, or any special thematic connection either to Kalidasa's own play or to Goethe's. Despite the lack of any positive evidence that Goethe knew *The Beggar's Opera*, the extreme popularity of the piece in England and Schiller's reference to it (n. 14) show that *The Beggar's Opera* must have been generally known in German intellectual circles in Goethe's time. The parallel Goethe would doubtless have recognized between Kalidasa's and Gay's prologues would certainly have appealed to his sense of universality. Indeed, one might well argue that Goethe's prelude, with its director, author, and player amalgamates those of his predecessors, for Kalidasa has a director and a player, while Gay has an author and a player.

from the "Prelude," who must agree, like Gay's Beggar, to a last-minute change in the ending of his play? Both plays have, in effect, a double ending—the tragic ending that could have been, the ambiguously happy ending (for what is Gretchen saved?) that is. This doubleness pervades *The Beggar's Opera* at all levels, leading to considerable disagreement as to how to take it. In 1777, for example, in two simultaneously running productions in London, Lucy was played in the one as tragic, in the other as comic. The play constituted a concerted challenge to neoclassical principles of decorum in two senses—in the social sense because its characters are from the bottom of the social scale but are indistinguishable from those at the top and in the generic sense because of its parodic, but not too parodic, mixture of tragedy, opera, pastoral, ballad, and comedy.[16] But surely the same is true of the Gretchen tragedy. Faust's association with Mephistopheles and the transformations he has undergone at the latter's hands render him in an important sense classless, and thus the class distinction on which the potential for tragedy at first appears to depend becomes irrelevant. Similarly, the generic identification of the play as sentimental love tragedy is undercut by the operatic structures, as well as by the double end. *Faust* is a play that deliberately violates conventions and repeatedly calls attention to this fact. The refusal to adhere to specific conventions results in a new kind of realism—a realism that depends, paradoxically, on the insistent staginess and artificiality of the play. This is, then, still the realm of the "Prelude in the Theater"; the Gretchen tragedy is precisely the love intrigue described by the clown for the ultimate play within the play (ll. 160–65)—chance meeting, sentiment, involvement, happiness, hindrance, ecstasy, pain—and its idiom is not, ultimately, that of eighteenth-century tragedy or of Shakespearean tragedy but of opera.

In this doubleness my reading deviates furthest and yet comes closest to traditional readings, which see this part of the play as a sentimental love tragedy on the tragic destruction of simplicity and purity by the attempt of the theorist or idealist to experience the real world—or, at an even more traditional level, on the way an alliance with the devil necessarily spoils Faust's efforts to achieve the good,

---

[16]For a detailed analysis of how this works in Gay, see Ian Donaldson, "'A Double Capacity': *The Beggar's Opera*," in *The World Upside-Down: Comedy from Jonson to Fielding* (Oxford: Clarendon Press, 1970), 159–82, esp. 164–65.

the beautiful, and the true. Such readings depend ultimately on a naïve response to Gretchen as the pure ideal projected upon her by Faust. But Gretchen is, after all, a sensualist who poisons her own mother, and what is more, up to the last moment would do it all again. I speak crassly here to make a point, but Jean Hagstrum's sensitive history of the sentimental love tradition in *Sex and Sensibility* will no longer allow such naïve responses to any of Goethe's heroines.[17] For indeed, the tradition of seduction drama outlined above is but one strand of a much larger tradition of the tension between sexual and ideal love in the eighteenth century; one could just as well situate the Gretchen tragedy thematically in the context of Rousseau's *Julie*, as Shelley does, and Richardson's *Clarissa*.[18] And surely no serious reader of either of those texts would think that the moral question would begin to exhaust their significance.

Hagstrum's more sophisticated view of the sentimental love tradition offers a larger context for the standard interpretive issues on the Gretchen tragedy. Hagstrum, for example, comments about *The Fair Penitent:* "The absence of Christian order presages century-long developments that will substitute instinct for institutions, emotion for conscience and creed. The fear of sexuality by the good and its embrace by the bad, who are given moments of power and persuasiveness, seem to comment on the potential loss of morally directed energy in modern man."[19] What Hagstrum offers here is a specific historical framework for the moral issue in the Gretchen tragedy, for in the famous credo scene ("Martha's Garden") Faust makes precisely the substitution that Hagstrum describes. Faust cannot say he believes in God but asks Gretchen to accept as the equivalent the assertion "Feeling is all!" (l. 3456). And Gretchen does indeed respond that the parson says almost the same thing, with slightly different words. Both Faust and Gretchen substitute instinct for institutions, then, and the language of the play validates the substitution by relating the feeling upon which both depend to the weaving presence of *natura naturans*—heavens, earth, stars "weave in perpetual mystery, invisi-

---

[17]Jean H. Hagstrum, *Sex and Sensibility: Ideal and Erotic Love from Milton to Mozart* (Chicago: University of Chicago Press, 1980).

[18]Shelley connects *Faust* to *Julie* in a letter to John Gisborne of April 10, 1822, in *The Letters of Percy Bysshe Shelley*, ed. Frederick L. Jones (Oxford: Clarendon Press, 1964), 2:407.

[19]Hagstrum, *Sex and Sensibility*, 120.

ble-visible (ll. 3449–50). This is "spirit," or divinity, as it has been defined by the play. The amorality of the play's conclusion is thus not a personal aberration of a particularly unconventional mind; rather, here as in *Werther* Goethe clearly displays the implications of the sentimental love tradition, which must lead to the paradox that human sexual love is good, even divine, yet leads to death. The Gretchen tragedy is thus in this sense the culminating love story of the eighteenth-century tradition. The nineteenth century, in adopting it, failed to see how it mercilessly uncovered the innate ambiguity of that tradition.

We can now return to the question of why Goethe added the story of Gretchen to his metaphysical drama. As the play within the play, as the play described by the clown, the Gretchen tragedy is what "Night" was working toward, the embodiment of the ideal in the real. And the extraordinary achievement of the Gretchen tragedy is precisely that its apparently simple realism is yet the vehicle of "higher meaning." As we saw repeatedly in "Night," this synthesis can only take place in the transient moment of play. Thus it is central to understanding the Gretchen tragedy to recognize the intrinsic theatricality provided by the use of the operatic mode. All the rest of *Faust* works much more openly in this framework. In the very next scene, the first scene of Part II, Faust will finally articulate his own version of this insight. As we shall see, Faust's affair with Helen insists repeatedly on its own theatrical nature, which has, indeed, long been recognized, and the illusory nature of the Helen sequence will be elaborately prepared for by the "Classical Walpurgis Night." The "Walpurgis Night" of Part I does not prepare for the Gretchen tragedy in the same way, but it does interrupt it right at the climax. Our recognition of the staginess of the Gretchen tragedy thus requires that we also ask after the theatrical nature of the "Walpurgis Night," to which we now turn.

7

The Illusion of Reality:
The "Walpurgis Night"

The great witches' sabbath on the Brocken, a peak in the Harz Mountains, was and is famous independently of both Goethe and the Faust
legend. The result: everyone knows that the "Walpurgis Night" constitutes the great orgiastic climax of *Faust*, the final overwhelming
eruption of the demonic powers in the play. It is also, of course, the
great climax of most *Faust* operas, where the music explodes and the
stage is filled with wild dancing. Indeed, the same is often true of
performances of the play itself. It is, then, both the operatic and the
demonic high point of the play. And yet I have never taught the
"Walpurgis Night" to a class that has not—at least at first—been
disappointed, or even bored, by this famous climax. For to tell the
truth, much of it seems to be devoted to vapid satire of Goethe's
minor contemporaries. The reader sinks, not into primal ecstasy, but
into a morass of footnotes. The difficulty arises from the same misap-
prehensions that have concerned us all along, and it evaporates as
soon as *operatic* and *demonic* are understood with the special resonance Goethe has given them in *Faust*. Therefore I will explore how
these two terms should be applied to the "Walpurgis Night," then
try to show what the special coherence and interest of the scene
actually is.

Nineteenth-century composers were certainly correct in focusing
on the "Walpurgis Night." The text calls for music and dancing: in its
"prologue," the scene "Cathedral," a choir sings the requiem mass; in
the scene itself choruses of witches and warlocks engage in elaborate

ensemble numbers; there is even a trio *sung* (we are explicitly told) by Faust, Mephisto, and a will-o'-the-wisp. The "Walpurgis Night's Dream" is accompanied by an orchestra of insects and other grotesques. And although the "Walpurgis Night's Dream" is to be read basically as an allusion to Shakespeare, nevertheless the reconciliation of Oberon and Titania was the subject of a popular operetta that Goethe had staged in Weimar in 1796.[1] Furthermore, both *A Midsummer Night's Dream* and *The Tempest* (the source for Ariel) were performed in the eighteenth century only as operas.[2]

But opera in *Faust* functions consistently as one of several related nonillusionist forms, and its importance here signals yet again the non-Aristotelian nature of the scene. Like so many other scenes in *Faust*, it is structured basically as a processional masque. This is obvious in the "Dream," where each figure has the obligatory single speech; but as soon as one recognizes it in the "Dream," the rest of the scene also begins to look less strange. It, too, has essentially no plot and no real interchanges among characters. What really happens is that Faust and Mephistopheles wander past a number of curious figures; the scene is a procession inside out, so to speak. At line 4092 Mephistopheles suddenly appears very old as he parodies the old fogies sitting around the campfire. By emphasizing the continuity between essence and appearance the stage direction points to the importance of this fundamental technique of the processional masque. That the "Walpurgis Night" is operatic, then, only calls attention to its "significance." We are not to descend into orgiastic ecstasy at all, but rather to read the higher meaning in the allegory.

Demonic also has a special resonance, which can be approached most directly by considering a poem by Goethe called "The First Walpurgis Night." The poem was written in 1799; Goethe worked on the "Walpurgis Night" scene 1798–99 and then again 1800–1801. Thus the poem is likely to be relevant to Goethe's conception in

---

[1]*Oberon; Oder der König der Elfen* by Paul Wranitzky (Pavel Vranický, 1756–1808). The opera remained popular until it was supplanted by Karl Maria von Weber's *Oberon* in 1826. Goethe knew and respected Wranitzky, who was to have composed his continuation of *The Magic Flute*.

[2]In fact, *Macbeth* as well (associated, as we have seen, with the "prologue" to the Gretchen tragedy, to which the "Walpurgis Night" can be seen as a kind of epilogue) was performed with elaborate machinery, music, and dancing in the late seventeenth century.

Faust.[3] It consists of a series of speeches by four solo voices (a Druid, one of the people, a watcher, a Christian watcher) and four choruses (Druids, Women, Watchers, Christian Watchers). The Druids call upon the people to come with them to the forest to celebrate the arrival of spring with the traditional bonfires in honor of the Father. At first the people hesitate for fear of their Christian oppressors, but they eventually carry out their duty while some of their number keep watch. The watchmen decide to trick their persecutors by pretending to be the devils that the Christian priests talk about so freely. Duly terrified by the watchers' antics, the Christians run away and the Druids perform their pure rites in peace.

The first point about this so-called ballad is that it is conceived as a kind of oratorio, or primitive opera, with single voices and choruses responding to one another.[4] It is, therefore, operatic in the same sense as is the "Walpurgis Night" in *Faust.* Second, this proto-opera thematizes Goethe's now familiar subversion of the demonism of the Faust legend. What to uncomprehending orthodox Christian eyes seems a dangerous witches' sabbath is in reality the peaceful celebration of the return of spring, pure worship of the Father in the flame. In *Faust* fire has the same ambiguity. On the one hand it is Mephisto's personal element, but on the other it also symbolizes the Absolute. What appears demonic is at bottom really divine, just as Mephisto is "A part of that power / Which always seeks evil, and always achieves good" (ll. 1335–36).

Finally, we must also consider the mechanism of the poem. The followers of the Druids protect themselves from Christian persecution by pretending to be the devils invented by the Christians themselves, in other words, by performing a play. Like Faust at the beginning of "Night," the Christians do not know how to "read." They mistake the illusion for reality and flee. The reader of the ballad, however, perceives the higher truth beyond the illusion, that demonism is nothing

[3]The poem is available in English in a translation by E. A. Bowring. I own it in *The Household Edition: The Poems of Goethe Translated in the Original Meters,* ed. F. H. Hedge and L. Noa (New York: Worthington, 1885), 151–54. It is readily available in German in any complete edition of Goethe's poems.

[4]It was indeed set as a cantata (op. 60) by Felix Mendelssohn. Evidently Mendelssohn understood what Goethe was really up to, for the writer of the jacket notes for my recording complains that the atmosphere of the music is too much like that of *A Midsummer Night's Dream* (also composed by Mendelssohn).

other than the creative power of nature, the force of life either in disguise or misinterpreted. This poem is important, then, not only because it treats the demonic in the same way that the play does but also because the mechanism of the subversion is the same. Both "The First Walpurgis Night" and the scene "Walpurgis Night" end with the performance of a play. Everywhere in *Faust,* performing a play is a significant act of mediation; this poem tells us how to look for the message beneath the surface grotesqueries in the play at the end of the "Walpurgis Night."

With this understanding of the implications of *operatic* and *demonic* in the "Walpurgis Night," let us turn to the scene itself. Clearly it is much more complex than the ballad; nevertheless, careful reading will show the same underlying structure, as well as the same fundamental subversion of the demonic. For the purposes of this discussion it is easiest to consider the scene in three major parts—the climb (ll. 3835–4023), wandering with Mephistopheles (ll. 4024–4222), and the "Walpurgis Night's Dream" (ll. 4223–4398). The brief scene "Cathedral" (ll. 3776–3834) functions as a kind of prologue to the "Walpurgis Night" and will be considered as such here.

"Cathedral" is a most astonishing scene. Gretchen, apparently attending the requiem mass for her brother (this is indicated explicitly in the *Urfaust*), is plagued by an evil spirit. It is the identity of this evil spirit that is so astonishing, for it would appear to be the voice of Gretchen's conscience. If this is so, it is not the voice of any kind of personal conscience, for Gretchen herself feels absolutely pure and secure in her love for Faust, as "Dungeon" is shortly to show so clearly. It is also not the voice of a false conscience sent by Mephistopheles. Mephistopheles avoids churches, never willfully torments in the play, and consistently takes pleasure in new life and creation. Rather, the evil spirit is an institutional conscience, for it speaks the language of the church. Its speeches intertwine with the choir singing the "Dies irae," and indeed at lines 3800–3807 the spirit summarizes some of the more lurid elements of the venerable Latin hymn. The hymn itself is quite a long one; Goethe has excerpted here only the most threatening and unpleasant stanzas. The evil spirit must thus be associated with a narrow Christian orthodoxy hostile to nature.

Given the generalized medieval setting of the play, the set here is presumably Gothic. "Night" has already attached a distinct negative meaning to a Gothic set: it is a prison. And indeed, Gretchen perceives herself to be imprisoned:

> I cannot move!
> The columns
> Imprison me!
> The vaulting
> Oppresses me!—air!
>   [ll. 3816–20]

When Gretchen prays to the statue of the Virgin outdoors ("By the City Wall"), she suffers neither from confinement nor from bad conscience; she seeks help on her way, not forgiveness or absolution. To follow Gretchen's way for a moment, she proceeds from the cathedral to the literal prison of the final scene. Thus the cathedral represents the same kind of spiritual imprisonment for Gretchen that the study represented for Faust. Small wonder its presiding spirit should appear as evil.

How is all this relevant to the "Walpurgis Night"? Gretchen calls for release and fresh air, she is shortly released into unconsciousness. We, who have shared her consciousness in the scene, are also released, perhaps into unconsciousness, into the demonic depths of the psyche. But more explicitly and on the literal level we are released into nature, for in the next scene we climb the Brocken with Faust and Mephistopheles. Thus the fresh air Gretchen calls for is the fresh air of the "Walpurgis Night," and the "Walpurgis Night" is introduced, not as evil, but as release from the explicitly evil spirit of Christian institutions.

This is the stance of "The First Walpurgis Night," and it continues in Faust's attitude toward what he sees as he climbs the Brocken. His first speech praises the pleasures of walking in the awakening spring landscape. Indeed, both his first speech and the third paragraph of the trio with Mephisto and the will-o'-the-wisp sound remarkably like the Faust of "Outside the City Gate" or of "Forest and Cavern." His interest is all in spring, flowing water, memory, rebirth, and—naturally—poetry. Even in the view of Mephistopheles, assuming the grotesque views of nature in the trio (ll. 3876–80, 3889–3905) are to be attributed to him, nature teems with life and activity. Whether this activity is seen as grotesque and threatening or as beautiful and inspiring, it is nevertheless the activity of living nature. In Faust's language we recognize yet again the positive idealist attitude of the poet or the macrocosm; in Mephistopheles' language, the chaotic realist view of the director or the earth spirit. Goethe's refusal to assign particular parts of the text to particular voices here emphasizes the fundamental identity of these opposing views; the trio is at bottom a celebration of the same creative nature we have seen all along.

Nature is not the only familiar motif here, for in trying to reach the top of the mountain the trio is striving. Their discussion parodistically reviews the modes of striving that were of such concern earlier. It is Mephistopheles, this time, who wants to take the straight-line path of direct transcendence. "Just go straight, you, in the devil's name!" (l. 3864), he snaps at the mischievous will-o'-the-wisp. But the will-o'-the-wisp, as a creature of nature, can only take the weaving course of the earth spirit.

> With all due respect, I hope I will manage
> To control my flighty nature;
> Our course usually only goes zigzag,
>
> [ll. 3860–62]

he assures Mephistopheles. Faust plays the mediator this time. He keeps his goal in mind, but is nevertheless willing to wander through the "labyrinth of the valleys" (l. 3841), in no hurry to shorten his way. *Labyrinth* recalls the language of erring from "Dedication," the "Prelude," and the "Prologue." It is the erring way that reconciles the direct jump to transcendence with the eternal circular motion of nature; it is that path into which we saw Faust forced in "Night."

The witches' choruses that accompany the later parts of the climb (ll. 3956–4015) are also probably best understood in this context, for the discussion centers on the various modes for reaching the top of the mountain. They range from sitting still to snaillike creeping, to tripping, to flying, to reaching the top in a single bound. In this case the witches mediate between the alternative patterns of the men. The two semichoruses of warlocks move in opposing patterns—the one creeping like snails, the other arriving in a single jump. The witches, by contrast, travel either by many steps or fly along by various detours. One passes the Ilsenstein; another has stopped to peek into an owl's nest. Here once again is the erring path. Since they travel like Faust, it is appropriate that the swarm of witches lands at the same place as Faust.

If the question is once more the proper mode of striving, there is also the question of the goal here. The travelers climb the mountain to celebrate the witches' sabbath. They expect to find Satan himself at the top of the mountain: "Sir Urian sits up on top" (l. 3959). Goethe engages once again in his customary subversion of traditional demonism. Satan stands in the place of the Absolute, of spirit, of the ideal. The switch is signaled by the euphemism for the devil used here, Sir Urian, which actually means an unexpected guest whose name is not known. Originally there was to be a scene with Satan at the top of the mountain, and there are still bits of it extant. However, there is nothing especially demonic about it at all; it smacks rather of the grotesque chaos of "Auerbach's Tavern." In any case, Goethe decided not to include a Satan scene. As a result, not only does the devil ironically represent the Absolute, but furthermore, Goethe elides the ultimate epiphany of evil. This elision is significant in two ways: first because it reinforces the pattern of the play as a whole to deny the existence of an evil principle, second because, to the extent that Satan ironically represents the Absolute, the Absolute cannot be directly perceived.

But it is a very *serious* joke that Satan takes the place of the Absolute here; we must understand that a witches' sabbath is as good a place to seek the Absolute as any other in the play. On the Brocken we are offered a view of the natural world equivalent to what we had in "Auerbach's Tavern" and "Witch's Kitchen"; this, too, is Mephistopheles' world. It requires only the creative, ordering vision of the human mind to perceive this world as Nature. And this is precisely what happens at lines 3916–31, when Faust sees the mountainside lit up by the gold within. Mephisto mythologizes the scene by describing it as the palace of Mammon, the traditional devil of wealth, who also builds the city of Hell in *Paradise Lost*. To the extent that we hear Milton in this reference (and most commentators do), it connects the speech to the subliminal classicism of the pact scenes and thus quietly undercuts Mephisto's northern-demonic interpretation of the vision. Faust's language—which yet again recalls the language of the speech to the moon with its glimmering, reddish dawn light, mists, flowing water, and delicate webwork—reveals the higher meaning of the vision. It is once again an epiphany of light, this time in the form of gold deep in the mountainside. It is a revelation of the Absolute in the darkness of chaotic nature—or better, a vision of the Absolute evoked by the now experienced eye of Faust. Ambiguous as this motif appears here, it will emerge as the single most important image of the manifestation of spirit in the world in Part II of this drama.

The opposing attitudes of Faust and Mephistopheles toward their climb, then, embody the tension they have represented from very early on between idealist and realist views of nature, between the tendency to see significance and the tendency to see chaos. In the second part of the scene Mephisto's view takes over in a return to the version of this tension we saw in "Auerbach's Tavern." Faust wants to continue striving (that is, climbing the mountain) but Mephisto insists on turning aside into a "small" world. Once again he becomes a kind of showman who offers Faust a parody of the real world. The line "There's dancing, talking, cooking, drinking, making love" (l. 4058) recapitulates the play proposed by the Merry Person in the "Prelude." And when Mephisto engages the old men around the fires, he parodies them in the most extreme way by even taking on their appearance. Indeed, everything about this scene is parody. The action parodies a village fair; Lilith appears as a female parody of the devil with no impact whatsoever. Faust dances with a young witch, who is, granted, grotesque, but who is anything but seductive or dangerous. Faust can resist this extraordinary temptress because of the red mouse that hops out of her mouth! Once again, the demonic appears absurd.

The scene is probably also to be recognized as parody of the early cantos of the *Inferno*. With its winding path, wild forms whizzing through the air and fires gleaming in the darkness, the setting is strongly reminscent of Dante. But it is inverted: Dante-Pilgrim descends toward Satan; Faust climbs. When Dante approaches the fire in Limbo (Canto 4) he finds the most distinguished figures of classical antiquity and the fire turns out to be light emitted from a great castle. The fires in *Faust*, by contrast, are indeed miserable little fires, and about them huddle not venerable sages but old fools. The ultimate relevance of the Dante allusion is once again the disappointment of expectation. The reader is led not to an epiphany of evil but to a highly mediated epiphany of creative spirit through the play-within-a-play motif from Shakespeare's *A Midsummer Night's Dream*. Dante is a peculiarly appropriate vehicle for this shift, for at the end of the

Inferno the world performs a similar kind of flip-flop, and the reader suddenly discovers that his descent has turned into a climb. In modulating from demonism to comedy, Goethe in fact repeats the structure of Dante's work, in which the *Inferno* is but the first part of *The Divine Comedy*.

In Goethe's play the climax of the Mephistophelean parody is the Proctophantasmiac. Any edition of *Faust* will explain the topical allusion, but it would be a mistake to think that a footnote of whatever length is the important issue here. We may or may not recognize the rationalist Friedrich Nicolai, who thought he had been cured of seeing ghosts by the application of leeches. Nevertheless, the Proctophantasmiac's rabid assertion of the Enlightenment position that spirits do not, cannot, exist questions the ontological validity of the entire preceding scene. This is of a piece with the ironic use of the supernatural everywhere else in the drama. Yet there is a double irony here, for the critic of the supernatural appears totally absurd in light of the obvious "real" existence of all these nonexistent spirits. What is actually real here? This question will be central to the last part of the scene.

We must also remember that the Proctophantasmiac is not the first character in *Faust* to lose his temper at nonexistent spirits. Although Faust participates good-humoredly enough in this elaborate spirit parody, earlier in the play he had no patience for the equivalent games staged by Mephistopheles in "Auerbach's Tavern" and "Witch's Kitchen." Ultimately, the hostility of the Proctophantasmiac must be seen as a grotesque reflection of Faust's own hostility to drama and play in his first dialogue with Wagner. The Proctophantasmiac raises once again the question of how to "read" illusion properly; the question is all the more important because it immediately precedes the illusory appearance of Gretchen and the play "Walpurgis Night's Dream."

Faust's vision of Gretchen, which is described immediately after the interruption of the Proctophantasmiac, plays an important role in the development of the thematics of reading. Normally this vision is understood as a warning that prevents Faust from succumbing to the distracting seductions of the "Walpurgis Night" so he can hasten to Gretchen's rescue. But this moralistic reading only holds if Mephistopheles is truly a principle of evil. It would also be more convincing if Faust expressed concern for Gretchen, rather than just desire, in response to the vision. In "Auerbach's Tavern" and "Witch's Kitchen," we remember, Faust did not hesitate to express his revulsion and to demand that they leave. Nothing of the sort happens here. How does the passage look if we do not immediately assume moral revulsion on Faust's part? Faust offers the vision as his second—and apparently true—excuse for breaking off his promising dance with the young witch. The figure *seems* to him *to be similar* to Gretchen. This is not by any means an absolute statement of fact; on the contrary, it is Faust's interpretation of the vision, as Faust himself realizes. He understands much better how to respond to spirit shows than does the Proctophantasmiac! Mephistopheles offers, however, a more sophisticated interpretation of the vision. He begins by explicitly identifying it as an image (l. 4190).[5] Then he suggests an allegorical interpretation for it. It is a Medusa, whose "frozen stare freezes a man's blood" ("Vom starren Blick erstarrt des Menschen Blut," l. 4192). The repeated German root *starren* has to do with fixedness, and if we ask about the implications of this concept in the play, we are immediately led back to the pact. The whole point of the pact is to resist fixedness, to force Faust to move with the flux of time and natural change. The real implication of Mephisto's warning about the vision is that for Faust to see Gretchen everywhere, to remain fixed on the past, will abort his striving. As we have already seen, in "Dungeon" Faust himself will beg Gretchen to let go of the past so that they can move on. Thus, as Faust's mediator to the world, Mephisto warns him to disregard the vision in good faith.

Furthermore, Mephistopheles continues, the creature appears to every observer as his own beloved. In the "Classical Walpurgis Night" of Part II Mephistopheles himself will meet several monstrous ladies of this type, who constantly change their forms. His comic classicizing here—that the vision is Medusa, who can carry her head tucked underneath her arm because Perseus once chopped it off—emphasizes that this vision is yet another of the many little shows in *Faust*. Thus the Proctophantasmiac and the vision of Gretchen render explicit the structure that has repeatedly appeared to be implicit in *Faust:* striving for the Absolute is inevitably transformed into the interpretation of play. We have also seen repeatedly how the search

---

[5]Paul Requadt (*Goethes "Faust I": Leitmotivik und Architectur* [Munich: Fink, 1972], 306) correctly compares this image to the image in the mirror in "Witch's Kitchen." In both cases the significant factor is the imaginative response of the beholder.

for transcendent meaning is transformed into the search for meaning within a concrete real world. Because Nature is now understood to be ordered by the transcendent meaning implicit within it (however paradoxical this formulation may seem), it is therefore the same as art. Henceforth in *Faust* art and Nature will stand freely for one another. Here the Neoplatonic and Kantian dialectics converge once and for all for Goethe.

The argument thus far should already be sufficient to dispel the widespread misconception that the "Walpurgis Night's Dream" is not an "organic" part of *Faust*. The original version of the "Dream" was conceived in 1797 as literary and political satire; when Schiller did not want to publish it, so the story goes, Goethe decided to publish it as part of *Faust*, so as not to waste it. The story is true, though the conclusion is patently absurd. Quite apart from the obvious fact that no one dumps unpublishable material into his acknowledged masterpiece, Goethe is known to have experimented with a Satan scene as an alternative climax. That he chose to revise the satire instead can only mean that he intended the delicate anticlimax he achieved here.[6]

The first step toward understanding it is simply an accurate description of the phenomenon. In their wanderings Faust and Mephistopheles stumble on a theater—an amateur theater, they are informed by the servile Servibilis. They join the group of spectators and the curtain immediately rises on a play within the play, the "Walpurgis Night's Dream; or, The Golden Wedding of Oberon and Titania: An Intermezzo." The play is introduced first by the stagemaster (compare the "Prelude in the Theater") and the requisite herald who normally introduces figures in masques. The figures introduced by the herald are Oberon, Titania, and their two servants, Puck and Ariel, who has been arbitrarily imported into this *A Midsummer Night's Dream* cast from *The Tempest*. They discuss their reconciliation, which is then celebrated in the rest of the play by the customary means of celebrating anything in seventeenth- and eighteenth-century courts—by a masque. The stagemaster and herald are thus the first frame; Oberon and Titania, the frame within the frame for the play that now begins. An orchestra of insects and other small creatures

---

[6]But Walter Dietze has offered a model reading of the scene in "Der *Walpurgisnachtstraum* in Goethes *Faust:* Entwurf, Gestaltung, Funktion," *PMLA* 84 (1969): 476–91. My reading is indebted to this one for its starting point.

accompanies and occasionally interrupts this elfin masque: it is the third frame. Once again we are reminded of the extensive preliminaries to *Faust* itself. It is evidently important that the "Dream" not be taken for reality.

The masque within the masque is a three-part satire of intellectual currents in the 1790s. The first part (through the speech of This World's Child, l. 4330) deals with *belles lettres;* the second (through the Sceptic, l. 4362), with philosophy; the third (through the Massive Ones, l. 4386), with sociopolitical trends. The specific references are explained in any good commentary to the play, but as in the case of the Proctophantasmiac, the essential significance of the masque for *Faust* can be understood without a detailed understanding of the topical jokes. The one action that happens over and over in this play is that it is interrupted, so frequently that it is scarcely coherent. There are several interesting things about the interruptions. First, there are interruptions that break the boundaries across all of the frames. Second, there are certain figures to whom we cannot unambiguously assign a place in this ménage. Is the Curious Traveler, for example, in the masque, or is he outside all the frames as another incarnation of the Proctophantasmiac, who threatens to become a traveler at line 4169? Then there are the will-o'-the-wisps, who are clearly allegorical figures in the masque, but who nevertheless confuse us because there was a "real" will-o'-the-wisp climbing the mountain with Faust and Mephistopheles earlier in the scene. Yet another important form of illusion breaking is represented by the Northern Artist, the Xenien, and This World's Child, who were, because of their names, immediately recognizable to Goethe's contemporaries as Goethe himself. Thus the work breaks not only the various boundaries between play and audience within *Faust* but also the boundary between *Faust* and the world. We are back once again to the importance of nonillusionist theater in *Faust*.

This makes it easier to understand why Goethe placed a seemingly irrelevant satire at the climax of his play. By definition satire must refer to something outside of itself, must have a real meaning beyond the text. It also cannot be simple imitation of reality or even very probable imitation of reality; otherwise it cannot achieve its purpose. Thus satire is an essentially non-Aristotelian form. Even in the eighteenth century satire was the one contemporary genre in which improbabilities and lack of realistic illusion were condoned. *Faust*, as we have seen, is centrally concerned with the interrelation of reality, illusion, and meaning. Satire is thus a particularly appropriate vehicle for the climax of the "Walpurgis Night," which summarizes the thematics of illusion and celebrates the ambiguous relationship of art to reality.

It is perhaps easier to see how the "Dream" plays with the relation between art and reality than how higher truth is involved. Nevertheless, the celebration of higher truth is an important aspect, no matter how indirect. It appears first in the fact that the masque celebrates the reunion of Oberon and Titania. These figures are to be recognized as borrowed, on the one hand, from Shakespeare's *A Midsummer Night's Dream*, where they embody the fertility of creative nature. On the other hand they were actually more familiar to Goethe's audience from a romance in *ottava rima* (the meter of "Dedication") by Christoph Martin Wieland called *Oberon* (1780).[7] Although Wieland explicitly acknowledged his debt to Shakespeare in the preface of his poem, his fairies are not simple fertility spirits like Shakespeare's. Rather they are the powers that translate the decrees of fate into concrete reality in the world. Oberon is comparable to the Zeus of the *Iliad* or, closer to home, the earth spirit in *Faust*. The restoration of order in Oberon's relationship to Titania thus means nothing less than the restoration of the orderly mediation of spirit through Nature in the world. It means the establishment of the connection between the man and the Absolute that Faust seeks through the entire play.

Because the "Dream" celebrates Nature in this sense, Oberon and Titania are accompanied by two servants who, with typical Goethean irony, ultimately turn out to be more important than the master for whom they mediate. Both Puck and Ariel are nature spirits (here and in their respective Shakespeare plays), but in their similarity they also embody some of the most basic tensions in the drama. In Shakespeare both Puck and Ariel are servants to rulers who take the role of stage managers in the action of their respective plays. Puck, however, is a trickster, while Ariel is a helper. Goethe preserves this distinction: Puck is the demonic nature spirit; Ariel, the beautiful, artistic one. This exactly echoes the opposing views of nature articulated by Meph-

---

[7]Wieland's *Oberon* was adapted as the libretto of Wranitzky's *Oberon* by Friederike Sophie Seyler, who maintained the importance of Oberon and Titania for the plot.

istopheles and Faust earlier in the scene and indeed all through the drama. At the same time Puck is the peculiarly English, local version of the nature spirit from a Shakespeare play preoccupied with its Englishness, while Ariel has an exotic biblical name (Isaiah 29:1) and comes from a play with a basically Italian setting. The two figures thus also embody the tension between the northern, or Germanic (Faust), tradition and the southern, or classical tradition; this tension is articulated explicitly within the masque by the Northern Artist (ll. 4275–78). Finally, these two spirits also embody the coming tension between the two parts of *Faust* itself. If Puck seems an organic outgrowth of the "Walpurgis Night," it is Ariel who invites the masquers (or is it the audience?) to follow him off into a spirit world, where we do indeed meet him in the first scene of Part II and where he remains an important figure, as we shall see. If Puck is the blunt nature spirit, Ariel is the nature spirit who is master in the realm of art, and it is this higher realm of Nature understood as art to which he beckons.

Lest this manipulation of frames and the relationship of art to reality seem hopelessly arcane, I would like to interrupt the argument here to emphasize once again that Goethe is really only trying to rescue in the post-Kantian world a tradition that was widespread if not absolutely commonplace in the Renaissance and the seventeenth century. Let us take as an example a painting by Rembrandt called *The Holy Family with Curtain*.[8] This painting is not a source for the "Dream," although Goethe was most likely familiar with it, but in it the categories of illusion, reality, and truth operate in ways that are exactly analogous to the "Dream." Thus it shows that there is nothing esoteric or unreasonably difficult about the scene once we have identified its proper ideological context. Inside the heavy frame of this painting (not reproduced here) the viewer sees a red curtain that has been drawn back to reveal, not the scene itself, but another frame—a painting within a painting. Within the inner painting the figures are symmetrically arranged on either side of the large windows at the back of the room; as happened with Oberon and Titania in the "Dream," the ostensible subject is reduced to frame. In this reading the "higher meaning" contained in the painting would be the light of God (appar-

---

[8] Now and in Goethe's time in Kassel at Schloss Wilhelmshöhe, which the poet first visited in 1779. Another obvious example of the phenomenon about to be discussed is the famous *Sistine Madonna* of Raphael in Dresden.

Rembrandt's *Holy Family with Curtain* was painted in 1646. Courtesy of Staatliche Kunstsammlungen Kassel, Schloss Wilhelmshöhe.

ently moonlight here) entering through the windows and embodied inside the room in the fire on the floor and in the Holy Child. But here again the interest in the painting is displaced from this central meaning to the frame. The light entering through the windows is feeble compared to the light falling into the painting from some unknown source in front and to the left (from the illuminating eye of the beholder?). This other light illuminates, not the next obvious center of meaning in the painting, the child or the mother, but rather the covers of the cradle and the ends of the mother's scarf. The strange lighting and the eager cat also displace the central point of the painting away from the windows (defined as central by the perspective) to the bowl of scraps before the fire. Thus the focus is all on the "insignificant" details of the real milieu, on the translation into a contemporary Dutch environment, and on the ways in which the higher meaning is framed. This is exactly analogous to the way Goethe focuses on contemporary satire in his elaborately framed "Dream." In both cases the obviousness of the displacement of emphasis artfully calls attention to the original locus of meaning, the divine creative force in the background.

I have touched as yet only briefly on that other creative force in the background, Shakespeare. The title of the "Intermezzo" conspicuously calls attention to Shakespeare, as does the presence of Puck and Ariel (who do not appear in Wieland's *Oberon*); the parallels between *A Midsummer Night's Dream* and Goethe's work emphasize and further illuminate the issues under discussion. Both plays are about night and moonlight, grotesque and demonic nature. The problematic reality of art and the way art calls the problematic reality of reality itself into question are fundamental themes in Shakespeare as well as in Goethe. In *A Midsummer Night's Dream* no one, except perhaps Hippolyta, is in full control of his or her thoughts or feelings; continuity of self is constantly interrupted by the manipulations of Oberon and Puck. The play within the play at the end translates these problems into the aesthetic realm by questioning the nature of dramatic illusion. Ironically, the mechanicals are much more "realistic" in their play than the rest but, as a result, much less a part of "real" life than any of the other characters, including the fairies. At the end of the play we finally return to the securely "real" world of the court of Athens, only to have Puck transform the entire proceeding into a dream in the last speech.

If the levels of unreality in Shakespeare are just as dizzying as in Goethe, the idea of marriage as resolution and affirmation is much more clearly foregrounded. At the end of Shakespeare's play Oberon and Titania come back together and the three mortal couples marry. Given the association of these marriages with midsummer night and with the elemental forces of nature represented by the fairies, they clearly affirm the creativity of nature and man's place in it. Goethe has telescoped this aspect of the play into the reference to the anniversary of Oberon and Titania and into the orchestra of natural creatures, who faintly remind us of Shakespeare's Peaseblossom, Cobweb, and Mustardseed. Most important, he telescopes it by having the amateur theatrical performed for Oberon and Titania themselves. The effect of this telescoping is to clarify that marriage is not the only form of resolution in Shakespeare's play, for marriage resolves only the fairy plot and the human plot. The clown plot, however, is resolved by the performance of a play. Thus a play is the equivalent of a marriage; it offers a similar opportunity for unity in duality. Shakespeare already emphasizes the tie by having the play be about a failed marriage; significantly, the marriage fails because Pyramus and Thisbe mistake appearances for realities and destroy dualities. The play within the play thus no longer displaces the true epiphany, the affirmation of creative nature, but is itself an equivalent one. The "Walpurgis Night" begins as a celebration of nature and ends as a celebration of theatricality. But the two are really the same.

One last question: How does all this material relate to the Gretchen tragedy, which it interrupts just before the catastrophe? In very basic ways, it turns out. Earlier parts of the "Walpurgis Night" were strongly reminiscent of "Auerbach's Tavern" and "Witch's Kitchen" ("Witch's Kitchen" explicitly looks forward to the "Walpurgis Night," l. 2590). These scenes thus constitute a frame around the Gretchen tragedy; indeed we read "Witch's Kitchen" as a prologue to the Gretchen tragedy, based on the witch scenes in *Macbeth*. The Gretchen tragedy is thus framed by Shakespeare allusions. The frame is skewed in the sense that the second part comes just before the end rather than just after it, but surely this skewing is yet another formal equivalent to the deliberately unclear relationship of illusion to "reality" treated so intensively in the "Walpurgis Night's Dream." More important, I think, is to observe the progression in the "frame" from the operatic tragedy *Macbeth* in the prologue to the operatic comedy *A Midsum-*

mer Night's Dream in the epilogue. In its course the Gretchen tragedy is transformed, we saw, from sentimental tragedy to comic opera. The frame objectifies and embodies this transition.

On this basis the location of the "Walpurgis Night" just before the end of the Gretchen tragedy becomes more important. If it identifies for us the true genre of the Gretchen tragedy, then it tells us how to read it. It is characteristic of multiple plotting to show different aspects of the same phenomenon. Shakespeare, for example, shows serious or comic, high or low versions of the same action; Dickens shows all conceivable variations of the same quality or phenomenon. But what Goethe does here is quite unusual, for the Mephistopheles plot provides in effect a hermeneutic for the Gretchen plot. It may partly be a function of the extended period of composition of the drama, but for whatever reason, it is a fundamental characteristic of *Faust* that later parts of the play unfold and interpret the implications of the earlier parts. Nowhere is this phenomenon more obvious than in Part II of the drama, where over and over again we shall see issues treated at full length which we were able to perceive in Part I only by dint of very careful reading. Part II is above all an effort to unpack and properly display the implicit riches of Part I.

8

The Reality of Illusion:
"Charming Landscape"

The scenario of "Charming Landscape" is prepared by Ariel's last speech (*the* last speech before the dissolution) in the "Walpurgis Night's Dream":

> Whether loving Nature,
> Whether Spirit gave you wings,
> Follow my light track
> Up to the hill of roses!
> [ll. 4391–94]

In the context of the "Dream" the speech is a clear invitation to flee the realm of natural reality embodied in Puck for Ariel's realm of higher art. Here now is Ariel's realm. "Charming Landscape" stands in the same relation to the "Walpurgis Night's Dream" as Ariel does to Puck. This is also the relation of the macrocosm to the earth spirit, of the great world of Part II to the small world of Part I. In the "Dream" natural reality was transformed into play; this scene proceeds from play—a spirit ballet—to the higher meaning of natural reality. "Charming Landscape" is thus a *réplique* to and, in a sense, continuation of the "Intermezzo" of the "Dream." Like the "Dream," it interprets what has come before. There have already been numerous occasions in the analysis to look ahead to "Charming Landscape" as Faust's first articulation of his true relation to the Absolute. But the scene also maps out what is to come; both formally and thematically

"Charming Landscape" defines the unique aspects of Part II as well as its continuities to Part I. For the *Faust* initiate the scene is undeniably the heart of the play. Since the scene offers few interpretive difficulties, the discussion here will focus on the general significance of its centrality. [1]

"Charming Landscape" is, then, Ariel's intermezzo. What does this mean? It is a world of art, for it begins with a ballet. But since the performers are nature spirits, it is a world of Nature, that is, nature under the sign of spirit. The spirits magically heal Faust of the wounds inflicted by the Gretchen tragedy, so that, they say, he can get on with the business of life. We understand: so that *we* can get on with the business of the play. There is nothing demonic about the magic of this scene; Mephistopheles is not even present, although it would be difficult to distinguish these nature spirits from those whom Mephisto sent to Faust in Part I. As a result, "Charming Landscape" explicitly confirms our interpretation of the true significance of magic in the play as authorial artifice.

If this world is magical according to the same rules as Part I, it is also natural in the same way. For the Nature that Ariel and the other spirits weave about Faust is nothing other than the Nature he sought in that perennial speech to the moon, where he longed to hover and weave with the spirits in the moonlight. In that speech and in the vision of the macrocosm Faust longed to bathe; here the elves actually do bathe him, in order, as they say, to return him to the light. The symbolism of bathing as an act of rebirth is even more open here than in those early passages. There we had to hear the religious overtones in the language, but here they are explicit: Faust rises as a new Adam in Paradise. This is perhaps the purest but by no means last instance of the fulfillment of Faust's first wish in the play.

That wish had been fulfilled before—in Gretchen's room, for example—but never quite so literally with the moon so fully and actively present. It may seem surprising that the moon should play an important role, since otherwise the sun has long since succeeded the moon as symbol of the Absolute. Indeed, nowhere is this symbol more powerfully incarnated than in the sunrise at the end of this scene. Yet the moon will again succeed the sun as the dominant light in the

---

[1] A good close reading and thematic analysis may be found in Stuart Atkins, *Goethe's "Faust": A Literary Analysis* (Cambridge: Harvard University Press, 1964), 101–5.

"Classical Walpurgis Night" as it already was in the "Walpurgis Night" of Part I. The moon is a weaker light and has been associated until now with the obscurity and inaccessibility of the Absolute. But the moon is weaker because it is reflected. The moon mediates the light of the sun as art mediates perception of the Absolute.[2] The renewed importance of the full moon here thus retrospectively illuminates a previous hidden level of meaning in that first moon to which Faust turned in "Night." From the perspective of "Charming Landscape" that moon not only embodied Nature but prefigured the insight that Nature was the equivalent of art. The "Walpurgis Night's Dream" first clearly identified these two manifestations of the Absolute with one another; "Charming Landscape" translates the insight into the symbolic vocabulary of the drama.

The way in which the wish of the moon speech is fulfilled here takes account of the developments of Part I, for the scene shows a series of rebirths into nature and light. Ariel defines the program in his first speech, then the incantatory spirit song moves the world from darkness to light, from sleep to new activity. After the sunrise Faust repeats the process in his own monologue. This speech recreates the world around him, then renounces direct vision of the sun-Absolute to accept the world as the proper sphere of activity for man. When Faust turns from the brightness of the rising sun, he repeats his earlier inability to face the earth spirit. The line "The colorful refraction, that is life" (l. 4727), surely the most famous line of Part II, affirms Faust's acceptance of the lessons of Part I: knowledge of the Absolute is accessible only through the mediation of the world.

It is impossible to overlook the triumphant affirmative tone of this scene; nevertheless it would be naive to equate the triumph with a simple glossing over or erasure of the moral issues inevitably raised by the Gretchen tragedy, however little those issues may need to be at the center of discussion. In fact, this scene is the first in the play that allows ethics really to come to the fore. The scene uses religious vocabulary intensively—holiness, Paradise, eternity—as well as the imagery of bathing. The action of Nature becomes indistinguishable from the action of Grace. The scene thus enacts a ritual purification,

---

[2]The moon is consistently associated with art in Goethe's moon poems. See, for example, "To Luna" (1768), "To the Moon" (1778), "Darkness Settled from Above" (1827).

the very possibility of which admits a need for such purification. As the elves finish their work, they add a new dimension to the concept of activity that also takes account of this moral sense:

> All is open to the noble
> Who understand and swiftly grasp.
> [ll. 4664–65]

This passage makes explicit the two preconditions that morally validate the restless activity of a Faust—innate nobility and comprehension. In the "Prologue in Heaven" the Lord had indeed long since said, "A good man in his dark urge / Is ever conscious of the proper course," (ll. 328–29). On the one hand, this vague assurance is now sharpened; on the other, the restatement in "Charming Landscape" calls attention to these important preconditions at a time when we may well be worrying about the morality of the play.

Finally, when Faust awakens, he is immediately ready to strive. This larger pattern of loss, rebirth into the world, and new striving is of course familiar from Part I. To understand fully why it is not a moral failure to begin striving again so quickly after the destruction of Gretchen, we should consider for a moment what Faust's alternative would be. Suppose for a moment he awakened to grief for Gretchen, repentance and breast-beating for his part in the affair. This would be to adopt the stance of Gretchen herself in "Dungeon," to refuse to let the past be past; it is a stance that is unacceptable in *Faust*. But to let the past be past is not to erase it. The poet in the "Prelude" and Faust himself, after the Easter chorus and in "Forest and Cavern," have articulated the process by which the past, as memory, becomes inspiration. And indeed this concept will be nowhere more important than in Part II, where Goethe will ransack the memory of Western culture to create Helen and where the memory of Gretchen herself will appear to inspire Faust both before and after his death. The elves do not obliterate Faust's unsavory past; under their influence, as under that of Shakespeare's Ariel, the experienced reality undergoes "a sea-change into something rich and strange."

Not only the past but all of nature undergoes such a sea-change under the influence of the spirit world. This is the profoundest of the many senses of the rainbow image at the end of the scene. The influence of the sun transforms the water droplets into an orderly array of color. Contrary to the accepted Newtonian theory of color, Goethe did not believe that the prismatic effect of the water droplets simply dispersed and made separately visible the different kinds of light that constitute white light. According to his *Theory of Color* (1810)—the single achievement of which Goethe was probably most proud—color was generated by the interaction between pure white light and material bodies. To translate this into the terms of our discussion, color is the result of the combination of spirit and world; it is Nature, the only realm through which perception of spirit, of the Absolute, is possible.

This new image for Nature carries a multilayered message. First, because of its scientific basis, it yokes spiritual or philosophic to scientific truth. The implication, then, is that *Faust*, addressing itself to all aspects of knowledge, is truly cosmic in its significance. Second, because the rainbow encompasses all possible colors, it offers an infinitely variegated Nature. Faust is now offered the possibility of much more detailed perception of the world around him and, therefore, of the Absolute. And indeed, in Part II, Faust's quest is articulated in an amazing wealth of geographical and historical detail. Third, the reader can scarcely overlook the biblical significance of the rainbow, the sign of God's promise that there would never be another flood (Genesis 9:8–17). As in *Faust*, so too in the Bible, the rainbow signifies that previous crimes are now washed away. More important, the rainbow signifies the existence of God (or spirit) somewhere outside of the world. This is not to suggest a traditional religious significance in *Faust*. To see a rainbow at sunrise Faust must look west, but to see the place of God's presence in church one must look east. Spirit is not to be mistaken for God. What is important here is the *signifying* aspect; the rainbow is referred to three times as a "sign" in the biblical account. This signifying aspect relates the rainbow as natural phenomenon to the realm of art. In the rainbow Goethe has formulated a symbol that is simultaneously nature and art, Puck and Ariel.

Faust reads the symbol not in terms of these ultimate profundities but, as we have already seen, as a kind of summary moral to Part I. For him the rainbow embodies his renunciation of direct transcendence and his turn into the world. Faust must turn away from the sun as he had to turn away from the earth spirit; the colored refraction mediates his perception of the sun just as, in effect, Mephistopheles mediated his perception of the Absolute. In this respect Faust's rainbow has a predecessor that further contributes to the richness of the image, Byron's *Manfred,* written in 1816 under the impact of *Faust, Part I.* Byron's exposure to *Faust* appears to have been limited to an ex tempore oral translation of parts of the play done for him by Monk Lewis in the summer of 1816. Nevertheless the limitations on Byron's knowledge of the text are less important in this context than the fact that Goethe documentably perceived the play as a deliberate response to *Faust.*[3] For our concern here is with the way "Charming Landscape" responds to *Manfred.* The setting of "Charming Landscape" repeats the setting of Act II, scene ii, of *Manfred:* "A lower Valley in the Alps.—A Cataract." Bryon's waterfall also generates a rainbow (sunbow, as Byron calls it), and from this sunbow Manfred conjures the spirit of the place, the Witch of the Alps. Like Ariel, the witch is an exquisitely beautiful spirit, who mediates between the powers of immortality and the earth, and from whom Manfred seeks healing. But here the similarities end. The sympathetic witch can only help Manfred if he subordinates himself to her; however this is the one thing Manfred cannot do. Having once commanded spirits he refuses to serve this spirit of nature or any other spirit. And in the next scene he ascends—indeed, transcends—to the summit of the Jungfrau to confront Arimanes, ruler of the destinies and apparent guardian of the boundary between life and death. In his refusal to subordinate himself to the spirit of Nature, Manfred is much more "Faustian" than Faust. That Manfred still insists on transcendence must have appeared to Goethe as either a misunderstanding or a perverse distortion of the essence of his *Faust.* Thus when Faust accepts the message of the rainbow, he undoes Manfred's perversity. The rainbow not only recapitulates the message of *Faust I;* it also reiterates it in the face of what was only the first in a long series of misreadings of Goethe's subversive conception of the Faust theme.

Once the rainbow is understood as an implicit critique of Byron's presumed rejection of *Faust I, Faust II* gains a whole new level of complexity. Now it must be recognized as a work that reflects on its own meaning and upon its own status as an ambiguous sign. *Faust I* raised questions on the epistemological function of drama in general; the "Walpurgis Night's Dream" ruminated in sophisticated ways on

---

[3]See, for example, his review of *Manfred* (1820). E. M. Butler offers an extensive but unfortunately hostile analysis of the relations between the two poets in *Byron and Goethe: Analysis of a Passion* (London: Bowes & Bowes, 1956).

the relation of drama to reality. But nowhere does *Faust I* obviously take account of a real, particular audience. Now, however, this possibility has been opened to the second part; drama, too, will be perceived now in much more distinct detail and variety than in Part I.

The rainbow also has another predecessor in the Faust chapbook itself. The expanded 1599 edition of the chapbook contains a brief anecdote in which Faust reaches out the window and catches hold of a rainbow.[4] Here the rainbow demonstrates Faust's supernatural powers, not his renunciation of direct access to the supernatural. The rainbow would appear to be yet another example of Goethe's subversion of the Faust tradition, but there is more to it than that. The idea of catching hold of the rainbow introduces a new way of understanding the Faustian problem. The Absolute is to be perceived, we are shown, not in transcendence, but in nature or in art, in the rainbow. Yet as the "Walpurgis Night" most vividly demonstrated, Nature and art, like the rainbow, are illusory; they cannot be grasped. The word *grasp* bridges the gap, in a sense, because it involves both literal and figurative implications: it means both "catch hold of" and "comprehend." German however, separates the cognate root *greifen* into literal and figurative meanings by the use of prefixes: *ergreifen* means "catch hold of"; *begreifen* means "comprehend." The chapbook uses the word *ergreifen*. Faust's act is supernatural because it is literally impossible. The earth spirit had rejected Faust in Part I with

> You resemble the spirit you comprehend [*begreifst*],
> Not me!
>
> [ll. 512–13]

But now Goethe uses the same word as the chapbook at the end of the spirit song:

> All is open to the noble
> Who understand and swiftly grasp [*ergreift*].
> [ll. 4664–65]

The separation of the concept of understanding emphasizes the literal concreteness of the grasping here. Yet what does Goethe offer for

---

[4]Chap. 72 in the edition of Richard Benz, *Historia von D. Johann Fausten* (Stuttgart: Reclam, 1966). This chapter is not available in English.

Faust to grasp in the scene but that elusive, ungraspable rainbow! The contradiction reveals what the skeptical reader has suspected all along: Goethe's elegant symbolic solution to the romantic quest for transcendence in the world raises more problems than it solves. If Faust cannot grasp the rainbow, then he cannot perceive the Absolute in the world. What, then, does it mean to grasp a rainbow? And how do you guarantee that a rainbow will be there to grasp? These are precisely the forms that Faust's quest takes in Part II: how does one generate a rainbow at will, and how does one grasp it? The Helen that Faust literally embraces in Act III is only the most obvious solution to this problem. There will be others, as we shall see.

Nothing undergoes a greater sea-change under the influence of spirit in *Faust* than the drama itself. The reader perceives immediately that he has entered a different world in *Faust II*, yet it is not so easy to find a language to describe the difference. We might start with the absence of Mephistopheles. In Part I, Mephisto summoned the spirits of nature onto the stage to lull Faust to sleep; here they come of their own accord. The elfin chorus is accompanied by an Aeolian, or wind, harp. This instrument, which sounded in response to the breeze with no human agency, was conceived in the romantic period to be the voice of Nature itself. This chorus, unlike the spirit chorus of Part I, does not so much describe Nature as speak with its very voice. It does not generate an interlude separate from the action of the play but itself generates the action of the scene, the passage of the night. The elliptical and ambiguous grammar of the essentially untranslatable spirit song has an incantatory effect. As the language shifts from lullaby to exhortation, from ambiguity to clarity, it seems itself to generate the light, which grows brighter from stanza to stanza, and to evoke the climactic sunrise. This passage, one of the great masterpieces of German lyric, enacts what is described at the beginning of Genesis, the voice creates light. There are few places in literature where one has such a strong sense of the *logos* at work.

Furthermore, if we compare the scene to Faust's sunset speech in "Outside the City Gate," we see that now the light descends on its own accord into the world; no human subject has to transcend the world to follow it. Nature exists and acts in and of itself in Part II, without being perceived or described or invoked by the mind of a character. Both the sunset speech and the song of Mephisto's spirits structured their descriptions of the world, we may remember, in terms of the four elements. In "Charming Landscape" the visible world is actually made of these elements, especially of water and fire. The world in this scene is one of mists, moisture, and waterfalls; it is lit up by a sea of fire (ll. 4707–10). The rainbow is the synthesis of fire and water literally visible to the spectator. Henceforth in Part II fire and water will remain the organizing categories. The cosmos is no longer just invoked in the play, it is manifestly present on the stage.

Faust's monologue reveals the same pattern. This is really the first time in the play (although the speeches at the beginning of the "Walpurgis Night" tend in this direction) that Faust speaks objectively about Nature and not about his reaction to it. His magnificent speech generates the Garden of Eden around him. As in the spirit song, Faust does not describe a created or existing world but lists attributes at the moment of their coming into being. Indeed these attributes only exist for Faust in that they are perceived and articulated. This is a paradise in the process of becoming, as line 4694 says: "A paradise comes into being around me." Faust thus repeats the creative act of the word in the spirit song. The reaction to the rainbow in the waterfall is typical in this regard. Here Faust questions the waterfall in search of a valid generalization. How different this is from his description of the waterfall at the end of "Forest and Cavern," where it is the image for titanic Faust destroying innocent Gretchen. That was a projection of a highly individualized Faust in a very particular emotional state; this waterfall objectively embodies an impersonal truth.

Nature is now not only manifestly present on the stage but also manifestly symbolic. It is not subjective projection but impersonal sign. The human realm is explicitly subordinate to the cosmic, natural order, and this order is no longer personified in the anthropomorphic Lord of the "Prologue in Heaven." Faust's monologue is in *terza rima*, Dante's meter. This suggests that we are to understand the speech as a *réplique* to the Dante-izing observed in the "Walpurgis Night." If that reminded us of the beginning of the *Inferno*, this passage reminds us much more of the *Paradiso*, where the vision of God is a vision of light at the apex of the cosmic order. The important implication of the Dante reference here is the way Dante the pilgrim gradually evaporates in the increasing revelation of the order of the universe, the way the subject disappears before the objectivity of the cosmos. The drama has become openly and explicitly thematic.

But *terza rima* is not only Dante's meter; it is also used for dramatic monologue in the dramas of Calderón. The following contemporary description shows, in fact, how close the scene is to the great master of thematic drama:

> This blessed one has escaped from the labyrinthine wilderness of doubt into the security of faith, from whence he observes and describes the stormy course of the world with untroubled peace of mind. . . . Even his tears reflect each of them Heaven above, like dewdrops on a flower, glittering in the sun. His poetry . . . is an inexhaustible paean to the glories of the creation. Thus with eternally fresh and joyous amazement he celebrates the productions of Nature and of human art, as if he had only just seen them for the first time in yet unfaded splendor. It is Adam's first awakening paired with such fluency and skill of expression, with such penetration of the most profound natural laws as only sublime spiritual development and mature reflectiveness can generate.[5]

The passage seems a remarkably accurate reading of Faust's monologue, but August Wilhelm Schlegel, from whose *Lectures on Dramatic Art and Literature* (1809) it comes, is talking here about Calderón. Schlegel's translations first inspired Goethe's enthusiasm for Calderón. Whether this particular passage was present to some level of Goethe's consciousness as he composed "Charming Landscape" seems less important to me than the fact that Schlegel's description of Calderón is so extraordinarily appropriate to it. It documents the profound affinity between *Faust* and the Spanish dramatist, even where there are no explicit borrowings, as there are elsewhere in Part II.[6] Until now in the argument, Calderón has been present as the embodiment of a model of a less familiar form of drama that, I have been trying to show, underlies Goethe's conception of drama, even in his early years. It is in this sense only that I argued that Calderón was present in Part I. But in Part II he emerges as a consciously accepted "ancestor" of Goethe's play. The drama is implicitly a thematic drama in the first part, even though it often looks like an Aristotelian mimetic drama. In Part II now there is never the danger of taking the surface

---

[5]A. W. Schlegel, *Vorlesungen über dramatische Kunst und Literatur: Zweiter Teil*, Lecture 35 in *Kritische Schriften und Briefe*, ed. Edgar Lohner, 6 (Stuttgart: Kohlhammer, 1967), 266; translation mine.

[6]In a seminal essay, "Goethe, Calderon, and *Faust: Der Tragödie zweiter Teil*," Stuart Atkins extensively documents motifs borrowed from Calderón in Part II (*Germanic Review* 28 [1953]: 83–98). Atkins also suggests that the form of "Charming Landscape" is, in fact, imitated from Calderón in *Goethe's "Faust*," 102n.

illusion to be the poet's prime concern; everything that happens will clearly reflect some higher meaning.

It would be misleading to think that this stylistic development is unique on Goethe's part or that Goethe was being intentionally esoteric in Part II. Mozart's *Magic Flute*, surely one of the most popular texts of any sort at the turn of the century, stands in exactly the same relationship to its source, Wieland's *Oberon*, as Part II does to Part I of *Faust*. In both texts a human couple must prove its superior virtue through trials by fire and water in order to reconcile the warring rulers of the cosmos (Oberon and Titania, Sarastro and the Queen of the Night). In Wieland this plot is clothed in probabilistic, albeit exotic, detail. The quarrel between Oberon and Titania is motivated; the couple is shipwrecked then almost burned at the stake; Oberon and Titania are shown together at the end. In Mozart's opera, by contrast, the plot is consistently allegorized. The hostility between the Queen of the Night and Sarastro has no superficial motivation, only cosmic significance, the trials are reduced to symbolic passages through the portals of the respective elements, the forces of light and dark are reconciled only symbolically in the marriage of the younger generation (the Queen of the Night herself is driven off at the end, not reconciled). Although Wieland's *Oberon* does not lack orientalizing elements, it contains no ritual. By contrast almost all of the oriental elements in *The Magic Flute* appear in ritual contexts, Masonic and other. *The Magic Flute* is by no means so complex or difficult a text as *Faust II*; nevertheless the parallel shows that the tendency of the second part to an explicitly thematic mode is hardly unique.

"Charming Landscape" evokes a particularly relevant parallel development in the visual arts. Goethe certainly knew Guido Reni's fresco *Aurora*, on the ceiling of the Casino Rospigliosi in Rome. It might be assumed, then, to have influenced his conception of the sunrise, where Phoebus thunders out in his chariot, accompanied by the Hours. Guercino's related fresco of 1621–1623 in the Villa Ludovisi is perhaps slightly more dramatic and includes a few *putti*, some of whom might be construed to be hiding themselves in the rocks like Goethe's elves. But neither painting contains the crucial motif of the noise, and neither seems to be an especially significant model for the scene. Nevertheless, if we compare either or both with another dawn picture that Goethe certainly knew, *The Morning* (1803) by the German romantic painter Philipp Otto Runge, we observe a

Guido Reni's fresco *Aurora* was painted in the ceiling of the Casino Rospigliosi, Rome, in 1613. Courtesy of the Istituto Centrale per il Catalogo e la Documentazione, Rome (E 34489).

significant stylistic shift.[7] Both Reni and Guercino show a chariot taking off from the earth into the sky; Runge shows groups of spirits on a lily between earth and heaven. Barely visible in the mist beneath them are the earth and some roses, the flowers of earthly love. The lily, the flower the angel always carries in paintings of the Annunciation, signifies heavenly love. The topmost spirits support the morning star. Thus the spirits are enclosed in a significant—symbolic—cosmic framework; the whole is framed by another allegorical network of flowers and spirits that move from death and darkness at bottom center through water up to the heavenly hosts worshiping the holy name of God inscribed in Hebrew at center top. In 1808 Runge did a more elaborate oil version of this theme. The later version has the figure of Aurora in the center, so that it is at first glance more comparable to Reni's and Guercino's treatments. But in all other respects the painting is even more intensely preoccupied with figures, objects, and tonalities *only* as signs of higher meaning, with essentially no importance attached to their existence on the literal level. Again, I have no intention of arguing that Runge's *Morning* ought to be considered a source for the sunrise in "Charming Landscape." But I do want to show that whatever language we use to describe the difference between the two parts of *Faust* describes an important aspect of what we might call the romantic sensibility. Where *Faust* at first appears to be unique and esoteric is where it is in fact most typically romantic.

But we still need language to describe that difference. The most obvious word to use would appear to be *allegory,* but that term presents several problems. The first is that Goethe himself used the word mainly negatively in contrast to his own conception of *symbol.*[8] Sec-

---

[7]Goethe expressed considerable reservation toward the mystical Christian allegorizing of the school to which Runge belonged. Nevertheless, he owned and prominently displayed etchings of the *Times of Day* cycle to which *The Morning* belongs; in 1817 he called in print upon the unknown owner of the plates of these etchings to issue more copies (in *Über Kunst und Altertum,* 1 (1817), 2; *Gesamtausgabe der Werke und Schriften in zweiundzwanzig Bänden,* 17 [Stuttgart: Cotta, 1962], 517).

[8]Goethe's so-called theory of allegory and symbol is to be found in a letter to Schiller, August 16, 1797 (*Briefwechsel mit Friedrich Schiller,* ed. Karl Schmidt, *Gedenkausgabe,* 20 (Zurich: Artemis, 1964), 394–97) and in scattered aphorisms (*Maximen und Reflexionen,* nos. 279, 314, 1112, 1113). Essentially the difference is that allegory substitutes an image for a concept (*Begriff*), which is accessible to the understanding, while a symbol is a specific concrete example of an idea (*Idee*), which is not accessible to the human understanding and therefore incommensurable. Goethe's language here is Kantian; in the terminology we have been using, Goethe's *symbol* can represent the Absolute or ideal; *allegory* cannot. *Symbol* is therefore more truly poetic for Goethe.

Philipp Otto Runge drew this allegorical version of the dawn, titled *The Morning*, in 1803. Courtesy of the Hamburger Kunsthalle. © Ralph Klein-hempel.

ondly, allegory implies the presence of an idea behind the poetic text, and in a notorious utterance Goethe asserted there were no ideas behind his texts.[9] I do not think either of these objections needs to be taken very seriously. Allegory had fallen on evil days in the eighteenth century, and Goethe uses the word in the eighteenth-century context; however he had nothing but respect for the greatest allegorical dramatist of our tradition, Calderón. If we use allegory in a broader sense than simply poetry that clothes abstractions in bodies, we will mean something quite different from what Goethe did when he used the term in his polemics.

And indeed, I use *allegory* here to mean any text that consistently calls attention to the fact that it does not mean just what it says. This is essentially Angus Fletcher's definition in *Allegory: The Theory of a Symbolic Mode*, and as Fletcher himself points out, almost all literature is to some extent allegorical.[10] This insight raises problems from the other side. Certainly *Faust I*, read as I have been reading it, is already allegorical in these terms. This is not so much of a problem as it seems, however, for in Fletcher's thinking about allegory, which I would like to exploit here, allegory is a *mode* of writing, fundamentally opposed to what he calls the mimetic mode (and what I have been calling the illusionist, or Aristotelian, tradition). In effect Fletcher offers a scale ranging between these two poles. A given author or a given work may be more or less allegorical, more or less mimetic. The various criteria for what one might call the allegoricity of a text enable us to distinguish the relative positions of the two parts of *Faust* on such a scale and to distinguish in useful ways between the styles of the two texts.

Many of the qualities Fletcher finds normally associated with allegorical texts have already been identified repeatedly in *Faust I* and will continue to appear in *Faust II*. The more important of these are the quest structure, a tendency to be operatic, episodic construction, and a fundamental underlying dualism.[11] Though richly present in

[9]To Eckermann, May 6, 1827: Johann Peter Eckermann, *Gespräche mit Goethe in den letzten Jahren seines Lebens*, Gedenkausgabe, 24 (Zurich: Artemis, 1948), 636.

[10]Angus Fletcher, *Allegory: The Theory of a Symbolic Mode* (Ithaca: Cornell University Press, 1970), 8.

[11]In essentially all the allegories Fletcher deals with, this is a Manichean dualism of good and evil; romantic allegory may well be unique in replacing the Manichean structure with an amoral dialectic. In the interests of saving space, I have rather arbitrarily chosen but a few of Fletcher's rich selection of characteristics of allegory; the

Part I, these qualities will be even more obvious in Part II, especially the episodic construction, which is often a stumbling block to inexperienced readers.

Nevertheless, there are two very important aspects of allegorical presentation that distinguish Part II from Part I. Both of these have to do with the imagery utilized in the allegorical mode. The first point is that allegory prohibits our normal sense of the world. Fletcher's illustration is the isolation of objects in surrealist painting; a relevant literary term that comes to mind is *alienation.* I argued that there is already some alienation in Part I in that we are constantly offered plays within plays and elaborate framing devices. This is true, but the framing devices are necessary because the plays within the play in fact do not violate our normal sense of the world. The Gretchen tragedy, for example, without the context of the frames is easily read as the great love tragedy of the modern world; without the frames, "Night" is easily read as a penetrating study of the modern mind. The use of the supernatural is consistently ironized; for those who prefer to overlook the irony (which, as Fletcher argues, is itself a relative of allegory) the supernatural can be readily psychologized and thus explained away. Although I have tried to forestall this kind of normalizing reading, *Faust I* can be—and all too often is—read in a way that keeps our sense of the probable from being too badly violated. It is not possible, however, to read *Faust II* this way. From the unmediated appearance of the elves and the miraculous healing of Faust on, the play constantly violates our sense of the normal. Indeed, it frequently violates the characters' sense of the normal as well, as we shall see in Act I, where the members of the emperor's court and the master of the emperor's revels are unsettled by the incursions of uncanny forces into their world. Strangely enough, it is Mephisto's relative unimportance in Part II that brings about this alienation. His presence in Part I serves as a convention to explain deviations from the norm of probability. Without him the work suddenly looks very peculiar. In retrospect we realize that Mephisto was a mediator not only to the real world but to spirit as well, for he made all of its incursions into *Faust I* appear somehow normal.

The second quality with regard to which Part II is more obviously

---

ones listed seem to me to apply to *Faust* with a minimum of explanation, but they are by no means the only ones.

allegorical than Part I is perhaps Fletcher's single most important category, one he calls *kosmos*.[12] This is the term Aristotle uses for ornament in the *Poetics*, and it has two connotations—first, as an ornament (e.g., object of dress) or symbol that implies rank in a hierarchy; second, as a reference to the whole order of the universe. *Kosmos* thus refers to a kind of imagery that connects its referent to a larger context or to several contexts at once. The theocentric nonillusionist drama of a Calderón is obviously "kosmic" (or "cosmic") in a way that the anthropocentric drama of the Enlightenment is not. The implicit meaning of *universe* in the term also calls to mind the whole structure of microcosm-macrocosm relationships that pervade Renaissance thought. Once again, I would not deny that *Faust I* is cosmic; but the cosmic moments in *Faust I* are self-consciously stagy (the "Prologue in Heaven" and the invocation of the macrocosm are good examples). In *Faust II*, by contrast, there is scarcely a moment that is not explicitly cosmic. Faust proceeds from the emperor's court, where figures are identified only by their places in the hierarchy to the "Classical Walpurgis Night," peopled entirely by known mythological figures, to a love affair with Helen of Troy. He travels through an impersonal world defined by traditional coordinates. The relation to myth in each part clarifies this difference with regard to *kosmos*. In Part I, we remember, the rejection of Faust by the earth spirit was a veiled replay of the story of Zeus and Semele. The important point here is that the classical reference is veiled. In Part II, Faust confronts a fully unveiled mythological world. He converses with sphinxes, griffons, and river nymphs; rides on the back of a centaur; begets a child on Helen. The cosmic connections are no longer veiled or at best referred to; they are always openly present on the stage. One wonders if this is not perhaps the one thing Goethe really learned from Calderón—to write openly cosmic drama.[13]

Might one then call Part I symbolic and Part II allegorical? One might, but only, I think, if one uses the terms in Fletcher's sense, as

[12]Explicit discussion of this term is to be found in Fletcher, *Allegory*, 108–46.

[13]Goethe is traditionally considered not to have been influenced by Calderón because he once said as much to Eckermann (May 12, 1825 [Eckermann, *Gespräche*, 158]). But like so much else in the conversations with Eckermann, Goethe's bald assertion that Calderón had no influence on him must be taken very circumspectly. Among other things, we might note that almost all of *Faust II* was written *after* the remark in question, which does not disallow the possibility of future influence. On this question see also Atkins, "Goethe, Calderon, and *Faust*," 83–89.

extreme points that define a continuum. In this case the distinction between them is that "in the case of allegory there is no intention of ultimate paradox, whereas in myth and 'symbol' the poet refuses to admit that reason or perception provide the highest wisdom."[14] Even in this case there is a special wrinkle induced by the historical circumstances. Ultimately, allegory is not paradoxical, because it is cosmic; it contextualizes itself in the accepted order of the cosmos. But in *Faust*, as we have seen, and indeed in the romantic period in general, the fundamental problem was that the cosmos was inscrutable; the Kantian dilemma arose precisely out of the recognition that the cosmos was unknowable. But if romantic allegory can contextualize only in an inscrutable cosmos, it must be ultimately paradoxical, and thus, at bottom symbolic. All romantic allegory will necessarily waver between symbol and allegory. The traditional discomfort of Goethe scholars with the word *allegory*, or the English-speaking reader's sense that reading *Faust II* is not quite like reading *The Faerie Queene*, is thus not entirely unfounded. It is this wavering that, on the one hand, makes it so difficult to specify the differences between the two parts of the play and, on the other, makes the second part of the play such a challenge to its readers.

[14]Fletcher, *Allegory*, 322.

9

The Spirit of Fire:
Act I

Act I has scarcely been the most popular part of *Faust II*. Its usual fate is to be considered in pieces. "Charming Landscape" becomes (to some extent properly) a prologue to all of Part II; the Helen sequence, from the Mothers to the end of the act (again, to some extent properly), part of a unit formed by Acts II and III. The rest is turned in some way into a precursor of the Helen sequence. Nevertheless, there is much to be learned from Goethe's arrangement of the parts of *Faust II*. Act I has a coherent and significant structure of its own; it makes important statements about how to read the rest of the play and about the nature of history and art, the central concerns of Part II.

If we begin with the assumption, then, that Act I constitutes a functional unit, let us consider its structure. First, "Charming Landscape" stands alone in a world entirely independent of the plot of Act I, as a prologue at a higher level of abstraction. It poses the problem that Act I deals with but that is not solved until much later in the play; in this sense it is the prologue to all of Part II as well. The rest of Act I falls readily into three parts: an introductory scene at the imperial court (ll. 4728–5064), a masque (ll. 5065–5986), the return to the court with shows of various sorts, most obviously the paper-money scheme and the dumb show. The masque itself, again, readily divides into three parts, and it turns out that the three parts of the masque correspond to the three parts of the act itself. The task now is to understand the significance of the structure.

"Charming Landscape" clearly formulates a new level of understanding of the Faustian problem. The Absolute is to be grasped, we have seen, not in transcendence but in nature, in the rainbow generated from the sun's rays (pure spirit) shining in the real drops of water. In this formulation the Absolute may be grasped only figuratively: it can be *begriffen* but not *ergriffen*. This necessary renunciation of the literal is all the more curious because only sixty lines earlier the elves had triumphantly concluded their song, "All is open to the noble / Who understand and swiftly grasp" (ll. 4664–65). The problems posed by this scene are: (1) how to generate the rainbow at will and (2) how to hold on to it (*ergreifen*). The obvious solution is the Helen of Act III, whom Faust can literally embrace. But in Act I the solution is first proposed in simpler terms. In effect, Faust digs for the pot of gold from which the rainbow is seen to emanate.[1] Let us examine our rudimentary structure for the rest of the act in these terms.

The first segment is the scene "Imperial Residence, Throneroom." The imperial palace is a world of magnificent appearances, but the problem is that it is a world only of appearances. The descrepancy between appearance and reality pervades the scene. Behind the splendid and luxurious facade of the court ritual the impoverished empire languishes in chaos. The figures all have roles rather than identities. Only Mephistopheles has a name as well as a function (and he here plays the *role* of court jester), while the astrologer speaks the part openly provided him by Mephistopheles. Similarly, the stylistic difficulty deliberately obscures the meaning to be conveyed and thus turns language into a kind of empty facade. The chancellor articulates this tendency of the style in a typically confusing formulation:

> I painted a black picture, but an even thicker veil
> Is what I would prefer to draw over it.
>
> [ll. 4807–8]

The difficulty stems here from the use of darkness in adjacent but opposing formulations. The first clause seems to imply that the speaker wishes his picture could have been brighter, but in the second line

---

[1] German folklore associates gold with rainbows in a variety of ways, including this one. See Hanns Bächtold-Stäubli, *Handwörterbuch des deutschen Aberglaubens*, 7 (Berlin and Leipzig: de Gruyter, 1935–36), 587–96. Rainbows are, incidentally, also understood in German folklore as bridges between heaven and earth by which angels cross into the world (ibid., 588). Here is yet another mediating aspect of the rainbow.

he wishes to obscure it even more. Furthermore, the scene seems to have no connection to what precedes it, for we move from "Charming Landscape" to the emperor's court with no warning or explanation at all. Without this causal connection the world presented here seems to have no grounding in nature or in the transcendent Absolute, the organizing categories of *Faust* up until now. As a result, finally, the Faust myth itself comes to seem a completely arbitrary vehicle for Goethe's play. And indeed, the thematics of the play will be determined even less by the Faust myth in Part II than in Part I. Although the episodes of Acts I and III are suggested by the chapbook, Goethe no longer bothers to subvert their original significance; instead he simply goes his own way. Henceforth the Faust theme, too, is completely divorced from what was once its essence.

The imperial officials within the scene all perceive the emptiness of the appearance. Indeed, they define the state of the empire in terms of emptiness—empty coffers or empty wine casks. But gold and wine are the two most common metamorphoses in the play of the element fire, which in turn—although supposedly the Mephistophelean element—has been the most consistent symbol for the Absolute throughout Part I and in "Charming Landscape." We have returned once again to the chaotic world of "Auerbach's Tavern" and "Witch's Kitchen," reality uninformed by spirit. This world of empty appearances is, so to speak, a random collection of water droplets; it needs gold, the rays of the sun, fire, to be transformed into a rainbow and become significant.

The language of the scene reinforces this pattern. Mephistopheles proposes to solve the problems of the empire by recovering gold buried to protect it from the wandering hordes that destroyed the Roman Empire.[2] The way in which he talks about it, for example— "But wisdom can dig out the deepest things" (l. 4892)—uncovers the implicit significance of the gold, for "the deepest things" are also "the ultimate profundities." The qualities the gold evokes in its serious seekers are the familiar qualities of the Faustian search for the Abso-

---

[2]Indeed, the widespread belief that treasure is to be found at the end of the rainbow has been attributed to the fact that heavy rains often uncovered Celtic and Roman coins (Bächtold-Stäubli, *Handwörterbuch*, 594). A classic discussion of the broader significance of gold in Goethe's work may be found in Wilhelm Emrich, *Die Symbolik von "Faust II": Sinn und Vorformen* (Frankfurt am Main and Bonn: Athenäum, 1964), 188–212.

lute—wisdom and "The talented man's powers of Nature and Spirit" (l. 4896). Of course this language is in the mouth of the devil; perhaps we should share the position of the chancellor, who responds, "Nature and Spirit—you cannot talk this way to Christians" (l. 4897), and then, three lines later, "Nature is sin, Spirit is the devil" (l. 4900). But let us remember that in "Charming Landscape" the elves, with their "spirit power" (*Geistergrösse*, l. 4617), heal Faust and prepare one of the great moments of the play. Their leader, Ariel, is a nature spirit, a *Natur-Geist*. Mephistopheles thus speaks the language of the mainstream of the play; the expected irony is not there, and the chancellor is more correct than he knows when he says, "Spirit is the devil." Mephistopheles is indeed a nature spirit, for he enables Faust to perceive nature infused with spirit (or mind or the Absolute). Here he does it in the most obvious way possible, by revealing the gold shining in the depths, just as he had once before when he and Faust were climbing the Brocken to the Walpurgis Night celebrations. Furthermore, Mephistopheles offers the emperor the same *natural* alternative to his magic that he had offered Faust in "Witch's Kitchen." The emperor can take a shovel and dig for the gold himself, just as Faust can dig in a field for eighty years to maintain his health and youthful vigor. This parallel illuminates the identity of the forces that will rejuvenate the empire with those that rejuvenated Faust—the creative life force or the Absolute.

Thus the scene poses, like "Charming Landscape," the problem of validating the real world of appearances, of making it possible to see meaning in it. It is not surprising then that the rest of the act deals with *shows*, for Part I has already established such constructed, meaningful appearances as the appropriate manifestation of spirit in the world. The structure proposed for this act of validation is that of descent and recovery. By bringing up the gold, Faust (or whoever) brings significance and order into the chaotic world of appearances represented by the court. As earlier (and later) in the play, the ultimate symbol of the Absolute manifested in the real world is beauty, or the beautiful woman. Thus, after the masque the descent in search of gold will turn into the descent in search of Helen.

Let us move on, now, to the masque. Formally it is a radical modernization of the Jonsonian court masque, and the many Jacobean elements in this scene suggest that Goethe might have been aware of the provenance of this structure. The schematic Jonsonian masque would consist of: (1) a masque, presentation of a set of allegorical figures; (2) an antimasque, an interrupting dance or set of speeches by figures who represent the forces of disorder; and (3) the return of the masque, usually a new set of figures who reveal the presence of a higher order. The masquers (or actors) in this third part were often the highest members of the court, so that the king appeared as the embodiment of the order of the universe.[3] Here Goethe elaborates this form into a deliberately foiled dialectic that recapitulates the dialectic of Act I.

The first part of the masque is avowedly an Italianate processional masque (ll. 5065–5456). As commentators have long been aware, the idea of artificial appearance is the one aspect that connects the various figures. The gardeners offer artificial flowers; the mother tries, in effect, to sell her not very attractive daughter; parasites are by profession not what they seem; the drunk does not perceive the discrepancy between the situation as it really is and as he perceives it. The poets, who are clearly not what we would call serious poets and who have nothing to say, conclude this series of figures denoted, like the figures in "Imperial Residence," by their social roles. The mythological figures who succeed them appear updated into modern dress (the Graces and the Furies) or with their normal roles exchanged (the Fates, the Furies). In both cases the connection between real significance and appearance has been severed. If we regard the full succession of the masque—nature, society, poetry, mythology, allegory of the state (the elephant and its attendants)—we see immediately that this totality is presented in its artificial, empty, and negative aspects. The poets are given no speeches, because there is no spiritual voice here. This part of the masque thus recapitulates the phenomenon and problematics of the first part of the act; it presents once again, the realm of empty appearances uninformed by spirit.

The elaborate antimasque begins with the entrance of Zoilo-Thersites and continues until the approach of Pan. Goethe has converted Jonson's symbolic interruption of the masque into a real interruption. Zoilo-Thersites and the entourage of Plutus are evidently not ex-

---

[3]A description of the structure of Jonsonian masque and concise analysis of its development may be found in Stephen Orgel's Introduction to *Ben Jonson: The Complete Masques* (New Haven: Yale University Press, 1969). A less condensed analysis may be found in Stephen Orgel, *The Jonsonian Masque* (Cambridge: Harvard University Press, 1965).

pected participants in the show the court is putting on for itself; instead they put on a show for all the court, including the other masquers. In this way the antimasque fulfills the same function *within* the masque that the entire masque does for the act as a whole.

The antimasque is introduced by Zoilo-Thersites. Commentaries refer us to Zoilos, a hostile critic of Homer, and Thersites, a hostile and critical figure in Homer's *Iliad;* but Goethe probably did not have *only* the Homeric figure in mind. In Shakespeare's *Troilus and Cressida* there is a Thersites who cynically articulates the brutality and animality embodied by the Greek camp. But animality is a necessary aspect of the life force in Shakespeare as it is in *Faust*.[4] Goethe's Thersites is transformed into an egg, from which hatch an adder and a bat; but soon enough we will be reminded that Helen, too, hatched from an egg. Thus Zoilo-Thersites can unexpectedly introduce an allegory of creativity; Plutus (and there is a long-standing and fruitful ambiguity between Plutus, god of wealth, and Pluto, god of the underworld) brings the gold up into the world of the court, the world of appearances.

Why an allegory of creativity? Plutus, played by Faust, is the god of wealth. As the bringer of gold, which, we know, will restore the empire to order, he is the social manifestation of the mediator between spirit and reality.[5] He is accompanied by two figures, Boy-charioteer and Greed. Boy-charioteer identifies himself as the spirit of poetry; he lavishes his fictions—his ungraspable gifts that elude grasping hands—upon an eager audience. He is distilled from the spirit of Plutus. "You're spirit of my spirit" (l. 5623), Plutus says to him. Thus

[4]See G. Wilson Knight, "*Henry VIII* and the Poetry of Conversion," in *The Crown of Life* (New York: Barnes & Noble, 1966), 256–336, esp. 306–14. For a more extended discussion of Zoilo-Thersites in this vein, see Alan P. Cottrell, "Zoilo-Thersites: Another 'sehr ernster Scherz' in Goethe's *Faust II*," *Goethe's "Faust": Seven Essays*, University of North Carolina Studies in the Germanic Languages and Literatures 86 (Chapel Hill: University of North Carolina Press, 1976), 93–102. Ernst Beutler points out (in his note to l. 5457 in the *Gedenkausgabe der Werke, Briefe und Gespräche*, 5 [Zurich: Artemis, 1962], 773) that the emergence of a harlequin from an egg was a popular vaudeville number in Goethe's time. Zoilo-Thersites' egg is thus explicitly theatrical (and therefore mediating) as well.

[5]Aristophanes' Plutus, from the play of the same name, is also a restorer of social order. While Aristophanes' play doubtless lies behind both Shakespeare's and Goethe's conceptions at some level (the connection to Shakespeare will be discussed below), the particular affinities between the English and German dramatists are so strong here that any specific reference to Aristophanes remains invisible, at least to me.

he is the abstract version of what Plutus/Faust represents in social terms. Greed, played by Mephistopheles, creates indecent objects from the gold; he is but the most concrete, "animal" aspect of the creative force, the pole of nature, as opposed to spirit. What was previously a dialectic now appears as a spectrum. Not only do these three form a totality, but they share aspects. Boy-charioteer is a seducer (l. 5540); Greed, a sign maker and therefore a kind of poet. As master, Plutus takes responsibility for both and thus accepts them as part of himself.

Goethe did not invent this constellation of figures, and its source is part of the message here. The grouping Boy-charioteer–Plutus–Greed exactly reconstructs the trio Ariel–Prospero–Caliban in Shakespeare's *Tempest*, where once again we have the pattern of pure spirit, representative of social order, and erotic bestiality. Shakespeare's Ariel has already appeared in "Charming Landscape," where, as in Shakespeare, he is a poet as well as a spirit. Plutus, Prospero, and Faust are all speaking names with closely related meanings—wealth, prosperity, happiness. Indeed, Shakespeare's Prospero is a Faust figure who falls because of his love for knowledge, books, and magic. *The Tempest* turns on the restoration of individual freedom and social order. These appear in their highest form in the marriage of Ferdinand and Miranda, whose name means spectacle or show. This marriage is in turn a renewal of creativity and fertility, seen proleptically in Prospero's masque of Ceres. In other words, *The Tempest* is a play about the integration of the creative life force into the social order; Goethe's allusion to Shakespeare embodies the central problem of Act I. As a capsule repetition of the essence of *The Tempest*, the antimasque is thus the model for how pure spirit is to be retrieved from below. The vehicle is to be imaginative art, specifically spectacle drama, as it is in *The Tempest* as well. The entire masque, as an example of imaginative art, fulfills the same function in the act as the antimasque does in the masque.

In the third part of the masque the emperor himself appears, in good Jonsonian tradition. However, the restoration of order is not to be a simple revelation but a dialectical process. The emperor/Pan is to integrate the disruptive antimasque, the "irruption" of creative spirit, into the superficial order of the court-world to give it validity. The emperor's choice of role makes clear to what extent the restoration is to be understood as a dialectically higher order. To Renaissance Neoplatonists Pan, the god of nature, represents not simply lower, "animal" or lustful nature but nature in its most sublime form, truly the "all" (as the pun on the Greek name signifies) as the highest "one." The nymphs call him here, translating literally, the "All of the World" (l. 5873).[6] Goethe gives him gnomes as followers because they burrow underground to find the gold, symbol of spirit, which Pan, as Nature, is to infuse into the real world. For Nature is not itself the superficial reality of the world of appearances but reality infused with spirit.

The emperor as Pan, then, is to complete the transformation Plutus/Faust has begun. With the chest of gold Plutus/Faust has given him access to spirit; emperor/Pan must somehow descend into the chest and actually bring it forth. He fails, and in his failure his disguise, and thus the identity of the emperor with the god of Nature, is lost. Spirit is not infused into reality, and the result is chaos. The dialectic fails for perfectly obvious reasons. The gold is no more "real" than the bangles and trinkets Boy-charioteer scatters to the audience. To succeed, the emperor would have to "grasp" the gold in a figurative way; presumably he would have to be inspired by it in such a way that he became a more effective leader of his empire. But instead he mistakes it for real gold. He has not learned the lesson that Boy-charioteer and Plutus tried to teach the crowd—that the manifestations of spirit can be comprehended but not grasped, *begriffen* but not *ergriffen*. It is the problem of the rainbow again. Unmediated contact with the Absolute is not more possible now than it was when Faust confronted the earth spirit in Part I. Only by remaining aware of the fictional aspect of his activity would the emperor have been able to make effective use of the gold of Plutus.

The first two sections of the masque have been condensed, or rather distilled, versions of the first two sections of the act; the same is true for the section that follows the masque. The last part of the act consists basically of two shows, or masques, in which spirit fails to be integrated into the world of appearances. In both cases, as in the emperor's masque, the disruption arises from failure to respect the integrity and autonomy of the fiction. The first of these shows is the paper-money scheme. The emperor's complete incredulity at the acceptance of the scheme portends its ultimate failure clearly enough. Act IV shows that the new currency is indeed unable to guarantee the sta-

[6]Edgar Wind, *Pagan Mysteries in the Renaissance* (New York: Norton, 1968), 191.

bility of the empire. Why does it fail? Because no one, particularly the emperor, whose responsibility it is, remembers that the bills (note the telling ambiguity here of the word *Schein*, which means both appearance and banknote) are not real gold. It is already worrisome that the emperor signed the enabling act unawares. The models of creative imagination in the masque of Plutus were self-conscious, but the emperor's creative act is uncontrolled. The unselfconsciousness of the drunk in the first part of the masque was a specific example of the emptiness of that world. When the money is then duplicated by "men of a thousand arts" (*Tausendkünstler*, l. 6072), the whole process becomes charlatanism. Faust as co-treasurer of the empire is still seen in his role as Plutus; the emperor treats his mask as if it were real. But the most important indicator of failure is the apparently comic scene where the emperor asks his courtiers what they will do with their new wealth. All but the fool intend to prolong the joys of court life; none has any new projects in mind. The emperor is depressed that it will be business as usual, but the failure is really his. This is the moment for creative leadership, when the emperor should be directing the growth of new enterprises that would be stable in themselves and obviate the need for soft currency. Instead he behaves as if he had a permanent source of real income, which of course he has not.

The dumb show of Paris and Helen, together with the preparation for it, occupies the rest of the act. While the scene contains important philosophical statements, the mode of presentation should not be overlooked. It is important for us as readers to realize that even from the beginning, from the famous Mothers scene, we are dealing with a kind of masque or fiction. The scene "Dark Gallery," is the first return in Part II to the Faust–Mephistopheles relationship of Part I. Because of all that has come between, this scene cannot be read as anything but an almost nostalgic reevocation of Part I. Mephistopheles appears here as the ironist, as the prince of paradoxes, and finally, as liar. Faust explicitly recognizes that Mephisto's bombastic nihilism is a fiction, indeed a fiction which he will transform into his "All." Faust is able to enter into this fiction and to exploit it by consciously becoming an actor in it. When he shudders after line 6264, we must notice that Mephisto has already given him this cue at line 6216, the last part of which reads, "Does it make you shudder?"; when he sets off, "Faust strikes a distinctly peremptory *attitude* with the key" (l. 6293; emphasis mine), an "attitude," or stance, that Mephisto thoughtfully evaluates. Faust's exit in this scene ("Faust stamps and sinks out of sight") is nothing if not theatrical.

Like Faust's later descent to the underworld, this visit is elided. Goethe follows the same principle as Faust here and observes the limits of his own fiction. In place of this elided scene is a little entr'acte by Mephistopheles. With his cures for freckles and the like, we are in the realm of charlatanism—pure show—and old wives' tales (*Altweiberrezepte*). The last word gives pause for thought: Mephisto's old wives' tales take the place of Faust's visit to the old wives. Thus Mephisto's little performance parodies Faust's elided descent. Evidently an important function of the scene is to preserve the profundity of the Mothers by parody. In fact, in this scene Mephisto parodies himself, for the fiction of the Mothers and Faust's accompanying theatrics were Mephisto's creation. Nevertheless, like Mephisto's formulation "Nature and Spirit," the Mothers articulate the central issues of the drama.

What are these central issues? The iconography of the Mothers derives from late classical and Renaissance descriptions of Eternity, hoary but prolific mother of the years.[7] Goethe makes them into the sources of all forms, and in particular of the forms of Helen and Paris for the show at court. In this respect they function as his Muses, as the sources of his creative power. As the creative powers that generate forms, they are functionally identical to the earth spirit of Part I, who wove "the living garb of the Godhead" (l. 509). They are, therefore, *natura naturans,* the original version of the Absolute, which now returns to join the sun/fire/gold imagery. This continuity with the beginning of Part I might seem astonishing, but it is less so when we notice significant references to "Witch's Kitchen" in this part of Act I. Mephisto's initial paradoxical description of how to find the Mothers reminds Faust himself of the visit to the witch in Part I (ll. 6229–32). This is already the second reference to "Witch's Kitchen" in Act I and underlines the similarity of the situations in the two scenes, the apparent meaninglessness of the world of superficial appearances. When Helen appears in the dumb show Faust compares her to the figure in the mirror in "Witch's Kitchen" (ll. 6495–97). Here is the ideal that

---

[7]The classical sources for Goethe's conception have been extensively explored by Harold Jantz in *The Mothers in "Faust": The Myth of Time and Creativity* (Baltimore: Johns Hopkins University Press, 1969).

suddenly infuses the real with significance; it appears in the form of Gretchen in Part I, in that of Helen in Part II. In the midst of his affair with Gretchen, in "Forest and Cavern," we remember, Faust thanks some lofty spirit (ll. 3217–34), apparently the earth spirit, for all his gifts. The parallel gift in Part II comes from the Mothers. In retrospect the subliminal classicizing associated with the earth spirit (Goethe suggested modeling him, we remember, after the Zeus of Otricoli; the encounter reenacts the myth of Zeus and Semele) is enhanced by the parallel to the Mothers, who introduce the central classicizing sequence of Part II.

Nevertheless, while the figures are functionally identical, there is a significant difference, which accords with the differences between the two parts of the play. Although the Mothers are the conferrers of form, it is not strictly accurate to call their forms the "living garb of the Godhead." Rather, they give Faust the power to conjure ghosts and shadowy forms, but forms, Faust explicitly says (l. 6430), without life. The dumb show is nothing but a "goblin play" (*Fratzengeisterspiel*, l. 6546), in Mephisto's terms, and keeps relapsing into traditional pictorial themes—first "Luna and Endymion" (l. 6509), then "The Rape of Helen" (l. 6548). The Mothers create a world of art, not of living nature. This is implied not only by Helen's ghostly and iconological aspects, but also by the choice of the particular icon "Luna and Endymion," for the moon is identified in *Faust II*, as we have seen, with art. But as we have also seen, art and Nature, while not identical, occupy the same mediating position in Goethe's dialectic. The Mothers are thus an equivalent for the earth spirit adapted to the changed focus and more abstract character of Part II.

The dumb show itself is staged so as to remind us, the real audience, that it is not real, but rather a spirit play. For indeed the only way spirits can appear "directly" is through the mediation of play. The discrepancy between the decor of the room and the setting of the play (Greek set within Gothic set), the accompanying music, the presence of Mephisto and the astrologer as commentators—all remind us of the artificiality of Paris and Helen. Yet the audience reacts to the spirit figures as if they were real figures in their own world of banal appearances. It has still not learned the lessons of Boy-charioteer and Plutus. Far worse, Faust has also not absorbed the lesson he himself gave. In Part I he had been completely blind to the representational nature of the earth spirit and could not face him. In his encounter with the Mothers he was more successful, because, as we have just seen, he accepted the play aspect of the situation and entered into it. But now, like the emperor, he oversteps the boundary of the fiction with catastrophic results. He grasps Helen and she fades, touches Paris with the key and he explodes. He has recovered the Absolute, spirit from the depths, but he has not successfully integrated it into the real world of appearances.

We are back, once again, to the problem of the rainbow. This was first formulated as a double problem—how to generate the rainbow at will and how to hold onto it. Faust's difficulties at the end of the act must not obscure the recognition that Act I has emphatically answered the first part of the problem. To create art is to generate the rainbow. This is, perhaps, less a lesson (it does not teach anyone how to be an artist) than it is a statement about the epistemological function of art. Nevertheless, this insight underscores the fundamental change in direction of the play that began with the "Walpurgis Night's Dream." The locus of Faust's quest is no longer the world but his own creations.

Thus the attitude toward artificiality and appearance shifts in the course of the act. In the first part it appears to be negative, to judge by the court and by the figures in the first third of the masque. But with the appearance of Boy-charioteer everything changes. Boy-charioteer is effective and important because he is an artificer. Furthermore, his significance and his status as mediator between spirit and nature depend on his being an allusion to Shakespeare. The Herald, we remember, is told that he can understand Boy-charioteer by describing him. Appearance is no longer separate from essence but provides access to it. Henceforth, then, artificiality is less important than the response of the observer to it. Those who take it for what it appears to be are burned. But to those who penetrate to its essence a new world of achievement opens. In good Shakespearean fashion the only character to possess this wisdom in Act I is the fool, who converts his paper money to land. Significance lies, so to speak, in the eye of the beholder. This is once again the message of "Witch's Kitchen" translated from the terms of nature, where Faust's vision brought beauty into chaos, to the terms of art. And now it is the reader of *Faust* who is warned of the descent that he himself must make in search of essence.

But descent has many meanings in this text, and not least among them is the temporal one. Up until now in the play neither time nor particular historical setting has been especially important. The Faust theme presumes a sixteenth century setting, although nothing in Part I really exploits or demands it. But from the throneroom scene until the middle of Act V, the historical setting will be everywhere obtrusive as history and historicity become central concerns in the play. Act I is set at the court of the German emperor, evidently sometime in the Renaissance, for the emperor has brought back the new fashion of masking festivities from his visit to Italy to be crowned. Commentators have long since realized that Goethe exploits the techniques of Shakespeare's history plays to portray this court; the Jonsonian aspects of the masque also help to localize the historical setting. Two important motifs further suggest a specifically Elizabethan setting. The first is the explosion when Faust tries to rescue Helen; in the source for this motif, this event occurs at the court of Queen Elizabeth.[8] The second is the fire that almost destroys the entire court at the end of the masque; it was common knowledge at the time that the Globe Theater had burned down in 1613 during a performance of Shakespeare's *Henry VIII*.

And indeed, *Henry VIII* is particularly relevant to the representation of the court in Act I, for of all of Shakespeare's histories, *Henry VIII* is the only one that consistently exploits the techniques of Jonsonian masque.[9] This tendency is so strong in the play that Samuel Johnson argued that Ben Jonson himself had refurbished the play for its ill-fated performance.[10] Regardless of the validity of this argument, the play shows the king himself masking (I, iv); it begins with a description of a luxurious royal pageant (I, i) and shows three lavish royal processions on stage (II, iv; IV, i; V, v); furthermore, an allegorical vision is enacted on stage (IV, ii). There are also central thematic connections. For half the play Henry is an irresponsible ruler like

[8]Heinrich Düntzer, *Goethes "Faust, Zweiter Theil": Erläuterungen zu den deutschen Klassikern*, Erste Abtheilung, 13, 14 (Leipzig: Ed. Wartigs Verlag Ernst Hoppe, 1900), 134. The source in question is Antoine Hamilton's "L'Enchenteur Faustus," published in F. M. Leuchsenring's *Cahiers de lecture* (1789); Elizabeth causes the explosion by trying to embrace the shade of Rosamunde, which has appeared with those of Helen, Cleopatra, and Mariamne.

[9]It has recently been argued that the play makes sense only if it is understood as a masque; see John D. Cox, "*Henry VIII* as Masque," *ELH* 45 (1978): 390–409.

[10]Apart from the popularity of Johnson's work on Shakespeare, this argument was widely disseminated through the commentary in the edition of Edmond Malone, the major Shakespeare edition in Goethe's time (*The Plays and Poems of William Shakespeare*, 2 [London, 1821], 395, 399). Malone's edition first appeared in 1790.

Goethe's emperor; the play turns on the relation of order to disorder. Ultimately, however, Henry emerges as the ordering force in the play as Wolsey (another prelate-chancellor) is toppled. Henry also transforms what at first appear to be undisciplined animal forces, like his desire for Anne Bullen, into a glorious orderly future, embodied in infant Elizabeth.[11] In this respect *Henry VIII* appears as the equivalent of *The Tempest*, which, as we saw, deals with the integration of creative power into the social order. This integration never takes place at Goethe's court, as it does at Shakespeare's. It is the divergence from Shakespeare in the "real" world of Act I as much as the convergence with him in the masque that tells us that such integration can only be represented in the mediating realm of art.

Thus the presence of Shakespeare in Act I is both more pervasive and more complex than had originally appeared. Clearly Shakespeare is already the great ancestor in Part I; in Part II there will be other ancestors as well. Shakespeare is the gate through which we enter and return from the journey to those other ancestors. That framing gate tells us the journey can never be other than a journey of the imagination, can never be "real." Just as our descent into the Renaissance world to which Faust is native is mediated by Shakespeare, the return to those earlier ancestors will have its appropriate mediators.[12]

The actual problems of Goethe's emperor have as much to do with historical models as with Shakespeare's *Henry VIII*. The salient characteristics—the combination of luxurious ostentation and poverty, the struggle with the rival emperor in Act IV, and the distribution of the empire to the vassals in Act IV—all derive from the career of the emperor Charles IV (1316–1378). As he began work on Act IV, Goethe consulted an eighteenth-century study of the Golden Bull, which was promulgated by Charles IV in 1356 after his victory over the rival emperor Günther von Schwarzenburg and after his coronation in Italy. This document defined the functions and relative powers of the seven electors of the empire; its real effect was to destroy the emperor's centralizing power and to distribute it among the electors. This is precisely what Goethe's emperor does after the defeat of the

[11]On the tension between order and life forces in *Henry VIII*, see Knight, "*Henry VIII* and the Poetry of Conversion."

[12]This problem has recently been treated from a different but interesting point of view by Heinz Schlaffer, "*Faust: Zweiter Teil*": *Die Allegorie des 19. Jahrhunderts* (Stuttgart: Metzler, 1981), 99–123.

rival emperor in Act IV. Indeed, the Golden Bull and the rival emperor are the two topics Goethe associates with Charles IV in his autobiography.[13]

Edward Gibbon devotes three pages to Charles IV at the end of Chapter 49 of *The Decline and Fall of the Roman Empire*.[14] His central concern there is the appalling discrepancy between the lavish appearances of Charles's court (his example is the pageantry of the banquet at which the Golden Bull was promulgated and at which the electors appeared in their roles as steward, chamberlain, and so on, as in *Faust*) and Charles's essential powerlessness and even poverty. He was arrested, according to Gibbon, and detained in an inn by a butcher of Worms as hostage for the payment of his expenses. The context in which Gibbon introduces this central theme for *Faust* is significant. Charles IV is introduced to illustrate the nadir of the fortunes of the Roman Empire; he and the state of his empire are compared at length to Augustus and the state of the empire at its height. Thus along with Shakespeare, Charles IV is another gate that opens the way into the past and frames the descent into history in *Faust*. *The Decline and Fall of the Roman Empire* pursues the history of the empire through the fall of Constantinople in 1453. That brings us up into the Renaissance, almost to the time of Shakespeare, and the modern rediscovery and idealization of antiquity. In fact, Gibbon reports the belief that Roman gold was buried in Rome by the Goths when they sacked the city and that centuries later their heirs, who knew the secret, dug it up and carried it off.[15] The parallel to *Faust* suggests—and this suggestion is clearly borne out in the course of the next two acts—that buried gold represents the Absolute in a particular form, namely, the

---

[13]*Dichtung und Wahrheit*, pt. II, chap. 1; *Gesamtausgabe der Werke und Schriften in zweiundzwanzig Bänden*, 8 (Stuttgart: Cotta, 1959), 27.

[14]We cannot document precisely when Goethe read Gibbon, but he borrowed a late volume of the *Decline and Fall* from the ducal library in 1806. Since Schiller's wife's eighteen-year-old cousin was reading it in the intervals between her singing lessons in Weimar in the late 1790s, we may safely assume it was widely known in contemporary German intellectual circles.

[15]Edward Gibbon, *The Decline and Fall of the Roman Empire*, ed. J. Bury (New York: Heritage Press, 1946), 3: 2432n. Pietro Citati (in *Goethe*, trans. R. Rosenthal [New York: Dial Press, 1974], 437) identifies the importance of a passage from Tacitus' *Annals* (XVI, 1–3) for the buried gold plot in Act I. Tacitus is there concerned, like Gibbon, to evoke the decay and sense of lateness of imperial Rome; thus the *Annals* appears here as the Roman step in the chain of texts and allusions leading back to earliest antiquity.

form into which it was minted by classical antiquity. Gibbon represents finally, the highest achievement of the eighteenth-century idealization of Roman society; as such he appropriately introduces a descent into the past that explores antiquity in its role as ancestor of modern culture.

This descent proceeds apace in the rest of the act. The masque moves us in imagination across the Alps to Italy, to the Roman world implicitly evoked by the hints about the buried gold of the empire. Italy is also, as commentators have often noted, halfway to Greece and to Helen. The appearance of Zoilo-Thersites moves us both farther east to the Greek world and also deeper into the past. Yet Goethe's odd combination of Homer-critic with critic from Homer and his choice of a classical figure who is also a character in Shakespeare maintain the same "framed" perspective on the past that we have already observed. The Mothers, supposedly very ancient goddesses, move us further back yet, while the references to dolphins (l. 6244) and tripod (l. 6283) are unambiguously classical. Nevertheless, the historical framing continues. Although the Mothers are supposedly very ancient, they are known to the modern world through two essays of Plutarch, one of which is entitled "De defectu oraculorum." The Mothers are transmitted by a historian for whom classical greatness is already in the past and in a work about the disappearance of the divine voice from the world. Finally Helen and Paris themselves appear—or rather, their shadows appear. It is not just that our literary tradition begins with the story of Paris and Helen, but that our entire history begins with the equivalent story, as Herodotus pointed out at the beginning of his *Histories*.[16] Helen embodies in *Faust* not simply beauty and not simply manifest Spirit but also the beginning of history.

The descent in search of spirit and of history has yet another dimension. If we trace the succession of images for the Absolute in Act I, rather than their significance, we arrive at yet another level of signification. The progression begins in "Charming Landscape" with the fiery sun, an image familiar from Part I. "Throneroom" shifts to the image of gold in the twin forms of buried treasure and money. In the masque these forms are shown to be labile at best. The treasure of

[16]Herodotus, *The Histories*, trans. Aubrey de Selincourt (Harmondsworth: Penguin, 1976), 41–42.

Boy-charioteer turns to insects, the gold in Plutus' chest is given arbitrary and obscene shapes by Greed. When the emperor peeps into the chest, the gold appears to boil; it is formless potential. At the same time Boy-charioteer defines himself as a poet, so that poetry is understood as another shape in which gold manifests itself. The final shape is that of Helen, invoked through the tripod Faust has re-covered from the depths. When Faust reaches for Helen, he is not burned as the court and emperor were; instead he falls into a faint. Faust does not return to the heights again until the beginning of Act IV, when Helen has disappeared for good. The progression of images, then, moves toward increasing spiritualization and abstraction. Descent into the depths to fetch gold ultimately becomes descent into the self to fetch inspiration.

The implicit model of creativity here is thus a psychological one. Access to the Absolute is no longer to be found in the world, as in Part I, but in the world re-created by the mind. It would be wrong to understand this position as a rejection of Part I, for only the mind that is open to the world has this capacity to recreate its own world; we remember again the final words of the spirits in "Charming Landscape":

> All is open to the noble
> Who understand and swiftly grasp.
> [ll. 4664–65]

It is a commonplace of *Faust* criticism that Part I deals with the private or small world, the microcosm, and Part II with the great world, the macrocosm. And so, indeed, they do. But it is nevertheless important to remember what Part I already demonstrated, that the macrocosm cannot be perceived directly. It can only be perceived as a show, in this case as a show projected by the mind of Faust himself.

We have now explored at some length what it means to generate a rainbow at will. The second part of the problem, how to generate a rainbow that can be *ergriffen* as well as *begriffen* is the subject of Acts II and III. The creative act in Act I is subjective. Spirit is mediated through the creator, the one who descends to fetch it. Acts II and III deal with the process of objectification, which locates the act of cre-ation in a historical continuum, both natural and cultural. The last two acts explore, then, the consequences of the historicization of spirit. It is not a coincidence that we begin to think of Hegel here. The very possibility of writing literary history would be undermined if there were not a level of discourse that could comprehend *Faust* and *The Phenomenology of Mind* together. Despite Goethe's notorious hostility to abstraction, it is necessary to read *Faust II* at this level of abstraction to perceive the order implicit in his own structuring of the work.

10

The Spirit of Water:
Act II

If Act I was an effort to conjure Helen through the forces of fire, Act II is the attempt to conjure her from the water. At bottom it deals with the same problem as Act I, how to generate a graspable rainbow, how to bring up creative force or spirit from the depths to validate appearances. Now that we have moved into the realm of myth and art, now that we are in some sense inside the allegories created in Act I, this attempt will be more successful. Act I characterized the goal in terms of fire, gold, myth, imagination, antiquity, and the beginnings of time. In Act II water imagery will predominate over fire; this represents a significant shift in focus. The emphasis will no longer be on the descent and the buried treasure, but on the ascent, on the continuity between lower and upper worlds, on how to go from spirit to concrete form. This is where both Faust and emperor/Pan failed in Act I. The emphasis will appear to be less on creating art than on creating life; but we understand, of course, that the fundamental identity of art and Nature in the play makes the distinction spurious. Furthermore, both art and Nature have become, through the process of descent in Act I, projections of the seeking human mind. At least Acts II and III, if not IV and V as well, are continuations of the "show" begun with Faust's descent to the Mothers. It is a show created by Faust and stage-managed by that experienced director Mephistopheles.

The act begins with a series of "plunges," which indicate that it begins in the equivalent of the realm of the Mothers at the end of

Faust's descent. The curtains open to reveal Faust in the state of unconsciousness into which he had plunged at the end of Act I. But he has also returned to his study, which the audience has not seen since Faust's departure into the world. He—and we—have thus plunged back into his past. Faust's old robe is still there; Wagner is still there; the student Mephisto led on is still there as well. As the travelers proceed to the "Classical Walpurgis Night" the act slips into a much deeper abyss. Erichtho's prologue takes us back to the origins of the Roman Empire in the battle of Pharsalus, fought between Caesar and Pompey in 48 B.C. Erichtho is the witch Pompey consulted before the battle; the poet of whom she complains is Lucan, who portrays her most dreadfully indeed in his epic, *Pharsalia*. Lucan is important here, because he identifies the Thessalian setting both as a land of witchcraft and as the cradle of history.[1] Here Erichtho mediates the transformation of the historical world into a poetic or spirit world by reporting that the fires change color from red to blue (spirit fires burn blue). But this transformation plunges us even deeper into the abyss of time, into the prehistorical world of mythology. This is, in fact, mythology at its very oldest levels, for the sphinxes identify themselves as the oldest of mythological creatures, too old ever to have seen Helen.

The relative antiquity of the sphinxes may seem obvious to us, but it was a new idea in the eighteenth century. The first significant periodization of ancient art was made by Johann Joachim Winckelmann in his *History of Ancient Art* (1764). Previously, antiquity had been considered a permanent ideal, not a transient historical phenomenon. Winckelmann was widely admired, often revered, in mid-eighteenth-century art circles, and he profoundly influenced the historicist theories of the later part of the century and of the nineteenth century. Thus this apparently innocent reference signals a genuine historical beginning to the act and at the same time a genuinely historical pattern of organization for this re-creation of antiquity. But a historical view of antiquity is not only one from a modern perspective; it is also a view that recognized the existence of historical change and the impermanence of any single manifestation of the ideal.

---

[1] On the legendary beginnings of Thessaly and the association of Thessaly with the beginnings of war, see Marcus Annaeus Lucanus, *De bello civili (Pharsalia)*, bk. VI, ll. 333–410, esp. ll. 395–410, and on Thessaly as a land of witchcraft, ll. 434–506.

As in Act I, this plunge into antiquity is mediated by the Renaissance, again in the form of Shakespeare. Any reader familiar with *Henry V* will immediately recognize the fundamental elements of Goethe's prologue—the hideous witch surveying the fires of the hostile armies by moonlight and the transformation into a spirit world—in the chorus at the beginning of Act IV. This eve of the battle of Agincourt might well have suggested the eve of the battle of Pharsalus to Goethe, because Fluellen, the pedantic captain who is fixated on military history, discusses Pompey and his camp within seventy lines of this chorus. Now, all the choruses in *Henry V* have as their main topic the need for the spectator to engage his imagination and supply what the stage can only hint at, "Minding true things by what their mock'ries be" (IV, pro., 53).[2] Indeed, *Henry V* is preoccupied with imaginative projection and the need for valid role-playing. Henry is a great and effective king, not because he is especially honest, but because he plays his role well. The Shakespearean echo is significant, then, on at least three levels. *Henry V* explores, like this part of *Faust*, the function and effectiveness of imagination. As a history play it is an especially appropriate source for a prologue to the most historically minded part of *Faust*. And finally, it provides once again a Renaissance gateway that opens up yet also frames our access to antiquity.

Homunculus, Wagner's curious creation (with a little help from Mephistopheles), identifies the significance of all these plunges into the past. The concept of the Homunculus comes from sixteenth- and seventeenth-century alchemy, which is a debased form of practical Neoplatonism.[3] But even without the Neoplatonic background the language of fire and light that characterizes the creation of Homun-

[2]I have already referred to the central importance of the spectator's imagination in Goethe's assessment of Shakespeare. The demands of the chorus in *Henry V* are clearly what Goethe had in mind with this part of "Shakespeare ad Infinitum" (1815, reissued 1826).

[3]Edgar Wind, *Pagan Mysteries in the Renaissance* (New York: Norton, 1968), 214–15. Even for Calderón, spirit (*Ingenio*) is the "unborn part of the soul" and thus a kind of Homunculus. See Calderón de la Barca, *A Dios por razón de estado*, in *Obras completas*, 3, ed. Angel Valbuena Prat (Madrid: Aguilar, 1952), 852. More discussion of the Neoplatonist aspects of Homunculus may be found in Pietro Citati, *Goethe*, trans. R. Rosenthal (New York: Dial Press, 1974), 233–34. Information about Goethe's knowledge of alchemy and use of alchemical imagery may be found in English in Ronald D. Gray, *Goethe the Alchemist: A Study of Alchemical Symbolism in Goethe's Literary and Scientific Works* (Cambridge: Cambridge University Press, 1952); on Homunculus see 205–20.

culus connects him to earlier manifestations of spirit in the play. The way he first appears in the test tube as glowing coal then glorious jewel, and the way Mephisto presides over his emergence are strongly reminiscent of the vision of Mammon in the mountainside on the way to the Walpurgis Night in Part I (ll. 3916–31). Wagner's pomposities—"So must man, with his great gifts, / Henceforth have higher and higher origins" (ll. 6846–47)—identify the significant truth about Homunculus: he is a spark of divine spirit, who will spend the rest of the act in search of incarnation. Thus we have plunged, like Faust, into the realm from which the spark of pure spirit may be retrieved into the world.

The act begins, then, in the realm of the Mothers, at the bottom of the descent. Since the problem of the act is to incarnate spirit, the fundamental gesture of the act is generation, and this gesture is repeated over and over again. It begins in the re-creation of *Faust I* in the first scene. The repetition of the familiar set and the negative attitude toward it (it is moldy and dusty) set the tone. The parodistic tone continues with the new famulus, who is a parody of Wagner, and the Baccalaureus, who parodies himself as a student. But beyond the level of parody, the presence of a *new* famulus and the promotion of the student suggest an underlying tendency to generation and development even in this musty chamber. The chorus of insects that are born from Faust's old gown and greet Mephistopheles as their father emphasize this pattern. The exchange between the Baccalaureus and Mephisto also holds an important place here. It appears at first to be an inserted satire of the more extreme forms of German idealist thought, especially of Johann Gottlieb Fichte, whose system derived the world from the ego's initial postulation of itself. Nevertheless, creativity is the central theme, for the discussion turns on the Baccalaureus' arrogant faith in his own capacity to generate the world. Lines like

> Human life lives in the blood, and where
> Is the blood in such commotion as in youth?
> That is living blood in lively strength
> That generates new life from life.
> There everything is in motion, something's getting done,
> Weaklings fall, the vigorous come forth.
>
> [ll. 6776–81]

parodistically celebrate youth, vitality, and creation—the very theme of the act. Furthermore, if we ask where else have we seen such language, the obvious answer is from Faust himself in Part I. The circulating energy of nature in the macrocosm speech, the emphasis on power in the invocation of the earth spirit, the vitalism of Faust as waterfall in "Forest and Cave" all come to mind. This parodistic aspect of the scene establishes the essential ambiguity of the creation that takes place in Act II. On the one hand, it is natural, even vitalistic. But on the other hand, it is anachronistic and self-conscious (Mephisto even turns to the audience for help at l. 6772). Whatever is created in this act will not be real or natural but, like Homunculus, artificial.

In this respect Homunculus again illuminates the significance of the basic patterns of the act, for the imagery associated with his artificiality organizes much of the play. Because Homunculus is artificial, he is enclosed in a crystal vial (l. 6884); he is, as Wagner suggests (l. 6860), a crystallized man. But Homunculus is not the only flame enclosed in crystal. Immediately after his crystallization (he is not yet "born" because he lacks a body), Homunculus articulates and interprets Faust's dream of the conception of Helen, the myth of Leda and the swan. According to the myth, Zeus took on the form of a swan to rape Leda; Helen was the offspring of this union. In this vision Leda sets foot in the water, and, we are told, "The pure life-flame of the noble body / Cools itself in the pliant crystal of the wave" (ll. 6909–10). During the "Classical Walpurgis Night" the dream is repeated as a waking vision articulated by Faust himself. Leda is invisible but the water is once again crystal, this time a mirror (l. 7284). Helen's mother is thus the equivalent of Homunculus, a spark of spirit protected in a crystal vial, the ideal not yet become embodied in reality. But Homunculus wants to become "real," to escape his crystal vial for a real body. In other words, he wants to proceed from artificial embodiment of the union of ideal and real (fire in crystal) to the living or natural embodiment of it (fire in water).

The image has already appeared once in Part I, in "Witch's Kitchen." It is not by chance that the fires, the fantastic apparatus and humming vessels of Wagner's laboratory recall the kitchen of Part I, nor that Homunculus recalls an important theme of "Witch's Kitchen" when he expects Mephisto to provide him shortcuts to activity in the world (ll. 6888–90). There, we remember, Faust saw the ideal embodied in the image of a beautiful woman in a magic mirror, spirit encased in crystal. After "Witch's Kitchen" Faust progresses from the mirror image to the living Gretchen. In Part II Homunculus will break his vial on the chariot of Galatea and pour his flame into the water. The next thing to follow this union in the play will be the appearance of Helen. Similarly the crystallized Leda will give way to her fluid (she will evaporate at the end of Act III), but nonetheless embraceable "living" daughter.

In this regard it is particularly interesting that Goethe seems to have based his descent/ascent structure on Aristophanes' *Frogs*. The wanderings of the three northern travelers among the classical ghosts are presented with broad Aristophanic humor. Especially when one takes account of the loftiness of the classical ideal in Goethe's time, the irreverence of his presentation must even have exceeded that of Aristophanes, who sends Dionysos and his servant Xanthias wandering through the Greek hell. The empusa Mephistopheles meets and the exchange of shape with the Phorcyads are both borrowed directly from *The Frogs*.[4] But the strong parodistic tendency of both plays is their most significant point of contact. As we have just seen, the Baccalaureus scene parodies, in a sense, the concern with creativity and generation in the act that is to follow. Similarly, the first scene of *The Frogs* parodies the play's concern for the social value of tragedy. In the first scene Dionysos' desire to recover Euripides appears superficial in the extreme, but at the end the impending return of Aeschylus is presented as the salvation of the state. At its most serious moments the play is comic, just as Act II is. The high point of the play, the dramatic contest between Euripides and Aeschylus is a series of parodies of famous or typical passages. In both plays parody serves the same function. It mediates—indeed, makes possible—the recovery of the past and of the spirit of poetry. In the first scene of the act Goethe parodies figures (Wagner, the student) who are themselves already parodies; in the larger structure of the act he parodies an author who is the arch-parodist of the Western tradition. The emphasis on art and

---

[4]The Phorcyads do not appear in *The Frogs*, but identity versus external form is a central issue in the play. One long comic sequence has Dionysos and Xanthias repeatedly exchanging clothing and identities; the theme appears on a religious level in the chorus of initiates, who have achieved some kind of higher existence in death. At the most serious level it appears in the progressive transformations of Dionysos from comic god of wine to god of the mysteries to serious god of tragedy.

artificiality does not, then, simply repeat what has come before. In Act II, Goethe specifies the kind of art that is to represent spirit in the world. And once parody has been identified as, in a sense, the highest art form for Goethe, the enormous collection of allusions we have already identified in *Faust* takes on yet another dimension of meaning. The allusions no longer simply identify or generate positions on particular themes or issues, nor do they simply place the play in contexts or traditions; now we see that allusiveness per se is the defining quality of art for Goethe.

The "Classical Walpurgis Night" shows each of the three travelers engaged in the creative act, each in pursuit of form. Before considering their quests in detail, it is worth reflecting briefly on the constellation. In the "Walpurgis Night" of Part I, Faust also quested as a member of a trio; the other two were Mephistopheles and the will-o'-the-wisp. Like Homunculus, the will-o'-the-wisp was a disembodied light; he followed, we remember, the zigzag pattern of the earth spirit. Although the will-o'-the-wisp melts away, the parallel between the two Walpurgis Nights is nevertheless significant, for the first one, like the second, is concerned with the generative power of nature. The trio returns in Act I, this time as Boy-charioteer–Plutus/Faust and Greed/Mephistopheles. Faust and Mephistopheles occupy their same places, while Boy-charioteer shares the element of fire with the two lights. Once again the third and most spiritual member is of a different, openly magical, order of being. In Part I, Faust needed to be turned away from too direct apprehension of spirit into the world; thus the will-o'-the-wisp evaporated and Faust never saw Satan. But in Act I the emphasis is entirely on the recovery of spirit, so that Boy-charioteer is the dominant member of the trio. Furthermore, as we saw, each of the trio in Act I shares characteristics with each of the others. Now in Act II this aspect becomes the most important. None of the three guides the others, but instead, each independently pursues the same goal—to locate his own appropriate form, to embody his own version of the Absolute. Faust, Mephistopheles, and Homunculus still occupy familiar positions in Goethe's dialectic; nevertheless, now that the Faustian quest has become the search for form in the temporal world instead of for the Absolute outside the world, all three are, in a sense, now genuine Fausts.

The "Classical Walpurgis Night" consists, then, of three parallel quests for the same thing. Goethe intertwines them to some extent, but basically they are arranged in three stages of increasing generality and illumination from dream to masque to ritual. The first quest is Faust's, and consists largely in the effort to realize a dream. This quest has already begun in the preceding scene when Homunculus described Faust's dream of the conception of Helen. Arrived in Greece, he first encounters the sphinxes, who, however, died out before the time of Helen. Now that he has gained entry, so to speak, to the history of Greek culture, Faust has no difficulty substituting spatial for temporal advance and can repeat the vision of Leda and the swan in his own words in "On the lower Peneios." We have already seen the significance of water in this vision; that Faust has moved from the upper Peneios, where he originally landed, to the fertile flood plain of the river, closer to the sea and surrounded by water gods, is a measure of his approach to the realm of Helen. The second dream is, significantly, both less abrupt and more "real" than the first. This time Faust is conscious; the actual set on stage corresponds to what Faust describes in his vision; the mystic union is realistically hidden (Leda is in a bower), not abruptly veiled at the last minute by the poet. The supernatural act, the mating of swan and woman, is displaced by the more natural water play of Leda's maidens and the attendant swans. This convergence of dream and nature continues when Faust meets Chiron. The wise old centaur generates a context for the existence of Helen by telling Faust first about the greatest of Greek heroes, then about the childhood of the greatest of heroines. This historical contextualization proceeds so rapidly and so effectively that Chiron must finally remind Faust that as a mythical figure Helen exists independently of pedantic conceptions of time.

Nevertheless, we must not overlook the importance of what has occurred. Subjection to history prevented the sphinxes from providing information about Helen, and having a particular place in history allowed Chiron to know her. It is true, in order to approach any nearer to her it is necessary for Faust to escape from time. The exchange between Manto and Chiron identifies Chiron's restless motion with the flux of time.

> MANTO: Do you still rove unwearied?
> CHIRON: You still dwell surrounded by peace,
> While circling is my joy.
> MANTO: I wait; Time circles me.
>
> [ll. 7478–81]

Manto's remark that she once smuggled Orpheus in through the same way similarly identifies her with the eternal world of poetic imagination. Faust himself has already made one such descent to the Mothers. There he departed, we remember, from the spatial realm to fetch the shade (spirit) of Helen; now he departs from the temporal flux to fetch a body for her. The problem in Act I, however, turned out to be not the departure but the return. For this reason, the path traced by Faust's quest is perhaps more important than the ultimate arrival at Manto's temple, for this quest establishes a particular, indeed unique, historical world to embody the spirit he will fetch. This is the lesson of historicism. Although the ultimate act of creation is a departure from time, nevertheless the substance of Faust's quest is to generate a valid historical context or matrix to contain his dream of the ideal.

As earlier in the first "Walpurgis Night" and in Act I, Faust's visit to the Absolute—here Persephone—is elided. And as before, it is replaced by Mephisto's burlesque of the same experience and, uniquely in this case, by the more abstract and illuminating parallel quest of Homunculus. Mephisto's burlesque quest reminds us, appropriately, more of the descent of Dionysos in *The Frogs* than of Orpheus. As always, Mephisto is especially drawn to the grotesques—the sphinxes, griffons, ants, and arimasps. The latter three, according to Herodotus (and indeed, according to the most bizarre and fanciful sections, Books III and IV, of Herodotus' thoroughly Mephistophelean book), were collectors and guardians of gold. Mephisto has in fact plunged here to the very realm of buried treasure he himself promoted so vigorously in Act I. This is the role Mephisto has played all along in *Faust*. As the reality principle he has led the way to the Absolute.

Mephistopheles does, it is true, at first feel considerably out of his element. These classical monsters are rather too high-spirited for the poor northern devil (ll. 7086–87). And yet this world that worries Mephisto actually replays the issues of Act I at a more intense level. Mephisto, who was in his element in the world of empty appearances at court, cannot keep up with the constantly shifting forms of the Lamiae or the empusa, much less the appalling shifts from natural to artificial landscape brought about by Seismos. The masque of Seismos—and it is a masque, for none of it turns out to be real—presents once again the retrieval of gold from the depths. As at the emperor's court the gold generates social inequity and chaos. At the height of the disorder a meteor falls out of the moon and destroys the whole appearance. We are reminded here, first, of the fire that engulfs emperor/Pan and that Faust extinguishes by invoking the power of water; second, we think of Helen in the dumb show, identified with Luna, and of the explosion she sets off.

Mephisto does not, however, remain to witness the catastrophic end to this spirit masque, but sets off in the middle to pursue form, first in the shape of the Lamiae. When he fails to catch one, he rejects this mummery and masking (ll. 7795, 7797), as he significantly calls it. He turns then from the artificial mountain of the masque to Oreas, the living or natural rock. In this respect he repeats the pattern of Faust's quest, which moved from dream to historically grounded natural reality. The parallel continues when Mephisto approaches the cave of the Phorcyads. These three weird sisters, also known as the Graiae, were supposed to live off beyond the edge of the world, where neither sun nor moon shone; in this respect they embody the same kind of goal as the Mothers or, for that matter, Persephone. It is not surprising that they identify their cave as a temple, for Faust's way to the underworld led through Manto's temple. Furthermore, these three hags were the daughters of Ceto, a daughter of the primal sea, and Phorcis, the old man of the sea. Thus, like Faust and later Homunculus, even Mephisto arrives at the principle of water in this act. Nevertheless Mephisto makes one concession to his role as eternal negator: he does not descend to the Phorcyads but climbs. Once there he finds the burlesque version of what Faust seeks to give reality to his spark of the Absolute. Instead of the most beautiful woman who ever lived, Mephisto chooses for himself the ugliest hag. Yet there is still a subtle strand of identity between Helen and the Phorcyads. Helen is associated with swans by her heritage, but so are the Phorcyads;[5] swan imagery will remain important in the play all through Act III. In the Phorcyads, Mephisto thus finds his own Helen. Faust has already donned his role as poet in Act I; as poet—a second Orpheus in this context— Faust creates a Helen apart from himself. Now Mephisto dons his garb for the play in which both are to perform in Act III.

Homunculus also seeks a role in the "Classical Walpurgis Night," but as has been typical of him thus far, his adventures illuminate the action at a more abstract level. Faust and Mephisto have sought specific, historical forms for the "sparks"; Homunculus seeks the general equivalent of this, a body to enclose his light and replace his crystal

---

[5]Aeschylus, *Prometheus Bound*, ll. 794–97.

vial. Like Mephisto he briefly works through the problematics of Act I in that he watches the second part of the masque of Seismos. In his conversations with the two Greek philosophers, Anaxagoras (who believed the earth was created by the forces of fire) and Thales (who believed in the creative power of water), the masque is now explicitly interpreted as creation from fire. And like the others he turns from the fire to descend to the water, this time beyond the point Faust reached to the sea itself. There his flame attracts two old men of the sea, Nereus and Proteus—the first a prolific father, the second a god of transformation. These two embody the generative power and the form-giving capacity represented in the principle of water. But they also embody something more. When Thales approaches Nereus for advice, Nereus replies that neither Paris nor Ulysses took his advice and in the process gives a capsule summary of the history encompassed by the Homeric epics. In his next speech, where he explains that Galatea has replaced Venus, he opens up the later history of classical religion. Thus Thales completes the sense of historical context begun by the sphinxes' inability to talk about Helen. We have moved from the beginning to the end of the history of antiquity. Proteus offers the ultimate generalization of this theme. To become, he tells Homunculus, it is necessary to begin in the sea as the tiniest of living things and to evolve up the great chain of being. This is the historical flux enlarged to the cosmic scale of modern biology. And yet, like Faust, Homunculus is to gain a form from the great wealth of time only by the gesture of leaving time, of death. He breaks his vial on the chariot of Galatea, the historicized goddess of beauty and therefore the spiritual equivalent of Helen and embodiment of perfect form. In this moment we see on stage the merging of fire and water, of spirit and form.[6] Crystal is exchanged for water; art paradoxically becomes life in the moment when Homunculus passes out of the world and through the looking glass.[7] This epiphany of ultimate harmony is the moment of the creation of the rainbow, and it is properly

[6]In the Renaissance and post-Renaissance tradition Galatea is one of the standard embodiments of water in pictorial cycles of the four elements. Documented in Christof Thoenes, "Zu Raffaels *Galatea*," in *Festschrift für Otto von Simson zum 65. Geburtstag*, ed. Lucius Grisebach and Konrad Renger (Berlin: Propyläen, 1977), 237 and note.

[7]The reference to Lewis Carroll is not inappropriate here. As early as 1778 in the poem "The Fisherman" Goethe used the image of passing into the water for passing out of the real world into the realm of fantasy.

hailed as the triumph of Eros.[8] The epiphany that Faust expected in the embrace of Gretchen is now celebrated on stage for all of us to experience.

Like every other fulfilled moment in the play this triumphant epiphany can only take place in some kind of show. Nevertheless, it is a show that requires less interpretation than some of the previous ones, for Nereus explicitly tells us that the scene is the annual momentary epiphany of Galatea. It is thus a kind of ritual, the high point of which is explained for us. The other parts of the ritual are less clear at first glance. They do, however, all contribute to the epiphany of Galatea as the ultimate form in which life can be embodied. Before considering the series of figures we should note the importance of the moon in this scene. It remains, according to the stage direction, at the zenith throughout. The presence of the moon identifies the world of the "Classical Walpurgis Night" yet again as a mediating, artificial realm, especially since the sirens describe the Aegean inlets of the last scene as the place "where Luna shines double" (l. 7513), that is, where both moon and its reflection are present. That the moon remains at the zenith is especially important, though perhaps astonishing in view of the importance of history in the act and in view of the necessary transitoriness of Galatea's appearance at the end. If the moon stands still, this ritual is, like Faust's descent through Manto's temple, out of time. As a moment out of time the scene in some sense replaces Faust's scene in Hades, which Goethe attempted but never actually wrote. This final festival must thus be understood as the fulfillment of Faust's earlier dreams, as the creation of Helen. Homunculus as spirit is Zeus, the descending god, and Galatea is Leda, the woman in the water. The moment of union is ineffable; in the two earlier dreams it was veiled, here it passes in a rush. But this ineffability is associated, curiously and ineluctably, with the temporal flux. To keep the terms of Faust's old bet with Mephistopheles and to accept the transitoriness of the moment is no longer simply a matter of a disciplined imagination; that discipline is rendered profoundly necessary by the nature of human existence, which is poised between the historical rush of the world and the permanence of transcendence. The historical nature of the world requires that any manifestation of transcendence, because it must be in the world, be transitory. Only the affirmation of mutability

[8]Cf. also Wind, *Pagan Mysteries in the Renaissance*, 131–37.

enables anything approaching a truly fulfilled moment in time. And that affirmation takes place, we are shown, in the infinitely repeatable ritual of the act of love.

The succession of figures in this ritual would appear at first to be a philologist's dream (or perhaps nightmare). However, none of these figures really comes from any more arcane a source than Ovid's *Metamorphoses* or Herodotus' *Histories*, and both these texts would have been thoroughly familiar to any tolerably educated contemporary of Goethe's. Even the allegorical harmonization of fire and water at the end was a cliché of the period. Metastasio's *Dido Forsaken* ends with the sea rising to douse the flames of Carthage, then a calming marine procession; an example closer to home would be the trials by fire and water in *The Magic Flute*. Furthermore, all of the speakers, in good masque tradition, tell the reader everything he needs to know about them. All it really takes to read this scene is self-confidence.

The larger shape of this progression of figures is the development of the representation of divinity (spirit in the world) from mixed human and animal form to the beauty of the pure human form. The sirens had first appeared among the sphinxes and griffons. Goethe follows classical and Renaissance tradition in conceiving them as women with the legs and wings of birds. Indeed, the sphinxes warn Faust about their hawklike claws among the twigs (ll. 7162–63). They embody the irresistible allure of the water, an allure that in this play it is proper not to resist, like Ulysses, but to follow, like Homunculus. Already at the beginning of the masque of Seismos they call upon all present to flee the earthquake for the safety of the sea, where Luna shines double; now they serve as the heralds to the final ritual masque.

First to appear, then, are the Nereids and Tritons—the latter explicitly identified as sea monsters (probably to be understood as humans with horses' bodies and fishes' tails). Their arrival identifies and starts to pull together the major themes of both the ritual and the play as a whole. They come in response to the song of the sirens. Their assertion "Gracious song draws us onward" (l. 8049) is echoed, it turns out, in the very last lines of Part II, "The eternal feminine / Draws us upward" (ll. 12110–11). (Both predicates in German are *zieht uns hin/heran*). The sirens, the water, Galatea are all what will be finally identified as the eternal feminine, the power of love. But the Nereids and Tritons have not come empty-handed, and their gifts are of great significance. They bring gold and treasure from the depths of the sea where it has lain in ships wrecked by the singing of the sirens. This is, of course, the gesture of Act I, the recovery of gold from the depths. Now it seems to be much easier to bring the gold back. But there is more. In Act I it was suggested that the gold in the depths had been buried at the fall of Rome, as the result of catacylsmic historical events. The mythical equivalent here, shipwreck, is less than cataclysmic. Indeed it is a repeated, common event for the sirens. Destruction, as well as generation, belongs then to the force of love. This is a perspective that readily embraces the Gretchen tragedy; indeed, from this point of view Mephisto's comment that Gretchen is "not the first" ("Dreary Day. A Field," l. 15) appears rather less cynical. The power of love is the power of nature, which encompasses death as well as birth. This is scarcely an original insight with Goethe, but it is one that *Faust* reinvests with profundity. Finally, the Nereids introduce the theme of evolution; they go to fetch the Cabiri to prove that they are more than fishes (ll. 8063, 8069), that the direction of development lies toward their human half. The theme continues in the exchange between Nereus and Homunculus that follows. Our attention is shifted to fully human forms, but more important, Nereus defines humans as beings who ever strive to become like gods (l. 8096), though they consistently fail to transcend themselves. We are reminded of Faust and the earth spirit. Once again a major theme of the play is placed in a much larger context. Striving seen from the larger context of the temporal flux becomes evolution, while the circular motions of the cosmos become the cycles of repetition brought about by the complementary generative and destructive powers of love.

The discussion of the Cabiri confirms this reading. Goethe summarizes with extraordinary virtuosity the various views as to the number and nature of the Cabiri, a topic of some discussion in the period.[9] The Cabiri seem to have been the most primitive form of divinity, for they were worshiped in the form of clay jugs (l. 8220). However, our sources are unable to agree upon either how many there were—three (l. 8186), four (l. 8187), perhaps seven (l. 8194) or eight (l. 8198)—or whether they were indeed so primitive as all that. Some were conceived as Olympian gods, therefore in human form (l. 8197), or even

---

[9]Goethe satirizes here a treatise by Friedrich Schelling, *On the Gods of Samothrace*. A brief but good discussion may be found in Cyrus Hamlin's interpretive notes to the Norton Critical Edition, 333–34.

as fully transcendent (l. 8199). They are seen as burlesque strivers—
"Yearning starvelings / For the unreachable" (ll. 8204–5). But if the
Cabiri comically represent striving as evolution, they also comically
combine fire and water. On the one hand, they have a special relation
to Neptune (ll. 8180–81); on the other, they are the equivalent of the
golden fleece (ll. 8212–15). The connection to gold is significant here,
for Herodotus identifies the Cabiri as the sons of Hephaestus, god of
fire. Small wonder, then, that the approach of the Cabiri precipitates a
preliminary climax with double chorus that is exceeded only by the
final epiphany.[10]

The Telchines focus both these concerns—the synthesis of fire and
water, and history as evolution—onto the specifically human form. As
the smiths and temporary bearers of Neptune's trident, they enjoy a
special relationship to the water god. Similarly, they enjoy special
protection from Helios, god of the sun. As smiths they would also
belong to Hephaestus. All of these gods belong to the stage of Olympian religion in Greece, which means they were consistently conceived in human form. And indeed, the Telchines emphasize at the
end of their speech not only that they have portrayed their god in
hundreds of human versions but also that they were the first people
ever to do so. The burlesque of the Cabiri hints, indeed, that one
might transcend the conception of human form for the gods, but
everything else in the scene insists upon the superiority of human
form. This is the turn into the world of Part I, now focused into one
precise image that yet takes account of the subjective basis of artistic
inspiration in Act I. The transcendent Absolute is to be sought not
simply in the world but in the beauty of the human form.

There can be no question that Galatea is one such manifestation of
the Absolute. Even before Homunculus empties his vial at her feet
she is accompanied by the powers of spirit in the form of doves with
wings "as white as light" (l. 8342). The scene abounds in traditional
tags of Renaissance Neoplatonism, all of which identify Galatea as the
ultimate *coincidentia oppositorum*, the embodiment of the harmony
of all conceivable pairs of oppositions. The sirens, for example, call

---

[10]Citati discusses the equivalence of Eros and the Cabiri (*Goethe*, 295), a reading
that I find fully compatible with mine. Altogether Citati's interest in the arcana of the
"Classical Walpurgis Night," the back alleys of classical mythology, which I argued are
not strictly necessary to understanding it, is very interesting and leads to a reading
with which I fully agree.

upon the Nereids to approach "in moderate haste" (l. 8379). The phrase refers to the widely popular paradoxical motto *festina lente* (hasten slowly), a motto that was, probably not incidentally, often illustrated by dolphins.[11] In the same speech the sirens describe Galatea:

> Grave in aspect like the gods,
> In dignified immortality,
> And yet, like lovely human maidens,
> In alluring grace.
>
> [ll. 8387–90]

She is thus the simultaneous embodiment of both divine and earthly love.[12] At the sight of her, finally, Thales feels imbued with the beautiful and the true (l. 8434), concepts central to ancient as well as Renaissance Platonism. Goethe's source for his final epiphany comes also from this same context; it is Raphael's *Triumph of Galatea*.[13] Raphael's painting invests Galatea with all the attributes of Goethe's scene—the dolphins, the Nereids and Tritons, the scallop shell of Venus, the triple god of love above her head (replaced by Homunculus), the emblem of harmony (the bundle of arrows in the upper left-hand corner of the painting), the rapid motion past the observer and, above all, the intense excitement.[14] From all of *Faust* this scene offers itself as the most openly Neoplatonic version and resolution of Goethe's dialectic.

Nevertheless, Galatea has her uniquely Goethean aspects as well. Working less from mythological sources than—apparently—from his own reading of the tradition in the visual arts, Goethe makes Galatea the historical successor to Venus. He was well aware of the tradition of

[11]Wind, *Pagan Mysteries in the Renaissance*, 97–112.

[12]Ibid., 138–41.

[13]There was considerable interest in the painting among German romantic writers, including Ludwig Tieck and A. W. Schlegel. See Thoenes, "Zu Raffaels *Galatea*," 226. Thoenes also (242–45) offers a good example of a Neoplatonist interpretation of the painting.

[14]Goethe also knew the ancient description of this motif from Philostratus (third century), whose treatise he translated and adapted with the title "Philostrats Gemälde" (The paintings of Philostratus) (1818). Under the topic "Cyclops and Galatea" he refers to the versions of Raphael in the Villa Farnesina and of Carracci in the Palazzo Farnese (*Gesamtausgabe*, 16 [Stuttgart: Cotta, 1961], 495).

Goethe's depiction of Galatea shares much of the iconography of Raphael's fresco *The Triumph of Galatea,* painted ca. 1512, in the Villa Farnesina, Rome. Courtesy of the Istituto Centrale per il Catalogo e la Documentazione, Rome (C 9401).

representing Venus borne from the sea on a scallop shell.[15] We are
most familiar with this tradition from Botticelli's *Birth of Venus*, another monument of Renaissance Neoplatonizing.[16] The exquisitely
beautiful Galatea in her shell chariot described by Philostratus in the
third century is easily conflatable with this Venus.[17] The association is
much easier to make when one realizes, as Goethe doubtless did, that
the eighteenth century knew two Galateas. The first, the daughter of
Doris and Nereus, is the sea nymph of classical mythology officially of
concern here. The second is the statue created by Pygmalion and
brought to life by Venus as a reward for the sculptor's devotion.[18]
Their son was Paphos (site of an important Venus cult), their great-
grandson Adonis, later lover of Venus. Indeed, in some versions of the
myth Venus herself marries Pygmalion in the guise of the beloved
statue. Goethe's important innovation here is to shape these connections in historical terms, so that Galatea becomes the successor to
Venus.[19] Winckelmann had shown that classical art had a history,
Goethe generalizes this insight to the entire classical ideal. Classical
beauty per se is not recovered in Galatea; she is a version of it, a later
evolution of what Venus once represented. Thus the paradox of the
moon standing still but Galatea only flashing past is repeated; even in

[15]"Philostrats Gemälde," 467.

[16]Wind, *Pagan Mysteries in the Renaissance*, 131–37.

[17]Indeed, the major seventeenth-century interpreter of the Carracci frescoes in the
Farnese Gallery, Giovanni Pietro Bellori, could not decide whether the painting now
taken to represent Thetis and Peleus represented Galatea or Venus.

[18]At least since Rousseau's *Pygmalion* (1762, first performance 1772), the wife of the
sculptor has popularly borne the name Galatea. Rousseau's play was popular in
Weimar as elsewhere; Goethe mentions it in connection with his own monodrama
Proserpine, among other places. On Rousseau's influence on the naming of the statue
see Walter Buske, "Pygmaliondichtungen des 18. Jahrhunderts," *Germanisch-Ro-
manische Monatsschrift* 7 (1915–19): 345–54, and Meyer Reinhold, "The Naming of
Pygmalion's Animated Statue," *Classical Journal* 66 (1970–71): 316–19.

[19]Goethe is not, strictly speaking, the first to identify Raphael's *Galatea* with Venus.
In 1816 J. J. Haus argued that it was a painting of Venus, not Galatea. Haus sparked off
quite a controversy in Italy (described and documented by Thoenes, "Zu Raffaels
Galatea," 230–31). Haus's first polemic was published in Germany in 1815 as an
appendix to Elisa von der Recke's *Tagebuch einer Reise durch einen Theil Deu-
tschlands und durch Italien in den Jahren 1804 bis 1806*, ed. H. Böttiger (Berlin,
1815). I cannot specifically document Goethe's knowledge of this work, but von der
Recke was a long-standing acquaintance from Goethe's regular summer visits to Carls-
bad. In any case, the historical connection between the two figures is uniquely
Goethe's.

art there can be no permanent ideal. As in nature there can be only momentary manifestations and remanifestations of the ideal. And each of these manifestations will participate in the typicality of the eternal but will also have its own historical individuality.

Galatea is, then, a peculiarly historical manifestation of the ideal. Yet the connection of the name to the Pygmalion myth also ties Galatea to the other major precondition for all of Goethe's versions of the ideal, that they be artificial. For as the creation of Pygmalion, Galatea is the artificial come to life, nature outdone by art. In his *Italian Journey* (1817) Goethe uses the Pygmalion myth to clarify his own relationship to antiquity when he arrives in Rome:

> Wherever I go I find familiars in a new world; it is all as I anticipated and all new. I can say the same of my observations and my ideas. I have had no entirely new thought, have found nothing entirely foreign, but the old ones have become definite, so alive, so coherent, that they can count as new.
>
> When Pygmalion's Elise, whom he had shaped entirely according to his wishes and given as much reality and existence as an artist can, when she finally approached him and said, "It is I!" how different was the live woman from the worked stone.[20]

The tension between the astonishing liveliness of his new mental world (compare also Mephisto's distress when he first arrives at the "Classical Walpurgis Night") and yet its familiarity reflects again the dynamic mediation between the transitory real and the eternal ideal. Goethe quickly progresses from what he sees to the tension within his own mind. Thus Elise/Galatea represents here what is projected from the poet's mind, not simply antiquity in human form. The ideal beauty in "Witch's Kitchen" appeared in a mirror frame; Gretchen, in a play

[20]*Italienische Reise*, in *Gesamtausgabe*, 9 (Stuttgart: Cotta, 1960), 327; translation mine. Galatea bears the name Elise here from a widely popular mid-eighteenth-century retelling of the myth by Karl Wilhelm Ramler (1725–1798). This was probably the version of the story most familiar to Goethe when he went to Italy in 1786. Although the *Italian Journey* was not published until 1817, it was based on diaries. In the meantime Goethe had devoted much more attention to Rousseau's version; thus Galatea would have been the obvious name for Goethe as for everyone else by the time of the "Classical Walpurgis Night" (1830). For a good summary of the popularity of the Pygmalion story and its various incarnations in eighteenth-century Germany, see Buske, "Pygmaliondichtungen des 18. Jahrhunderts."

within a play; Homunculus, in his crystal vial. The epiphany of Galatea leads this theme back, in a sense, to its mythological analogue and original.

In retrospect it is possible to see that the entire act consists of figures who are really projections of the sculptor's imagination. Sphinxes and griffons are typical monuments of ancient Egyptian and Near Eastern sculpture; the grouping of Peneios and his nymphs is typical of classical sculpture. Seismos is characterized as a colossal caryatid (l. 7545); Goethe possessed a painting of the two-story caryatid from the temple of Zeus at Agrigento.[21] The multitudes of Nereids, Tritons, hippocamps, and other sea creatures are not uncommon in Roman sculpture. The language of the act specifically calls attention to this underlying tendency. Chiron talks about the inadequacy of the sculptors' attempts to represent Hercules (l. 7394); Mephistopheles spends ten lines expressing his amazement and regret that there has never been a statue of the Phorcyads. Not only does the act abound in well-known motifs of classical sculpture, but these motifs appear in roughly historical order from early (Egyptian) to late (Roman). Thus Galatea sums up the subliminal structuring principle of the act in both of her special aspects, as historicized and as "artificial" manifestation of the ideal.

And yet, if we consider this collection of sculptural motifs and the paths through which they would have been familiar to Goethe, a whole new dimension of significance emerges. It is obvious that Goethe knows that sphinxes belong to the oldest levels of ancient art and mythology, for they say as much (l. 7197). Nevertheless, if we ask what sphinxes Goethe actually saw, the answer is not Egyptian sphinxes but the Renaissance grotesques that ornamented doorways, picture frames, ceilings, furniture, and who knows what else. The same is doubtless true of griffons, which where still a popular pattern on candlesticks, crockery, and table linen into the nineteenth century. Doubtless Goethe also knew the motifs from ancient carved gems, as did every connoisseur of classical art from the Renaissance on. But although such gems are rarely so fanciful and grotesque as the Roman wall ornaments on which the Renaissance grotesques are modeled,

---

[21]The statue was not visible when Goethe visited Agrigento in 1788, but a painting of the recently excavated temple and colossus was sent to him in 1828. The "Classical Walpurgis Night" was written in 1830. The caryatid is now to be seen in the archeological museum at Agrigento.

they are nevertheless closer to these paintings than to the major monuments of sculpture. Similarly, though Goethe doubtless saw Roman sculptures of sea creatures on visits to the Vatican, in Rome he would have passed innumerable examples of late Renaissance and baroque fountain sculptures every day. Nor are fanciful sea creatures confined to the fountains of Rome; Renaissance painting abounds with them as well. Goethe knew that paintings of the triumph of Galatea were not uncommon.[22] In his first month in Rome he saw Raphael's *Triumph of Galatea* in the Villa Farnesina and, in the Palazzo Farnese, the Carracci frescoes that depicted—among a great multitude of Neoplatonist allegories surrounded by ornamental sphinxes and colossal caryatids—another Galatea (which owes much to Raphael's), as well as sirens sitting on the rocks. Goethe also knew and admired the tapestry by Raphael showing Saint Paul in prison (Sistine Chapel), in which the saint, a colossal bearded giant, bursts forth from underground with arms raised. In every instance, then, the implicit history of ancient sculpture is mediated by Renaissance images with which Goethe had had much more direct experience.

In the prologue to the "Classical Walpurgis Night" the mediation takes place, as we remember, through the Shakespeare references in Erichtho's speech. The finale also has a seventeenth-century literary mediator, this time Calderón, whose *Love, the Greatest Enchantment* Goethe admired in the translation of A. W. Schlegel.[23] The play dramatizes the Circe episode from the *Odyssey* as an allegory of the soul deciding between virtue and pleasure, that is, between higher love and profane love. The latter is embodied in Circe, the witch who rules the elements in their aspect of deceptive and constantly metamorphosing appearances. She can raise volcanoes, storms at sea or in the air, and is served by a giant named Brutamonte (bestial mountain). Ulysses finally tears himself from her toils and escapes to the sea, but Circe intends to block his escape by raising a great storm. At this critical pass Galatea appears in her sea chariot, accompanied by the requisite Tritons and sirens. She protects Ulysses by her superior power to keep the sea calm, she explains, because Ulysses punished

---

[22]"Philostrats Gemälde," 495. Philostratus was a significant source for Renaissance painters, as Goethe clearly knew. In using him then, Goethe repeats a Renaissance gesture.

[23]An English translation exists in several editions by Denis F. MacCarthy (e.g., London: Longman, 1861).

Giant caryatids and sphinxes surround frescoes on mythological themes on the vault of the gallery in the Palazzo Farnese, Rome, painted by Agostino and Annibale Carracci from 1595 to 1603 or 1604. Courtesy of the Istituto Centrale per il Catalogo e la Documentazione, Rome (E 37385).

the cyclops Polyphemos, who had brutishly destroyed her lover Acis. Her constancy to her dead lover represents a higher love opposed to Circe's lust. Goethe does not, of course, share Calderón's counter-reformation stance; nevertheless the glorification of love through the epiphany of Galatea clearly cites and builds on the triumphant conclusion of Calderón's masterpiece. Other parallels are also easy to find. The power of love as central theme, the structuring tension between fire and water, the consistent metaphor of water as crystal are all fundamental to Calderón's play. A crucial example of Circe's wickedness that appears twice in the play is the generation of fire from water. Goethe reverses this when Homunculus approaches Galatea to embody the wholesome blending of world and spirit (or, in Calderón's terms, profane and sacred love). When Circe is defeated by Galatea her palace sinks and a volcano—Mount Aetna—rises in its place. This extraordinary occurrence and her comic servant Brutamonte surely have some connection to the masque of Seismos. And indeed, Brutamonte brings a chest onto the stage in which live a dwarf and a duenna who perform what can only be described as a kind of Punch and Judy show. The apparently bizarre and certainly peculiar combination of elements in Act II becomes more comprehensible, if *Love, the Greatest Enchantment* is understood as a subliminal, perhaps even subconscious, program for Goethe. But the greatest significance of this program is to show not simply that the act is framed by Renaissance gestures but that the "recovery of antiquity" in the act is at every moment self-consciously modern.[24] Goethe's success in trapping his critics and explicators into reading his intensely Renaissance pastiche as a genuine recovery of antiquity is doubtless one of those "very serious jokes" in which the play abounds.[25]

Nevertheless, the concern for history and historicity in the play is anything but a joke. We have already, in effect, observed two important functions of the concern with history. It has first of all been seen as a way to gain access to the best or most effective embodiment of the Absolute in the world, the culture of classical antiquity. It has also successfully temporalized art, which process in turn makes it possible

[24]We should of course remember that in late-eighteenth-century usage *modern* comprehended everything from the Renaissance on.

[25]The formulation is Goethe's and comes from a description of the play in a letter to Wilhelm von Humboldt, March 17, 1832, (*Weimarer Ausgabe* pt. 4, vol. 49, 281–84). This is the last letter Goethe ever wrote and his final word on the play.

to accept the transience of the moment on the theory that each age will have its own peculiarly appropriate moments of insight. In other words, art constitutes the intersection of myth and history. This formulation enables us, I think, to understand something more about Goethe's choice of materials for the act. I pointed out earlier that the figures in the final ritual of the act were not really very esoteric, and indeed this is true for the entire "Classical Walpurgis Night." There is virtually no mythological information in it that was not much more widely disseminated in the eighteenth century and that could not be gleaned from either Ovid or Herodotus.[26] While *The Metamorphoses* and *The Histories* were indeed well-known sources of mythological information, Goethe certainly had other possibilities open to him that were equally well known, including Homer. Yet what Ovid and Herodotus have in common illuminates their importance for Goethe. For the most striking larger structural feature of both *The Metamorphoses* and *The Histories* is the way they proceed from mythology and legend to history. Ovid moves from the creation of the world to the Roman Empire; Herodotus, from the rape of Europa to the Persian War. And in Herodotus, the "father of history," there is further a persistent tension between mythological explanation and what might be termed rationalist or historical explanation. Herodotus is concerned, ultimately, to define and validate modes of knowledge. Ovid has somewhat different concerns; he seeks, like Virgil, to give the newly powerful Rome a cultural, historical, and spiritual context. Thus in their different ways both these works embody and are, I think, profoundly concerned with the intersection of mythology and history. If Herodotus tries to validate a mode of knowledge and Ovid to generate a cultural context, then Goethe surely attempts to do both. The advent of historicism requires that each age must interpret the past—antiquity, in particular—anew in order to "know" it. But this effort to know it is also an effort to validate it, to establish its importance for the present. Thus the "Classical Walpurgis Night" constitutes, ultimately, not a recovery of antiquity, but a validation (in the sense of establishing the

---

[26]Even the griffons and the arimasps, who seem quite arcane to us today, were well known to earlier generations. See, for example, *Paradise Lost* II, 943–47. The note to this passage in my edition (ed. M. Y. Hughes [New York: Odyssey, 1962]) identifies this story as "popular."

value of) antiquity for Germany at the beginning of the nineteenth century. It is, ultimately, the validation of Goethe's own classicism.

But if the play constitutes the intersection of myth and history, it is also surely the intersection of meaning (or significance) and history. And indeed, history, as it is conceived in *Faust*, is of itself meaningless. This is already communicated by the setting, the battleground of Pharsalus. Erichtho reflects about it,

> How often it has already been repeated! will always
> Be repeated into all eternity . . . No one yields empire
> To another; no one will yield it who has gained it by force
> And rules forcefully
>
> [ll. 7012–15]

History is meaningless violence, embodied later in the act in the restless circling of the centaur Chiron. The "historical background" in Act I, the state of the empire, was chaotic and dangerous; this pattern will persist in the rest of the play. And in retrospect, it was already true in Part I. "Outside the City Gate" showed us a world defined by love and war, and all Faust wanted from the pact was to cast himself into the "rush of time" (l. 1754); in the "Prologue in Heaven" the archangels described the eternal circular motion of nature (compare Chiron!) and its violence. The temporal flux can only be given shape, history can only be fixed by an effort of the mind. Angus Fletcher associates monumentality with allegory in precisely this respect: to set a monument is to fix history and to give it meaning.[27] One wonders, indeed, if this insight does not explain the emphasis on sculptural motifs in Act II.

Be that as it may, the need to shape history, to give it meaning from elsewhere, to marry the transient Galatea to Homunculus, illuminates the relation of the descents in *Faust* to perhaps the most important descent for European literature, the descent to hell in Book VI of Virgil's *Aeneid*. The parallel to *Faust* is inescapable since Aeneas is the only other seeker to be accompanied by a sibyl. Aeneas descends in search of his father, Faust in search of Helen; but in fact, both really seek the same thing, a meaningful past. Aeneas seeks his father to

---

[27]Angus Fletcher, *Allegory: The Theory of a Symbolic Mode* (Ithaca: Cornell University Press, 1970), 361–62.

learn the future of his race, but the real issue for Virgil is not the future of the mythical Aeneas but the past of Rome. Similarly Faust seeks in Helen a historically validated vessel for the spirit he has recovered from the Mothers; what this search means for Goethe is a historically validated form for his own poetic insight, a past for the masterpiece of the new German literature. Aeneas returns to the world through the gates of ivory, the gates of false dreams. He thus becomes himself a kind of false dream, a fiction, who henceforth operates in a world in which every single action has significance for the future glory of Rome. Aeneas has become an allegory. But the case of Faust is no different. He will return to the world in the role of the medieval German invader of Greece, and will enter into a marriage with Helen that will be a manifest allegory of the relation of modern German culture to the classical past. The parallel to Virgil here is all the more striking because Faust's original confrontation with nature was cast in Virgilian terms. For it turns out that Faust's speech in response to the sign of the earth spirit is very similar to the description of the storm in Book III of the *Aeneid*.[28] With Aeneas, then, Faust moves from the world as nature to the world as art. But the most profound sense of the parallel here must surely be that Virgil is the original "Western" poet, the greatest poet in our tradition who looks back to a classical past with longing and melancholy. What better model, then, for Goethe, when he attempts to assess his own relation to that identical yet of necessity profoundly different past?

However, we must never lose our Renaissance perspective. If Goethe argues with Virgil that history has meaning only when shaped by the mind, the imagery in which this argument is summarized is typically Renaissance. The ultimate embodiment of the multitudinous succession of forms that constitutes the temporal flux is Proteus, the god of transformations. In Act I the corresponding embodiment of the presence of spirit in the world was Pan. But the complementarity of Proteus and Pan, the many and the One, is yet another of the Renais-

---

[28]*Faust*, ll. 464–72; *Aeneid*, III, 192–99. In *Aeneid* III the advent of the storm that drives the Trojan fleet onto the coast of the Harpies (note the unexpected shipwreck motif in Goethe) is described in terms of the arrival of a dark cloud overhead, increasing darkness, then lightning—the same sequence of events as in Faust's speech. Aeneas emerges from this storm to confront the revolting Harpies, Faust the horrifying earth spirit. Both heroes are dismissed with reprimands for their inflated ideas of their own importance.

sance Neoplatonist clichés that structure this part of *Faust*.[29] Thus the marriage of Homunculus and Galatea has, once again, far more than natural or even cosmological significance. It is the marriage of fire and water, spirit and world, but also Pan and Proteus, meaning and history, the present and the past. And in this form it clearly adumbrates the coming marriage of the present and the past in the marriage of Faust and Helen.

[29]Wind, *Pagan Mysteries in the Renaissance*, 191–99.

11

The Spirit of Poetry:
Act III

The marriage of Faust and Helen is the last of those great high points in the play we always feel we have been waiting for. Given its literally central position in Part II and the ways in which Acts I and II seem to prepare it, we may well consider it in some sense the highest of those points. Like the equivalent episode in Part I, the Gretchen tragedy, it is a play within the play. At the end Mephistopheles will unmask on stage, while Helen and her son will evaporate, leaving their costumes behind them. And like all plays within the play in *Faust*, it represents the synthesis of real and ideal, here seen as the marriage of Faust and Helen. The act consists of three scenes—"Before the Palace of Menelaus at Sparta," "Inner Courtyard," and "Shady Groves"—in which the figures are increasingly conscious of their roles within a drama. Indeed, the final scene is not, strictly speaking, a separate scene, for Faust evokes a transformation of the set on stage, so that "Shady Grove" is really "played" in the "Inner Courtyard." But increasing staginess is not the only progression in this act. The three scenes represent the history of European literature in high points: classical tragedy, medieval lyric, modern pastoral opera. This history is viewed, however, not only progressively but also dialectically, for the three periods embody respectively the classic, the romantic, and their "marriage"—the three here being conceived as literary and epistemological modes. Thus we will need to explore each of these scenes in all of these different respects—as historical constructs, as generic constructs, as aspects of Goethe's various versions of the dialectic.

The first scene, "Before the Palace of Menelaus at Sparta," addresses above all the question "Who is this Helen on the stage before us?" The situation is confusing enough for the reader coming fresh from the "Classical Walpurgis Night," and by the end of Helen's very first speech, in which she supposedly introduces herself, Helen herself has become confused, recognizing already that she is the subject of fairy tales. In succeeding speeches she reassures herself that she had just returned from Troy and been sent ahead from the ships to prepare a sacrifice; but when she enters the palace she is driven from what she thought was her own home by the threatening stewardess Phorcyas, played of course by Mephistopheles. An energetic exchange of insults between Phorcyas and the chorus (ll. 8807–25) shakes Helen's confidence in her own identity.

> Can it be memory? is it delusion that seizes me?
> Was I all that? Am I now? Shall I be henceforth
> The nightmare image of that destroyer of cities?
> [ll. 8838–40]

Phorcyas completes the destruction by recalling all of the conflicting myths about Helen in succession, so that she finally cries out, "I faint away and become an empty image even to myself" (l. 8881), and faints. When she awakens she no longer expects to be anything but herself, a role player, ready to deliver herself into the hands of the newly arrived German barbarians (Goethe condenses some two thousand years into Phorcyas' careless "some twenty years or so" [l. 9004]) so as to save her women. She is even aware that Phorcyas, too, is but a role played by another, for at lines 9047–48 she notes that the mask has been momentarily dropped. This is a world in which identities are replaced by roles.

What, then, is Helen's role? We have already seen that the epiphany of Galatea reenacts the rape of Leda and is thus the realization of Faust's dreams about the conception of Helen. The Helen of Act III is the first character to appear on stage or to speak after this scene. Helen is thus projected in some significant poetic sense as the daughter of this Galatea/Leda. But Galatea is not simply a stand-in for Leda. She is the ultimate manifestation of form. The offspring of her mating with Homunculus—spirit in search of human form—can only be ideal beauty, the appearance of the ideal in the world. Thus the chorus repeatedly associates Helen with the sun (e.g., l. 8601) but at the same time recognizes that she is the ultimate form—"form of forms / Which the sun ever illumined" (ll. 8907–8). In the second scene Lynceus will equate her appearance with the rising of the sun. There can be no question that Helen, most beautiful woman who ever lived and most beautiful woman of antiquity, here represents one manifestation of spirit in the world, perhaps the ultimate one in our culture.

Her role is further determined by the mythological heritage. Helen is identified as "swan-begotten" (l. 9108) in the last chorus of the scene, and this last chorus invokes yet again the setting of Faust's double dream of Leda with its river, reedy banks, and swans. The mythological connection to Act II is strengthened by the other connections of Helen to the water. She has just arrived from the ships, by the grace of Poseidon and with the help of Euros, the wet east wind. The name of the river to which she has come, Eurotas, means "copiously flowing," and the Eurotas is in fact the river by which the rape of Leda took place. Faust's mythological dream has now been fully realized, and on a mythological level Helen's arrival from the sea follows logically upon the plunge into the sea at the end of Act II. But by the end of the scene Helen is understood to have come from the Underworld as much as from the sea. The chorus now identifies the swan's call as "death-heralding" (l. 9102); it turns out that it has been standard since Plutarch to conflate Leda with Leto, Night.[1] Furthermore, Goethe would have known from his mythological dictionary that some mythographers replaced Leda in the story with Nemesis, goddess of divine vengeance.[2] Thus the entire myth has strong associations with the Underworld. It is not surprising that to fetch Helen from the sea should be the equivalent of fetching her from the Underworld. In retrospect we understand better why Goethe laid such emphasis on the conception of Helen in Act II. He wanted to establish solid mythological grounding for the synthesis of ghost or spirit and physical form or world that he achieves in his Helen. Swans are already associated with poetry in mythology (and Goethe refers to the swan song in l. 9102); with that the mythological circle around Helen is closed. As

[1]See Edgar Wind, *Pagan Mysteries in the Renaissance* (New York: Norton, 1968), 153 and note.

[2]Benjamin Hederich, *Gründliches Mythologisches Lexikon* (Darmstadt: Wissenschaftliche Buchgesellschaft, 1967), 1447.

product of sea, underworld, and swan, Helen legitimately embodies nature, spirit, and poetry in her incarnation in this play.

But Helen's role is not exclusively grounded in mythology. Act II repeatedly called attention to the role of poets and other artists in transmitting our mythological heritage; Act III dramatizes this process. This scene is written in trimeter (basically a six-foot iambic line), the standard meter of Greek tragedy, and Helen's first speech is a typical Euripidean prologue, in which a character introduces himself and the situation of the play. As it turns out, Goethe's Helen owes a great deal to the heroine of Euripides' *Helen*. Euripides' play is set in Egypt, a land associated with death for the Greeks and their cultural heirs. Helen has been sheltered there during the Trojan War while an image of her ran off with Paris and lived in Troy; this is the myth Goethe's Phorcyas refers to at lines 8872–73. The rulers in Egypt are Proteus, a rationalized version of the god Goethe uses in Act II, and Psamathe, whose name means sand and who is herself a Nereid. The entire world of this play is defined by the water, from the opening lines—

> These are the waters of the Nile, stream of sweet nymphs.
> The river, fed with the melting of pale snows, and not
> with rain, rises to flood the flats of Egypt[3]—

through references to the river Eurotas at Sparta to the Leda myth and the final escape of Helen and Menelaus to the sea at the end. In addition to these motivic connections, the relationship of reality or essence to appearance is the central theme of Euripides' play. *Image* is a recurrent term. It is not only associated with the problem of the image of Helen, which Menelaus has brought from Troy and which evaporates upon his arrival in Egypt, but already pervades the Egyptian world as well. The sister of the current Egyptian king changed her name from Ido (idol or image) to Theonoë (knower of god) when her prophetic gifts developed. The play is preoccupied with the illusoriness of reputation and the capacity of language—whether as fame or as prophecy—to mislead. Indeed, all appearances are misleading in Euripides' play. The Greeks are constantly playing roles; ultimately only the servants do not lie. Man seems to consist of body,

---

[3]*Helen*, trans. Richmond Lattimore, in *The Complete Greek Tragedies*, 3 (Chicago: University of Chicago Press, 1960), p. 413, ll. 1–3.

spirit, and fame; but of these only the spirit, which manifests itself as justice, is truly dependable amid the shifting lies of the world.

Although Goethe does not adopt Euripides' moral stance, it is nevertheless evident that he exploits both the theme and the imagery of the *Helen* for his own use. The interesting point is that when Goethe chooses a classical model for his re-creation of Greek tragedy (and this first scene attempts nothing less), he chooses a tragedy with a happy ending (Helen and Menelaus escape together). This is neither by chance nor atypical; Goethe's first serious attempt to write drama on ancient models, the *Iphigenia in Tauris* (1787), closely follows another tragedy of Euripides with a happy end. Unlike *Iphigenia*, *Faust* even carries the subtitle "tragedy." By choosing the *Helen* as his classical prototype, Goethe thus constitutes a tragic tradition with legitimate classical ancestry but independent of conventional Aristotelian norms.

Goethe's modern source for the concerns of Helen continues these thematic and generic reflections. What happens to Helen in this scene is, I believe, a deliberate parallel to what happens to the heroine of Rousseau's *Pygmalion*, Galatea. The problem for Rousseau's Pygmalion is to recover his lost inspiration, which he does when Galatea comes to life. She is brought to life in two stages. First Pygmalion pours his own longing into her. "In my delirium I believe myself able to cast myself out of myself; I believe myself able to give her my life, and inspirit her with my soul."[4] Then he prays to the "soul of the universe, principle of all existence," who is also "sacred fire, heavenly Venus, through whom everything is conserved and reproduced without end!"[5] When Homunculus casts himself out of his vial to impregnate Galatea with his spark of a soul, he thus plays the role of Rousseau's Pygmalion. This is enough to identify the two Galateas.[6] But the real connection in Goethe comes through Helen, "daughter," as we have seen, of Galatea. Rousseau's Galatea, like Goethe's Helen, comes to consciousness of herself. When she descends from the pedestal her first word is *me*. She proceeds from consciousness of herself, then, to consciousness of what is not herself. This fascination with consciousness is typically modern, and will be identified as such in the

[4]Jean-Jacques Rousseau, *Oeuvres complètes*, 2 (Paris: Gallimard [Pléiade], 1964), 1228; translation mine.

[5]Ibid.

[6]The "Classical Walpurgis Night" was written three years after Act III. Thus it seems likely that the structure of the encounter between Homunculus and Galatea, perhaps even the initial choice of the Galatea motif, is determined by the importance of Rousseau for Act III.

last part of Act III, where the chorus will comment on the association of the music and new operatic meters with the way everything comes from the heart (ll. 9687–94). We have already seen the association of Rousseau and the nature of consciousness with Faust's original pact with Mephistopheles. It is therefore appropriate to find another work of Rousseau lurking behind the epiphany of Galatea and the marriage with Helena, the two most glorious fulfilled moments in the play.

Rousseau was not only present in the pact scene; he was revised, as well, and the same is true here. In the pact scene, we remember, Rousseau's solitary wanderer was implicitly criticized for reveling in consciousness rather than striving. Here, too, his Galatea and Pygmalion turn from the world into the bliss of pure self-consciousness. For when Pygmalion kisses her, she sighs, "Me again," submerging her newfound self-consciousness in consciousness of Pygmalion. Pygmalion likewise cries at the end, "Henceforth I shall live only through you," although previously he had shrunk from the thought of identity with the beloved. Goethe's Helen, by contrast, first gives up her consciousness of herself (she faints); but when she awakens it is to become conscious of herself not as a sentient but as an artificial being. Rousseau's Galatea steps down from her pedestal; Goethe's Helen does the reverse when she faints away and becomes herself a statue (*Idol*, l. 8881).[7] Later she actually *ascends;* she moves *forward* in time to meet Faust and joins him *up* on a dais. Finally, she *transcends* the limits of ordinary reality. Her consciousness is never Rousseau's pure consciousness of identity, but rather a completely outward-directed consciousness of herself as a role or a historical function. It is, if you will, a self-consciousness that transcends self. When Helen pronounces her equivalent of Galatea's *me*—"Here am I! Here!" (l. 9412)—the repetition of *here* already indicates the outward focus of her consciousness. And the context emphasizes this difference:

> I feel myself so far and yet so near,
> And but too gladly say: Here am I! Here!
> [ll. 9411–12]

Faust's conclusion to this exchange—"Existence is duty, were it only for a moment" (l. 9418)—reiterates the same sense of responsibility

---

[7]Indeed, in his autobiography Goethe explicitly criticizes the "false tendency" of Rousseau's play to dissolve art into nature (*Dichtung und Wahrheit*, pt. 3, bk. 2 [*Gesamtausgabe der Werke und Schriften in zweiundzwanzig Bänden*, 8 (Stuttgart: Cotta, 1959)], 573).

we saw in the pact scene. The lovers focus, not on themselves or one another, but on space (here) and time (moment). Consciousness for Goethe is spirit in the world.[8]

Once again Goethe uses Rousseau as a reference point whose meaning he reverses. But this reversal is, as it was in the pact scene, two-edged. Not only must Rousseau be corrected, but he is also worth correcting. On reflection, it is quite extraordinary that the full emergence of classical drama in *Faust* proceeds completely without reference to neoclassical drama, which could at least provide a historical frame equivalent to Renaissance sculpture in Act II. Why correct Rousseau but not even bother with Racine? The reason is that Goethe's interest in Rousseau is generic as well as personal. "In the beginning was the deed," Faust had translated. The spirit of classical drama as performance is revived not in the static psychological analysis of Racine but in the alternative dramatic tradition to which Rousseau's playlet belongs. This "lyric scene," as Rousseau called it, is operatic, for it alternated declamation with music. Thus when Goethe's chorus associates the musical accompaniment in the last scene with emphasis on the heart, it calls attention to the generic significance of Rousseau's play. The double determination of Helen here through Euripides and Rousseau serves as more than historical framing; it prepares the generic argument of the act that opera is the natural historical successor to ancient tragedy.

And yet, to make one last point about the sources for this scene, Euripides is not the exclusive classical model by any means. Commentators have pointed to language borrowed from Aeschylus and Sophocles, as well as from Aristophanes and Homer. Helen's description of her first encounter with Phorcyas inside the house, for example, owes much to the Pythia's description of the Furies in the *Eumenides*. Phorcyas' threat that the chorus will all be hanged goes back to the punishment of Penelope's maids in the *Odyssey*. The chorus's description of the gigantic gods destroying Troy is not even Greek; it comes from the second book of the *Aeneid*. The scene abounds in epic similes (e.g., ll. 8765–70) that are Homeric rather than tragic. But it is perhaps most important to be aware of the gradual modulation out of

[8]In fact, the celebration of the Cabiri in the festival of Galatea had already suggested this theme, for the passage satirizes an essay by Schelling that interprets the Cabiri as successive stages of consciousness. Goethe touches on this aspect when he refers to them as aware (l. 8200) and as seekers of the unreachable (ll. 8204–5).

the tragic mode into Aristophanic parody of tragic language. The tendency starts as soon as Phorcyas enters (her exchange of insults with the chorus is typically Aristophanic) and becomes extreme toward the end of the scene. There she parodies the sublime tragic mode (ll. 8974–81) in posturing that Helen recognizes as "well-known sayings" (l. 8982), and later uses very colloquial language (ll. 9010–30).[9] Here is the same historicizing tendency that we found in Act II but now applied specifically to Greek tragedy. It is also the same thing that is happening to Helen: just as Helen is separated in this scene from the historical and cultural context that brought her into being, tragedy too is untied from its original cultural moorings and set loose in the sea of history. Tragedy, then, has no more permanence than any other form; Goethe will pursue here its evolution. The analogy strengthens the sense that has already developed from other aspects of the discussion that the act is as much about the development of tragedy as about Helen, indeed that the fortunes of Helen are the fortunes of poetry.

The first scene begins with the specific historical reality generated by Act II and alienates that reality to transform it into poetry. Helen needs the context of ancient Greek tragedy to seem real, but then she must be divorced from that context so that she can marry Faust, who in turn comes from his own modern or "romantic" context.[10] At the very end of this scene Phorcyas describes Faust's Gothic castle in the midst of the Spartan setting. This repeats the situation of the dumb show of Paris and Helen from Act I, but in reverse. And this repetition of Gothic within Greek—or, as it will appear in "Inner Courtyard," Greek figures within Gothic—is a clear indication that the play is now ready to pick up where it was interrupted by the explosion at the end of Act I. Once again we have returned from a descent in search of spirit to a stage in the world; once again Faust has generated a "rainbow." But this one is better grounded in the real, and this time Faust will demonstrate more awareness of the artist's proper relationship to his work. This time spirit will be integrated into reality more successfully.

If the first scene was Helen's scene, the second would appear to be Faust's. We jump forward in time to a medieval setting, which would

[9]This argument is made *in extenso* in Emil Staiger, *Goethe*, 3 (Zurich: Atlantis, 1959), 373–75.
[10]The term *romantic* was often used in Germany around 1800 to refer to the medieval and Renaissance periods.

differ relatively little (in this context) from Faust's "proper" sixteenth-century setting. Goethe justifies the connection from the fact that during the Middle Ages, Frankish invaders and later crusaders established transient kingdoms in Greece. The style follows the change in set. The Greek trimeter gives way to the rhymed tetrameter often found in medieval German troubadour lyric. Indeed the central focus of the historical shift is the stylistic shift, for Helen self-consciously learns to speak in the new manner. Nevertheless, the stylistic development does not proceed linearly. Faust is the first "modern" to speak in the scene, and he speaks indeed in a "modern" meter, blank verse, which is the meter not only of Shakespeare but of Goethe's and Schiller's own dramas as well. Only when Lynceus enters do the medieval meters begin, and even so, Helen's first speech to Faust is still not rhymed but is in the more modern blank verse. It is crucial to recognize that in every scene the penetration of the past must begin anew, that we must move back through Shakespeare to the deeper past. Every reconstruction of the past is artificial and framed. Small wonder that Helen says so emphatically, "Here am I! Here" (l. 9412), for her journey thither has been tortuous in the extreme. Faust, too, has moved "backward," to rhymed couplets; it is a costume he must don like his medieval garb to alienate himself from his own reality and approach Helen. The emphasis upon culture and history as linguistic form implies that to conquer Greece is to take possession of its literature. Thus when Menelaus approaches and Faust distributes the provinces of Greece to his followers in prospect of their victory, he is distributing the classical heritage to the modern age. The real victory is the intellectual struggle to recover that heritage.

The measure of this victory is Faust's ability to create Arcadia by describing it. Having sent his army off to repel Menelaus, Faust describes Arcadia in a series of quatrains (ll. 9506–73). The speech proceeds from geographical identification to the birth of Helen to enumeration of the qualities more familiar to us from Renaissance pastoral. This Arcadia is a pure poetic world outside of normal space—"For where Nature in her pure circle reigns, / All worlds intertwine" (ll. 9560–61)—and out of time: "Let the past be put behind us" (l. 9563). In effect the speech recapitulates the generation of Helen by Goethe from the "Classical Walpurgis Night" through the pastoral in the last scene of Act III. But the astonishing thing about this concentrated poetic act is that it effects a total change of scene on stage simply through the power of Faust's language. At the beginning of "Inner Courtyard" the chorus had described the preparations for Helen's welcome as they occurred, but now Faust describes the new setting *before* it comes into being. Only in the spirit song in "Charming Landscape" have we seen a purer example of the creative power of the word. Faust has now become a full-fledged poet. Previously in the play the escapes from Gothic prisons (to "Auerbach's Tavern" in Part I, to the "Classical Walpurgis Night" in Part II) were stage-managed by Mephistopheles, who provided his magic cloak. Now the ultimate significance of Mephisto's magical shortcuts and of his mediation becomes clear. That mediating power which enables man to know the world and to know the Absolute is nothing other than the power of poetry. Faust has become, for the time being at least, his own mediator.

Faust is not the only mediator in this part of the play. The very next speech is the long tale of Phorcyas/Mephisto about the birth of Euphorion. This takes place in fairy-tale underground realms whose only existence in the play is in the language of Phorcyas. Mephisto, too, is a poet. Furthermore, the chorus immediately recognizes this tale as a modern version of the birth of Hermes. By clothing the ancient plot in new bodies and characters, Mephisto performs a mediation of antiquity little different from that of popular eighteenth-century writers.

There is a third mediating figure as well—Lynceus. In fact, the meaning of this scene turns on the identity of Lynceus, just as that of the first scene turns on Helen's identity. The name means lynxlike and refers to the sharp vision for which the animal was known in antiquity (cf. ll. 9230–31). It had already been given to the watchman of the ship Argo in the *Argonautica* of Apollonius of Rhodes. There the most important reference to Lynceus comes in Book IV where everyone searches for Hercules and only Lynceus can spy him at a great distance. Hercules, we remember, was mentioned in the "Classical Walpurgis Night" as the "fairest hero" of antiquity (l. 7397), the male counterpart of Helen. Here in Act III, Lynceus is blinded by Helen as Faust almost was by the rising sun in "Charming Landscape." As the worshiper of Helen, Lynceus thus embodies the visionary capacity directed specifically toward antiquity; he is Faust's "eye" for ancient beauty. The specific classical source is significant, for Apollonius is extremely conscious in the *Argonautica* of "looking back" to Homer. At the same time Lynceus is also the troubadour poet, as his eloquent verses testify. Thus he is Faust's mediator to the past in a more general sense as well.

Once again Goethe has reconstructed the trio of Act I: Lynceus now plays the role of Boy-charioteer/Ariel; the hideous Phorcyas/Mephisto, Greed/Caliban; and Faust, again, Plutus/Prospero. As the one who is blinded by Helen, Lynceus mediates to spirit while Mephisto has provided the antique forms (or realities). Faust has fully entered into the role of Prospero when he transforms the stage into Arcadia, but only Lynceus's spiritual capacity to "envision" antiquity enables Faust to become the creator of modern Arcadias. And indeed Faust's creation speech anchors itself firmly in the geographical center of Greece and touches, for the last time now, on the story of Leda and the swan, taking it finally up to the birth of Helen. This thorough grounding in the vision of antiquity is the essence of Goethe's classicism.

The play proceeds now to pastoral opera, which Goethe has selected to represent modern literature. But not only does the structure of the act follow the historical development of European literature; it is dialectical as well. Before the rest of Part II was written, Goethe originally gave Act III the subtitle "Classical-Romantic Phantasmagoria: An Interlude to *Faust*." Clearly the first scene is the classical part, the second scene the romantic part. The real synthesis comes in the last part, in the play within the play enacted on the set that Faust has just created in the courtyard of his castle. Mephisto's tale of the birth of Euphorion and the chorus's equivalent tale of the birth of Hermes repeat the poles of the dialectic at the beginning of the last scene. The double perspective not only adumbrates the final synthesis but also tells us a good deal about it.

Euphorion, the poet, is equated with Hermes the messenger of the gods. Both are mediators. Both grow up quickly, metamorphosing from infant to adult like a butterfly, embedded in the Protean historical flux. Furthermore, Hermes was the inventor of the lyre, which he then gave to Phoebus Apollo in recompense for having stolen the older god's cattle. But baby Euphorion is described by Phorcyas as "a little Phoebus" (l. 9620). Euphorion thus becomes, in effect, the direct receiver of the gift of Hermes; his poetic gift is the heritage of antiquity. The most important aspect of Hermes in terms of the space devoted to it, is that he is a rogue (l. 9652) and a thief. The German word here, *Schalk,* is the word God uses for Mephisto in the "Prologue in Heaven" (l. 339).[11] Euphorion, too, is a playful tease. The model of the poet is thus once again the clown or, as Act II has more profoundly defined it, the parodist. Even more important is that Hermes is a thief. This fact characterizes the modern poet's relation to antiquity, but it also puts that relation into perspective. All poets are thieves who exploit their predecessors. Goethe reveals that he himself is a thief in modeling the birth of Euphorion on that of Hermes. This is yet another perspective on the allusiveness of *Faust*.

But the importance of theft extends beyond the issue of poetry. In the previous scene Lynceus was, in effect, a thief as he amassed his extraordinary treasure. Menelaus, the legitimate—or perhaps *a* legitimate—possessor of Helen appears here as a pirate (ll. 8857, 8985). In fact, possession of Helen is always the result of a theft, whether through the wiles of Phorcyas or through the boldness of Paris or Theseus. As we have seen, the final epiphany of Act II must also be understood as a rape, in which Homunculus takes possession of Galatea. Furthermore, the subliminal violence of that scene increases when we realize that it is, as Goethe doubtless intended, a sanitized version of the birth of Venus. The goddess of beauty was engendered by the semen of Uranus, which fell into the sea when he was castrated by his son Cronus. In effect Cronus stole the creative power of his father; the result was beauty.[12] The symbol of creative power in the play, gold, provokes repeated thefts and war in the masque of Seismos. As the father of Euphorion by Helen, finally, Faust replaces Achilles in the myth; thus he stands in for the fiercest and most effective soldier in Western culture. From this point of view we can now see that the end of the spirit song—"All is open to the noble / Who understand and swiftly grasp" (ll. 4664–65)—functions as a prospective synthesis of the violence of history and the peace of eternity. The poet as thief, therefore, embodies a kind of theodicy, for he reinterprets violence and theft as manifestations of the creative principle in the world. Thus the final synthesis of Act III must be seen in a line with "Charming Landscape," the Gretchen tragedy, and the "Prologue in Heaven." What first appeared as essential amorality in

[11]Compare Pietro Citati, *Goethe*, trans. R. Rosenthal (New York: Dial Press, 1974), 181, who associates Mephisto with Hermes.

[12]We may also think in this context of Goethe's profound interest in the Prometheus myth, expressed in two fragmentary dramas (*Prometheus* and *Pandora*), where again the theft of fire results in the emergence of human creativity.

the prologue now emerges as a higher morality after all. It is important to understand this implicit theodicy because the last two acts return openly to moral issues, which must be understood, not in a traditional context, but in this moral context generated by the play.

The blending of the classical and romantic poet-thieves takes place in the form of an opera that begins right after the chorus on the birth of Hermes. From here through the lament for Euphorion there is full orchestral accompaniment and everyone, including the chorus, uses the short rhymed lines typical of Goethe's own libretti. Here Goethe's historical and generic concerns fall together. Because of its strong spectacular tradition, opera has always dramatized the kinds of epiphanies and manipulations that are central to *Faust*. But it is also the historical successor to tragedy, for it was born from the speculations of late sixteenth-century Florentine humanists who mistakenly concluded that Greek tragedies were essentially sung throughout. Their efforts to re-create true Greek tragedy are known today as the first operas.[13] We have already seen how the chorus associates the musical form with modern subjectivity; nevertheless it is the chorus itself that most clearly embodies the continuity between ancient and modern forms. This synthesis of ancient and modern, or classical and romantic, is the ultimate synthesis of opposites in the play thus far. The previous high point, the epiphany of Galatea, was less direct in that it merely represented all kinds of polarities in the play. But the opera in Act III is not only significant; it also *is* what it represents; it is explicitly the kind of show that the play has all along suggested would be the true locus of the synthesis of ideal and real.

As a result, the world of Euphorion seems a more stable construct than the brief moment of Galatea's appearance. Nevertheless, this world, too, dissolves, and the reasons for the dissolution illuminate the precarious nature of the blending. The irony of the parallels between Hermes and Euphorion, as well as the resistance of the chorus to the modern form into which they are pressed, suggests the problematic nature of the situation. The blending depends upon a fundamentally ahistorical gesture that denies the uniqueness of the classical period. It is possible to transcend this discrepancy temporarily, but not to overcome it permanently. Moreover, the blending is destroyed by the nature of Euphorion's own striving. He focuses his restless

[13]Interesting discussion of the parallel births of Greek tragedy and Renaissance opera may be found in Karl Kerényi, "Geburt und Wiedergeburt der Tragödie," in *Streifzüge eines Hellenisten* (Zurich: Rhein, 1960), 29–60.

activity first on a maiden from the chorus. He chases her as Mephisto pursued the Lamiae, but instead of turning into other forms, Euphorion's chosen one turns into a flame; Euphorion has been pursuing pure spirit. Once burned, he turns from the maiden to seek the world around him, for as he climbs the rocks, more and more of the world surrounding Faust's enclosed Arcadia comes into sight. And as Act II would lead us to expect, the world outside the realm of art consists of violence and war. In his striving to reach this worldly realm, Euphorion destroys himself. There is significance in the ironic reversal of the play's normal patterns here. Euphorion strives after pure spirit (fire) in the worldly mode of Mephisto, but he strives after the world with all the imagery of upward movement and flight associated with Faust's quest for the Absolute in Part I. The Absolute and the world have been so firmly mingled by now in the play that direction no longer matters; however, it does matter that Euphorion has separated his quest into steps. By separating the search for spirit from the search for the world, he unravels the synthesis achieved by his father in Act II. Another way of seeing this is to recognize that Euphorion is too much of a grasper. When he begins his chase he describes himself as a hunter (l. 9771), and soon his troubled parents hear hunting horns (l. 9787). Now, hunting horns and hunting are the ultimate clichés of German romanticism. Euphorion loses his balance and becomes too romantic. And this is associated with becoming too much of a snatcher, too much of a thief. In the terms of the spirit song the balance has shifted too far from understanding to grasping. The result is the dissolution of the "Classic-Romantic Phantasmagoria."

Discipline of the imagination has been long since defined as a central issue in *Faust*. Here the theme emerges as an open allegory. In his failure to control himself Euphorion is an Orpheus figure. Faust's descent was compared to that of Orpheus in Act II (l. 7493), but in fact Faust is not like Orpheus because Faust has succeeded in bringing his beloved back from the Underworld. Euphorion, however, is much more like Orpheus, though with the directions of motion reversed; the tragedy of both is the failure of self-control. Seventeenth-century Orpheus operas end with the apotheosis of the hero.[14] Goethe's opera

---

[14]E.g., Monteverdi's (1609). Gluck's (1762) ends with the restoration of Euridice to Orpheus in the temple of Amor, which is an eighteenth-century rationalized equivalent. The phenomenon would appear to be the modern version of the Euripidean *deus ex machina*, but devoid of its irony. On the widespread use of apotheosis for opera conclusions see Kerényi, "Geburt und Wiedergeburt der Tragödie," 58–60.

here ironizes such an apotheosis. Euphorion's aureole ascends to heaven, but his body disappears and his clothing and lyre remain behind to be exploited by Mephistopheles. Thus a full apotheosis is denied him; Faust, by contrast, is carried off in the clouds (a typical stage machine for apotheoses), and at the end of Act V indeed accomplishes a full-fledged baroque assumption into Heaven. In his constant recognition of the limits imposed by Arcadia, Faust is a better poet than his son.

But like Helen and Lynceus, Euphorion is more than his mythological determinants. Who is he really? Or rather, who else is he? In a suppressed stage direction to the masque in Act I, Goethe had told his readers not who Euphorion was but what role he played, which in *Faust* is, after all, more significant. Boy-charioteer was originally to have been introduced as Euphorion in the role of Boy-charioteer. Eckermann objected to the absurdity of a role played by a character as yet unborn, so Goethe struck the reference. Euphorion had already been born in the only sense in which he could be—that is, Act III had been written before the masque was begun—but Goethe must have despaired of explaining that to Eckermann, whom the poet seems to have taken—alas properly—as typical of the capacities of his audiences for the coming century. The connection between the two characters is obvious as soon as it is pointed out. Both are light-footed poets, poetic spirits. Euphorion's aureole connects him to the fire that has linked all of these spirit figures, from the will-o'-the-wisps in the "Walpurgis Night" on. Goethe also identified Euphorion with Byron.[15] Notorious for an aberrant sex life, Byron died in Greece on the way to join the Greek war for independence. On the basis of these parallels Goethe made the dirge for Euphorion also a dirge for the admired English poet. Byron, like Euphorion, is normally understood to embody for Goethe the spirit of modern poetry. And so he doubtless does. But in so doing, he also embodies what Goethe saw as the special danger of modern poetry. Right after Byron's death Goethe commented: "It is undoubtedly a misfortune that minds so rich in ideas should be so set on realizing their ideals and bringing them into real life. That simply will not do. The ideal and ordinary reality must

---

[15]In conversation with Eckermann, July 5, 1827 (Johann Peter Eckermann, *Gespräche mit Goethe in den letzten Jahren seines Lebens*, Gedenkausgabe, 24 [Zurich: Artemis, 1948], 256).

be rigorously kept apart."[16] This is precisely the error for which Goethe criticized Rousseau's *Pygmalion;* it is precisely the error of Euphorion himself. But as an error that places too much emphasis on reality, it is the error of Mephistopheles; and Euphorion is as much Greed/Mephistopheles as he is Boy-charioteer, even beyond his similarity to the demonic Byron. He chases after the girl as Mephisto does after the Lamiae; his fascination with the physical aspects of the girl, with war, with stirring up excitement is all Mephistopheles'. In fact, the interesting thing about Euphorion is that he embodies within himself the entire trio from the masque. Although within the scene he is different from Faust, his language of striving is exactly that of his father, as is his capacity to span both the poetic and the social realms. In this respect he is Plutus/Faust as well. Thus Euphorion represents yet another kind of synthesis, that of all the versions of the creative impulse into one figure. We are back again to the identification of the poet as thief. Faust's turn to political activity in the last two acts of the play is often seen as a problem or as a loss after the experience of Helen; sometimes it is seen as progress. What Euphorian shows us, however, is that it is neither the one nor the other, but simply an analogy to that experience. Mediation to spirit and mediation to the world are reciprocal, complementary, and identical all at the same time.

Given the play's clear recognition of Euphorion's mistakes, it is not surprising that the opera, the play within the play, should dissolve. It is in any case in the nature of aesthetic moments in *Faust* to be transitory. Nevertheless, the details of the dissolution make a series of important statements. Helen dissolves after her last embrace with Faust, which is, however, their first embrace on stage. We have come out on the other side of the thematics of the rainbow. The opera was a time when Faust could grasp the rainbow, but now it is no longer possible again. There will be no permanent rainbow, only a succession of transient ones. Unlike Gretchen, Helen does not seek to prolong her embrace of Faust indefinitely but accepts its necessary transience. Yet her abandoned clothing carries him off and upward; here would

[16]In conversation with Chancellor von Müller, June 13, 1824 (Kanzler von Müller, *Unterhaltungen mit Goethe,* ed. Ernst Grumach [Weimar: Böhlaus Nachfolger, 1956], 119). The relevance to Euphorion is unmistakable, for the comment is made with reference to Byron's death in Greece. I borrow here the translation of E. M. Butler in *Byron and Goethe: Analysis of a Passion* (London: Bowes & Bowes, 1956), 104.

appear to be the direct transcendence he has sought since the very beginning of the play! And what does it consist of but the memory of the fulfilled moment, of his transient encounter with the ideal. This is precisely what "Dedication," the "Prelude in the Theater," the reaction to the Easter chorus, "Forest and Cavern"—all identified as inspiration. Now, that memory has been extended to the memory of our whole culture. Euphorion's clothes by contrast, will provide inspiration of a different sort, for Mephisto looks forward to generating strife. Once again the synthesis dissolves into its two poles, the eternal ideal and the daily struggle of the real. But both poles carry with them henceforth the memory of the classical past. In some sense, then, in the memory of the synthesis, the past is rescued from complete oblivion in the flux of time. The world is somehow different as a result of this opera.

Yet what happens to the chorus certainly calls into question just how different. Panthalis remains loyal to her mistress. This spiritual quality participates in the permanence of the ideal and thus enables her to descend once again to the Underworld, that ultimate repository of spirit in *Faust II*. All of the rest, however, dissolve back into the four elements of which the world is made. Like the rainbow, they separate out into their original components, available to become another rainbow in the future. They return to the forms of Mephisto's spirits in Part I—earth, air, water, and wine. The parallel is not by chance, for the chorus ends with the chaos and tumult of wine pressing. We have returned to the real world embodied in the drinkers of "Auerbach's Tavern." And immediately after this speech Phorcyas disrobes to reveal herself as Mephistopheles. Thus the act returns us to the highly problematic, chaotic real world. Not only does this remind us that what has come before has all been play, but it further suggests that the play has had no effect on the real world.

What is the relation of art to reality? Is the world of *Faust* different now, or isn't it? Clearly the world itself is no different; world is after all one pole of the dialectic, a constant in the play. And yet individuals in that world clearly are different; the memory of Faust, at least, has been touched. But Faust is himself in this episode the poet, the creative mediator between world and spirit. The example of Panthalis now generalizes his position: any individual capable of spiritual effort becomes such a mediator and carries off the permanent mark of such mediation. Ultimately every individual must be this mediator for himself. In this respect, Goethe's position on the didactic value of drama in his later years illuminates the paradoxical end of this act. In an essay of 1827 on the meaning of catharsis in Aristotle, Goethe insists that "the complications will perplex [the spectator], the solution enlighten him, but he will not go home any the better for it at all. He will be inclined, perhaps, if he is given to reflection, to be amazed at the state of mind in which he finds himself at home again—just as frivolous, as obstinate, as zealous, as weak, as tender or as cynical as he was when he went out."[17] And yet in the same year he also wrote: "All poetry should teach, but unnoticeably; it should make people notice where something could be learned; they have to do the learning from it, as from life, by themselves."[18] It is not the poet or the play that ultimately changes the spectator. It is rather what the spectator or reader himself does with the memories that he keeps in his grasp. Ultimately, what we have from the work of art is what we learn from it by our own efforts. And this learning takes place through the act of recording, tracing in memory. All of us become, in effect, poets recreating the drama in our own minds as Goethe and Faust recreate antiquity in theirs. This is the only effect of the play in the world.

[17]"Supplement to Aristotle's *Poetics*," in *Goethe's Literary Essays*, ed. J. E. Spingarn (New York: Ungar, 1964), 108.
[18]"Über das Lehrgedicht," *Gesamtausgabe*, 15 (Stuttgart: Cotta, n.d.), 755; translation mine. The essay may be found in English under the title "On Didactic Poetry," in *Goethe's Literary Essays*, ed. Spingarn, 130–32.

12

The Spirit of History:
Act IV

Act IV has traditionally been considered the least accessible part of a generally inaccessible work. As the very last part of the play to be written—it was completed in July 1831, eight months before the poet's death—it has sometimes been seen as a kind of patch job to hold Act V to the rest of the play. Clearly, it connects Act III to Act V, but it does so in terms of the main issues of the play. Furthermore, it develops those issues in unique and significant ways, for Act IV counters Faust's incarnation of the ideal in the world in Acts II and III with Mephisto's parody of this creation in the real historical world.

Faust's monologue at the beginning of the act offers a final assessment of the previous action at the level of "Charming Landscape," but after that everything is presented entirely from the Mephistophelean perspective. "High Mountains" redefines both the relation of fire and water and the proper sphere of man, turning from Faust's idealizing view in Act II to the worldly perspective of the devil, familiar to us from "Auerbach's Tavern" and "Witch's Kitchen." Here we move out into the violent realm that had been the circumscribing background for the imaginative achievements in the preceding acts—out into Chiron's restless circling, Seismos's mountain realm, the world of pirate-Menelaus, the strife Euphorion so eagerly sought. Here the real historical world finally comes into its own. This is Mephistopheles' realm, and Mephisto returns, accordingly, as the generator of a series of shows that occupy the rest of the act, the scenes "In the Foothills" and "The Rival Emperor's Tent."

Faust's plays have focused on the representing of spirit in the world, but Mephisto's right the balance by emphasizing the "worldliness" of representation. These shows return to the relation of essence, or spirit, to appearance, or world, from Act I, but now are focused more explicitly on the problem of the spectator. Faust is a better reader than he was in Part I, but the rest of the audience on stage succumbs to the illusion of reality and thus makes possible the diabolical abuse of art in the service of political power. At the same time Mephisto's shows bring the history of European literature up through the neoclassical period, allowing the play's most open attack on neo-Aristotelian poetics.

The renewed importance of Mephistopheles has led most readers of the play to return here to the language of ethics, which, I have tried to show, is at best only marginally relevant to the earlier sections of the play. The way in which the Helen act returns openly to the concerns of the pact scene shows yet again that those concerns are epistemological, not ethical. Faust has not "escaped" Mephistopheles by finding Helen. In creating Helen he has rather fully exploited and internalized Mephisto's capacity to lead him into the world. Hitherto the play has insisted firmly on the transience of the fulfilled moment. Thus the synthesis of real and ideal embodied in Helen must unravel; Faust must return to the world to begin to *real*-ize his vision anew. He has not "fallen" back into the arms of Mephisto, nor was there any inherent flaw in his experience with Helen. It is in the nature of human existence to be subordinate to time, which it can transcend only momentarily. The chorus at the end of Act III raised the question of the permanent effects of the fulfilled moment; Act IV elaborates and explores the ramifications of this issue.

There is also a formal reason for the apparent return of ethical concerns, especially when we consider the apparent crime and repentance of the emperor in accepting diabolical aid. The strong closure of Act III and the lament for Euphorion as Byron appear to bring the history of European literature right up to the present of the play. This is not, however, really the case. Byron functions as the embodiment of the modern or romantic spirit in literature, but formally the act arrives only at the seventeenth century, at the pastoral opera with its climactic apotheosis and epiphany most familiar to us today in the work of Claudio Monteverdi. It remains to Act IV to continue the imitations or parodies of European literary forms into the eighteenth century.

Now, Act III defined opera, the modern revival of tragedy, as "inner," focused on subjective rather than objective experiences. The focus on individual psychology in drama is an Enlightenment development that accompanied the rise of neoclassical dramatic theory. The scene between the emperor and the archbishop parodies, as we shall see, eighteenth-century historical tragedy. Thus as *Faust* moves toward such forms in its internal development, it is not surprising that ethical concerns should appear to gain prominence. But because of the par-odistic element we must remain aware of how both the form and its concerns are subordinated to the broader view of drama developed by the play as a whole.

The setting for Faust's opening monologue symbolically adum-brates both the return to reality and the continuation of the history of European drama. Faust lands at the top of the mountains. At this height he has returned from the series of descents that have occupied him since Act I. At the end of Act III, we remember, Euphorion's ascent up the cliffs likewise initiated the return to reality. But the way Faust reaches the heights suggests the formal concerns of the act as well. The cloud that deposits him is the typical stage machine of baroque opera. Faust's preoccupation with clouds in his monologue lends special emphasis to this machine; it defines an operatic realm, or perhaps ambience, that the play will not leave again. In effect, this ambience has been defined by Act III as the precondition of all mod-ern drama. It will remain now as a matter of course, as a constant reminder of the essential form of drama, as a permanent ground on which even Mephisto's mordant parody of neoclassical drama will be played.

The cloud from which Faust emerges is, we remember, all that was left of Helen on earth after she dissolved in Faust's embrace. The formal equivalent is Faust's verse form, for in this monologue he still uses Greek trimeter. Faust safely landed, the cloud withdraws to the southeast, toward Greece, the origin of Western culture, where it remains, reflecting the greatness of days past but also, as brightness in the east, promising another sunrise. Here is once again an image for the abiding memory of the classical tradition and its persistent capaci-ty to inspire. As such the cloud is also a sign for the transcendent significance of the Absolute. The shape of the cloud—like a reclining Juno, Leda, or Helen—identifies it readily enough as the classical ideal and also as the eternal feminine. We must recognize the posture of the figure as an allusion to voluptuous Renaissance goddesses and mistresses of Jupiter, who repeatedly appear reclining outstretched in luxury. This is once more a mediated classical ideal diffracted through the Renaissance. It is also the same figure in the same posture as the one Faust saw in the mirror in "Witch's Kitchen." It is a measure of what Faust, as a model reader, has learned in the play that he can watch it withdraw with such equanimity.

And the figure becomes a mirror, reflecting the "profound significance of fleeting days" (l. 10054). The reflection awakens admiration and amazement, for it mirrors not the world before it but that world's "profound significance," the spirit that the play has seen beneath the surfaces of reality. In this respect it is the same kind of mirror as the rainbow in "Charming Landscape," and the shift in imagery from rainbow to cloud is another, more sophisticated measure of Faust's achievement. Both clouds and rainbows are visible because of the interaction between water and light. The difference is that clouds are more common than rainbows. Faust's ability, then, to read the cloud as a metaphor for his experience with Helen and all that it represents shows him as a more accomplished artist and reader, for he is able to perceive higher significance in more ordinary aspects of reality than he could in "Charming Landscape" or in Part I. On one level, the implication is, as immediately becomes clear in the second part of the monologue, that it is even possible to write a play on a modern subject (like Faust), not just on a classical one. But whatever the general accessibility of clouds, the spirit of this particular one, Helen, has now withdrawn to the distance of an ideal.

Faust has not, however, been entirely abandoned, for in reality the cloud has split and a shred has remained with him. This is the wisp described in the second half of the monologue. In a schema for this act Goethe indicated that the second cloud was to represent Gretchen, an obvious connection once it is pointed out. If the Helen-cloud embodies, as classical ideal, the memory of the culture, the Gretchen-cloud embodies Faust's personal memory—"long missed, highest prize of early youth . . . / The earliest treasures of the inmost heart" (ll. 1059–60). Personal memory as inspiration takes us back to the position and tone of "Dedication," the "Prelude in the Theater," the Easter chorus, "Forest and Cavern," while the rising treasures connect the passage to the imagery of Act I. The form of the second cloud is explicitly identified as "beauty of the soul" (*Seelenschönheit*, l. 10064). This is the modern spiritual "inwardness" of the opera at the end of Act III. Thus the two clouds again define the fundamental dichotomy of *Faust*—here as classical/modern, nature/spirit. The chorus at the end of Act III showed us one level of the dissolution of the synthesis achieved in the Helen act; Faust's monologue now shows us that dissolution in Faust himself. As the carrying, inspiring cloud breaks in two, so too Faust's inner synthesis of ideal and real, past and present dissolves as he reenters the historical world.

The classical dream is ended definitively by what is surely the most astonishing stage direction in all literature: "A seven-league boot clumps down; another follows immediately: Mephistopheles steps down. The boots hurry on" (after l. 10066). It is not simply the arrival of Mephistopheles that signals the break, but also the "Germanic" fairy-tale motif and the appalling independent activity of the object world. We have returned to a world of instruments and machines, a world that revels in the powers of manipulation, a world in which Mephistopheles can feel at home. We have returned to the "reality" of "Witch's Kitchen" and must now explore the new version of the world after Euphorion's fall.

The most striking quality of this world is that it is fallen. In a ludicrous parody of Milton, Mephistopheles explains that the mountains were created by the coughing of the fallen angels after they landed in hell.[1] It is easy to see how Goethe satirizes Vulcanism (the belief that the world was shaped mainly by the forces of fire) here, just as he did in the masque of Seismos. But more important, the Mephistophelean view of the world has again come to the fore. For Mephistopheles this world is like Auerbach's tavern or the witch's kitchen, all "tumult, violence, and chaos" (l. 10127). Human history has become Mephistopheles' realm.

If this world is associated with the biblical Fall, it is also associated with Euphorion's fall. Mephisto's landscape is the high mountain landscape glorified in *Manfred*, shown here to be the realm of the devil. When Mephisto offers Faust a rococo pleasure garden, Faust rejects it as "Tawdry and modern! Sardanapal!" (l. 10176). The play

---

[1]*Paradise Lost*, bk. I, ll. 670–730. The association of mountains with the fallen world in European thought through the seventeenth century and the impetus that came out of England to change that attitude are documented in detail by Marjorie Hope Nicolson in *Mountain Gloom and Mountain Glory: The Development of the Aesthetics of the Infinite* (New York: Norton, 1963).

Byron had intended to dedicate to Goethe (and for which he had sent
Goethe the dedication) was *Sardanapalus*. Euphorion's Byronism is
thus explicitly connected with this fallen world. But the fall of Euphorion is more than the fall of Byronism or modern poetry; because of
Euphorion's parentage, it is also the fall of modern classicism, that is,
of the Renaissance-baroque recovery of the classical tradition. This is
much more serious, and it explains, I think, the burlesque of Milton in
Mephisto's first speech. In the pact scenes we saw that Mephisto was a
Miltonic devil particularly with regard to this classicizing. In that
context Milton functioned as the Teutonic embracer of the classical
tradition who both justified a German classicism and identified immediate cultural ancestors for it. But in this new, fully historical world,
on the far side of the classical experience, Milton appears to be a fallen
classicist. If the weight in the pact scene lay on his classicism despite
his ambivalence, the weight here is much more on his commitment to
the Christian tradition. Indeed there is nothing classical at all about
the descriptions of hell borrowed and perverted from Milton. The fall,
then, is a fall into a Christian world.

The intense Christianity of Mephisto's fallen world appears most
clearly in the biblical language, much of which Goethe kindly identified for his readers in the margin. It is, I believe, intended to be
shocking that this biblical language is all in the mouth of Mephistopheles. The language is further undercut by the blasphemous parody of the temptation of Christ at lines 10130–34. In Matthew 4:8–9,
Satan tempts Christ by taking him to the top of a high mountain and
offering him the kingdoms of the world and their glory (quoted by
Goethe, l. 10131). Christ, of course, rejects the offers, but not so
Faust. He immediately responds, "But yes! Something great did at-
tract me" (l. 10134). To follow the logic of the play Faust must embrace the world, in opposition to traditional Christian doctrine. Yet at
the same time the way in which he does so also undercuts Mephisto's
position, for Mephisto has chosen to identify himself with that same
Christian position. Once again we have returned to the problematics
of the pact scene: Faust can only be saved by accepting all temptations. To reject temptation would be Christian, and hence Mephistophelean!

More confusing, perhaps, is the parallel between Faust here and
Homunculus in Act II. There Homunculus rejected Anaxagoras's offer
of Seismos's mountain and all its worldly glories to submerge himself

in the sea. He clearly chose the right alternative. Faust at first appears to do the reverse by accepting Mephisto's offer. Nevertheless, this is not the case, for what Faust has seen from the top of the mountain and really wants is nothing other than the sea. He wants, it is true, to control the sea, indeed to steal land from it, not to merge with it. Yet we have seen that Homunculus' plunge into the sea is, as a mating with Galatea, also a taking possession, even a kind of rape. The two are the same, but Faust's more "negative" attitude is part and parcel of the new world in which he finds himself. He will be aided in his first battle to earn the right to the seashore by three biblical mighty men, borrowed from II Samuel 23. Within the framework of II Samuel the mighty men are neither evil nor unacceptably violent; they are the warriors of the chosen of God, David. In *Faust* the figures emphasize the negative perspective that involvement in the world imposes upon all human activity. From the fallen, Mephistophelean perspective, biblical heroes are ruthless bullies, and the sea is sterile. Acts II and III, by contrast, took the larger and opposite perspective of eternal spirit. In this cosmological perspective, water embodied the temporal flux of generation and fertility. At the beginning of the scene Faust rejects Mephisto's Vulcanism, but he cannot reject the worldly perspective on existence and still act effectively in the world.

And act he will. Faust's desire to strive is the one constant in the radical reversal of perspective from idealist to realist. Until now in the play Nature has primarily served an epistemological function for Faust; in a long series of transformations it has remained the locus for perceiving the Absolute. Now for the first time it seems to be only itself. While Mephistopheles tries to people it with devils, Faust understands it rather as nobly mute (*edel-stumm*, l. 10095). Nature is founded only in itself (l. 10097) and closed (l. 10098). Faust lives now in the demythologized nature so lamented by other European romantics.[2] This is a nature in which—regrettably or indifferently, depending upon the perspective—one no longer searches for higher significance. This is, of course, the "modern" Enlightenment or scientific view, and Faust, true to his hard-won willingness to accept the transitoriness of the moment and live in history, embraces it. He sees the

---

[2]Schiller, for example, in "The Gods of Greece" (1788, 1800) catalogues the disappearance of divinity from nature in excruciating detail. English-speaking readers will think immediately of Wordsworth's sonnet, "The world is too much with us" (1806, 1807), in which the poet longs to see Proteus rising from the sea.

world now as essentially a theater for human achievement. Mephisto asks him if he wants the moon, but instead of the moon, in language reminiscent of his invocation of the earth spirit (ll. 464–67), Faust demands the earth:

> This earthly circle
> Still leaves room for great deeds.
> Amazing things shall come to pass,
> I feel strength for daring efforts.
> [ll. 10181–84]

And it turns out that what he really means by the world "leaving room" is that it can be operated upon; the new goal of his striving is to control the movement of the sea, that is, to rule the generative power of nature.

Has Faust somehow fallen, betrayed himself, betrayed us, betrayed the cultural heritage by passing from art to technology? Such a reading is, I think, too simple, for it ignores the fundamental validity of the real and of the temporal flux that the entire drama up until now has labored to establish. As reader-poets we must not renounce our cosmological perspective because Faust seems to have done so. Instead we must recognize that Faust's new view of a sterile sea does not constitute a rejection of the creative impulse. The point is rather that Faust has fully internalized that impulse. His sequence of translations for the biblical *logos*—word, sense, force, deed (ll. 1224–37)—before his first encounter with Mephistopheles already adumbrated this development. *Deed* was named there and has now become for Faust the ultimate manifestation of the power that created the universe. If Faust loses the balance between understanding and grasping articulated at the end of the spirit song, that will be only human. Nevertheless his consistent rejection of Mephisto's silly offers or rococo luxury, his vigorous rejection of war (l. 10235), and his criticism of the emperor's irresponsibility (ll. 10252–59) show that he has not lost full sight of the other pole of the dialectic, that he carries within him permanent traces of his encounter with the ideal, some spark of the creative power of the *logos*.

In effect, I am saying that social vision takes the place here of artistic vision. To the extent that what we have been calling the Absolute can be equated with the Platonic, "the good, the beautiful, the true," we can say that the play has moved through the Absolute as "true" and as "beautiful"; it remains now to explore the Absolute as "good," understood in this context as "social good." Clearly it is appropriate to read Acts IV and V as a commentary on the aftermath of the French Revolution. Nevertheless, whatever topical significance one might want to assign to these two acts, it is important to remember that here, as elsewhere in the play, such commentary is subsumed in the larger, cosmological context I have been outlining. Whatever local reasons might attach to the failure of Faust's projects, the context of the drama reveals them to fail because all human endeavor is ultimately subject to the flux of time.

While Goethe forces us to consider the violence of post-Enlightenment culture with less sentimentality than, say, Schiller or Wordsworth or Keats, nevertheless we must not overlook how typically romantic his position is. At the beginning of the play Faust was in the romantic prison of his own subjectivity. He needed to escape his prison and experience the objective world. Now the situation is reversed: Faust inhabits a hostile objective world over which his control is guaranteed only by his own internal creative power. Since the beginning of the play, Faust has gradually internalized what he had first projected in the macrocosm and the earth spirit. In Part II we have been tracing the process of this reversal in the emphasis on Faust's own creativity and the subjective model of creativity implied in Act I. Here is yet another shift in the categories and representatives of the dialectic. Yet the dialectic of subject and object remains, so that the fundamental structure of the play is still cast in the same terms.

Mephisto's astonishing dream battle in the final scenes constitutes a kind of coda to the reversal of values and the ambivalences of the rest of the act, for at one level the battle is Mephisto's parody of the earlier concerns of Part II. The triumphant appearances of fire and water, which turn the tide of the battle, parody the importance attached to fire and water as embodiments of the dialectic from the rainbow in "Charming Landscape" on. The difficulties of Grab-swag and Rapacious in looting the gold—the chest breaks, the apron leaks—parody at a more mundane level the difficulties of the stage audience in Act I when it tries to catch the gold strewn about by Boy-charioteer, and thus the entire concern with the recovery of gold from the depths. When the emperor divides the rewon kingdom among his vassals in what we have already seen as a kind of reenactment of the Golden

Bull, he repeats his failure of Act I to use the paper money to re-establish this realm on a more solid footing. The greed of the arch-bishop, who wore his chancellor's hat in Act I, cynically reveals the true motives for the prelate's original hostility to Nature and Mind. And in so doing it ironically establishes that Mephisto's absurd manip-ulations in the battle are no more than what this world deserves.

But the most important theme parodied here is the relation of essence to appearance, of spirit to world. It appears in the empty suits of armor animated by spirits, indeed by little flames. It also appears in the burlesque fairy-tale tone of the goings-on. The heralds, for exam-ple, report the sneer of the rival emperor.

> When we should recall [the emperor],
> A fairy tale says "once upon a time."
> [ll. 10495–96]

And indeed, the emperor's victory over his rival is a kind of fairy tale, full of magical surprises, presided over by Mephistopheles and his messenger ravens. Another aspect of this parody is the battle between the eagle and the griffon (ll. 10620–37), emblems of the emperor and the rival emperor respectively, which foreshadows the outcome of the real battle. If there is any meaning to this symbolic battle, it resides in the fact that the battle is a sign and therefore a kind of fiction. Yet then there is a profound irony in the fact that it is a battle between a real and a fictional creature, and one in which the real creature wins. Finally, signs are most profoundly problematized by the use of the semblances of fire and water to win the battle. Until now in the play fire and water have represented essences, the most basic principles of the dialectic; here, however, they are signs explicitly detached from their meanings. In Act I the problem was mistaking appearances for essences. Those who made this mistake were burned. The solution to that problem was seen to be art, a unique blending of appearance and essence, of real and ideal. Here, however, appearance is cynically divorced from essence to manipulate a naïve audience.

In fact, what is this whole performance if not Mephisthophelean art? The stage direction after line 10782, "A warlike tumult in the orches-tra, eventually changing to gay military tunes," tells us that the pre-vious trumpet blasts have been something more than the normal sound effects of, say, a Shakespearean history play. The presence of a full orchestra is already telling; the fact that the course of the battle to its successful conclusion is registered only in the orchestra is decisive. If the music carries the plot line, we are in the realm of opera. And once again, the presence of water and fire on stage as independently active or significant stage effects is known to us only from operas, such as *Dido Forsaken* or *The Magic Flute*. This is, of course, all burlesque here. Neither Mephisto's suits of armor, compared to empty snail shells (l. 10560), nor Faust's absurd interpretations of the flames above the helmets as the last manifestation of the Dioscuri nor his explanation of the logic of carrier ravens (wartime equivalent of carrier pigeons) can be taken seriously. In Act I we already saw Mephisto as a master of burlesque, entertaining the court with his old wives' tales; in Act III he chased Helen and the chorus through the ages with his off-stage threatening armies. Act IV is only his earlier talent run riot.

The use of sources here suggests that Mephisto's play is to be understood as a continuous and functional part of the extended meditation on the nature of art that constitutes Part II. Commentaries refer us to Walter Scott's *Letters on Demonology and Witchcraft* (1830), which Goethe was reading shortly before he began Act IV, as the source for Mephisto's phantom army. This may well be the case, but if so, Scott is only the most modern in a series of sources leading back to the Renaissance. Scott may well have reminded Goethe of the phantom army supposed to have presided over the fall of Constantinople to the Franks in 1204 mentioned by Gibbon.[3] In any case he would certainly have been reminded of the phantom army cum thunderstorms that Circe uses to defeat the rejected lovers, Lysidas and Arsidas, in Calderón's *Love, the Greatest Enchantment*. This is the reason that the description of the motions of this army (ll. 10640–63) suddenly switches from the four- and five-beat iambic lines that characterize the scene to trochaic tetrameter, Calderón's meter. One might even wonder whether the reference to the mirages for which Sicily was famous is not really subliminal reference to the explicitly Sicilian setting of Calderón's play.[4] It might seem just as strange that

[3]Edward Gibbon, *The Decline and Fall of the Roman Empire*, ed. J. Bury (New York: Heritage Press, 1946), 3: 2131.

[4]Commentaries refer us here to the *fata morgana* and to seventeenth-century descriptions of it by Athanasius Kircher. Goethe may well have known these, but the context of Calderón references in the play makes the connection to *Love, the Greatest Enchantment* both a more likely connection and a more meaningful one.

Circe should win any battles as that Mephisto should win any by such shabby means and get away with it. Circe represents the wiles of worldly love; men foolish enough to pursue her or to struggle with her on her own terms, as Lysidas and Arsidas do, deserve their punishment. Similarly in *Faust*, the emperor is scarcely a model emperor, but his rival has no claims to legitimacy at all and, to judge from the wealth in his tent, is not likely to be a less distractable, more responsible ruler. Neither side is very attractive in these struggles, and that is precisely the point in both works. In Gibbon, too, there is nothing to make anyone root for the Greeks, even though they are defending their own homeland. The sense of the phantom army is precisely the ultimate insignificance of the issues in dispute. But this is, as Erichtho pointed out before the "Classical Walpurgis Night," the very nature of history.

In this respect Mephisto's play is the exact complement to Faust's series of departures from history in Act II, which Goethe wrote shortly before he wrote Act IV. For the alternative to Circe in Calderón's play is Galatea, who embodies higher or spiritual love. Goethe maintains the complementary polarity of Galatea and Circe in the opposing approaches to play—idealizing and spiritual in II, real and worldly in IV. This connection is important, because it establishes not only a context in which Mephisto's play is typical of *Faust* but one in which it makes a special contribution. For if we recognize the battle of Act IV as a *réplique* to the triumph of Galatea, then the epiphany of Helen and her subsequent dissolution in Act III are framed by an analogous Calderónian situation, the epiphany of Galatea (in Act II) and her subsequent dissolution in the turn to her Circean alternative (in Act IV). This establishes a full Calderónian (i.e., Renaissance) frame to surround the classical centerpiece of Part II and gives Act IV an indispensable formal function in establishing the symmetrical, closed structure of Part II.

The implications of the sources for the epiphany—perhaps *counterepiphany* would be a better term—of fire and water at the climax of the battle are equally intriguing. The parallel that would immediately have sprung to mind in Goethe's time was *The Magic Flute*. The opera was extremely important to Goethe himself, who worked on a sequel to it in the 1790s. It was, however, so widely popular that in 1797 Ludwig Tieck had the poet of his play within the play in *Der gestiefelte Kater* rescue himself repeatedly from the hostility of the audience by pushing figures, whole scenes, and finally the fire and water setting from *The Magic Flute* onto the stage at crucial moments.[5] At the end of the ill-starred performance, only the fire and water get a curtain call. Like other modern determinants of Goethe's play, this one clearly points toward the operatic realm and, here at least, unmistakably toward the comic realm as well. But like so much of the rest of the play, the passage has an older determinant as well, this time an ancient one. Book XXI of the *Iliad* features a battle between fire and water. Achilles has finally returned to the battle, and in his rage has killed so many Trojans that the river Scamander becomes choked and attacks the hero. Achilles struggles against him but is finally driven back by the angry river. At this point Hera intervenes and orders her son Hephaestus, lord of fire, to drive back the river, which he does with his flames. This was evidently a part of the *Iliad* that appealed to Goethe, for in 1801 he set it as one of the subjects for his annual art contest. There are interesting points of contact to *Faust*. The passage is already a burlesque in Homer. The normal patterns of battle are taken to bizarre extremes; the gods become involved in most undignified fashion; the entire performance is finally described as a show put on to amuse Zeus.[6] As with the Phorcyads, once again Mephisto has found a congenial aspect of antiquity. But more important, the fire and water in Homer are not even signs for essences, but the very essences themselves, while the spirits who wield them, Hephaestus and Scamander, are rather mythological signs for the elemental realities. But Mephisto's fire and water are only appearances, not even genuine signs, for they are entirely invisible to spirit eyes. If they appear as parodies of earlier parts of *Faust*, they are complete perversions of their function in Homer, utterly ungrounded as they are in nature. The Mephistophelean view of the tradition thus not only runs counter to that of Acts II and III, but, at least as regards antiquity, actually perverts both the tradition and Faust's use of it.

If we take account now of just what literary tradition this Mephi-

[5]Available in English as *Puss-in-Boots*, trans. Gerald Gillespie (Austin: University of Texas Press, 1974).

[6]Immediately after the burning of the Scamander by Hephaestus, Athena fells Ares and coarsely attacks Aphrodite, while Hera boxes the ears of Artemis (XXI, ll. 394–426, 479–96). Zeus's amusement is referred to XXI, ll. 389–90. References are to *The Iliad of Homer*, trans. Richmond Lattimore (Chicago: Phoenix, 1961).

stophelean play represents, the perversion of the classical tradition
becomes all the more interesting. Act III followed the history of European tragedy from antiquity through the Renaissance. Act IV, as we
have seen, picks up the development with Milton (and *Paradise Lost*,
we remember, was originally conceived as an operatic grand spectacular and later adapted into one by Dryden), pursues it through
burlesque of the extreme forms of seventeenth-century opera, which
placed more stress on elaborate and spectacular machinery than on
any kind of coherence, to the typical political tragedy of the earlier
eighteenth century in the last scene. The final scene of the act is
written in alexandrines, the six-foot iambic line of the French neoclassicists that dominated the European stage in the eighteenth century. The unflattering picture of the church and, more important, the
willingness to exploit nature and its resources are typically Enlightenment patterns of thinking. Indeed the emergence of the unmistakably
neoclassical verse form reminds us again that the fallen, demythologized nature in which the entire act moves is the rapidly secularizing
world of the seventeenth and eighteenth centuries, the world after the
Cartesian fall into modernism, the world in which anthropocentric
neoclassical tragedy succeeds the cosmologically oriented drama of
earlier centuries.

In this, the very last scene of the play to be written, Goethe finally
allows the subliminal enemy to emerge—in a cacophony of ridicule. It
is a fallen, "after"-world, a very late re-creation of other worlds. Not
only is its re-creation of antiquity skewed and perverted, but its Christianity is false, if not downright hypocritical; even its revival of the
Middle Ages is seen as absurd parading in dusty snail shells (ll. 10559–
62). The whole thematic of appearances and the comic triumph of
literalism in the act constitute the heart of this attack. In the Aristotle
essay and the essay on didactic poetry referred to at the end of the last
chapter the focus of the polemical attacks is the poetics of the neoclassicists, which Goethe saw, to a large extent correctly, as taking
texts too literally, assuming too direct moral implications. The center
of neoclassical theories of catharsis was that the audience was somehow purged and improved by the experience of watching a tragedy.
Goethe's own understanding was, as we have seen, considerably more
sophisticated. Thus when the spectators of Mephisto's show in Act IV
are cruelly and cynically deceived by their own literalism, it is only

what they deserve. The gross manipulability of the public in this act reveals the inadequacy, indeed the profound danger, inherent in the form of drama that surfaces openly at the end of the act.

The emphasis here on parody and burlesque must not obscure either the literary or the social commitment of Goethe's attack, for Mephisto's "play" has much more direct effect on its spectators than any other play in the play. At the end of Act III we saw how *Faust* denied that art could be directly effective in the real world. Yet Mephisto's play achieves exactly what it set out to do—to win Faust the coastal territory he desired. Goethe has not changed his position here; once again, he has changed the perspective, with chilling effect. Up until now, our perspective on play has been strictly epistemological; the question has been how play mediates access to the Absolute. From this perspective it is wrong to take the play for reality. But in Act IV we view play not from the perspective of the audience, but from the perspective of the perpetrators. This is art, not in the cause of discovering truth, but in the frank service of power. This abuse of art in the real historical world, Goethe recognizes, is quite different from the ideal functions he has otherwise defined for it both in *Faust* and in his and Schiller's ambitious cultural programs of the 1790s, where art was to lead the way to the new society.[7] The fortunes of *Faust* in the last hundred and fifty years are, sadly enough, a prime example of such abuse, which is made possible by the gullibility of the audience, by its too ready acceptance of representation for reality. The Mephistophelean perspective on play leads to the same conclusion as the Faustian perspective, namely, that the position of the interpreter is pivotal. As Mephisto might put it, *Caveat spectator*.

---

[7]Almost any Goethe text of the nineties speaks in some way to the poet's ambitious program of social and cultural development through art, particularly through the stage. The key word in this program, which he pursued together with Schiller, was *education* in the sense of fullest personal development (*Bildung*). The idea was roughly that individual development and social development would somehow mutually foster each other and that art could play a leading role in furthering both. It seems clear, on the one hand, that Goethe always recognized that his hopes would never be more than partially realizable. On the other hand, it also seems clear that he was bitterly disappointed in just how obdurate the social and cultural realities of turn-of-the-century Germany proved to be.

13

The Spirit of Tragedy:
Act V

Whatever we may ultimately conclude about the achievement of a final synthesis at the end of *Faust*, there can at least be no doubt that Act V proceeds dialectically. The first half of the act seems to reject all of the positions the play has hitherto sought to affirm—the classical tradition, beauty, creative magic, activity—and to embrace what it earlier avoided—traditional models of tragedy and traditional ethics. In the second half of the act a sudden reversal in tone releases all of these concerns into a finale that exploits the full exuberance of the operatic stage. The extent to which this finale is understood as triumphant or bitter, genuine or ironic, dishonest or weak, will depend very much on how one reads the rest of the fifth act. I will follow the principle that a reading of the fifth act must depend on the context generated by the rest of the play. In this respect, we must understand the act as a genuine coming-together of the concerns of the drama, whether or not it successfully synthesizes the various polarities of Goethe's dialectic. It is necessary, then, to explore the dialectic of this act in some detail and to relate its various reversals to what has come before.

The first such reversal is Faust's wanton destruction of the idyllic world of Baucis and Philemon. Clearly more is at issue than the immorality of murdering the old people for their mite of land or than the brutality of their death by fire. Goethe's use of familiar mythological names invites us to compare his version with the treatment in Ovid (*Metamorphoses*, VIII, ll. 611–724). Not only the names of the old people but their love for one another, their simultaneous deaths, their close ties to nature (the linden trees), their piety (chapel/temple motif)—all connect Goethe's couple to Ovid's. Baucis and Philemon are the last remnants of the classical world, indeed, the last remnants of Faust's Arcadian idyll.[1] Not only does the couple live in primitive simplicity, in contrast to Faust's modern palace down below (the relative heights once again suggest the traditional relative positions of ideal and real), but they live in complete harmony with the elements: their hut is moist, while a controlled fire burns within. Yet if they embody again the synthesis of the elements, it is a synthesis on the brink of destruction, for just outside, the same elements in Faust's hands pose life-threatening dangers. This synthesis ties the couple to the world of Acts II and III. Indeed, the title of the scene, "Open Country," "Offene *Gegend*" in German, ties it also to the synthesis of the rainbow in "Charming Landscape," "Anmutige *Gegend*."[2]

There is, however, a very important difference between this world and the earlier ones: it is very old. Baucis and Philemon are very old; the myth deals with a time when the gods were no longer properly honored; the myth is itself a very late one (it first appears in Ovid); the gods are replaced by a demythologized wayfarer, whose appearance is probably suggested by the presence of a wayfarer to whom the story is told in the very late eighteenth-century version of the tale by Goethe's friend Johann Heinrich Voss. "Open Country" is written in trochaic tetrameter, again, the meter of Calderón. As in Act IV, the Calderónian meter serves as a recollection of the earlier Calderónian elements in the triumph of Galatea, now more distanced yet. At the beginning of Act IV, Faust's use of trimeter suggested an afterglow of the classical world. Here we are much further away; the afterglow comes not from the classical meter but from a late Renaissance meter that some-

[1]There are already affinities in Ovid's tale with the idyll tradition—the simple pleasures of the country life—but the connection had become more pronounced in Goethe's day. Johann Heinrich Voss, translator of Homer and author of popular contemporary idylls in hexameters, included his own elaboration of Ovid's story among his idylls. In *Was wir bringen* Goethe identifies the situation of the elderly couple explicitly as an idyll of the golden age as soon as they are identified as Baucis and Philemon (*Gesamtausgabe*, 3 [Stuttgart: Cotta, 1959], 1175).

[2]In *Was wir bringen* Goethe explicitly connects Baucis and Philemon to the theme of art. The opening scene of that play is a *tableau vivant* based on a well-known painting of the couple by Adam Elsheimer. Their hut is eventually transformed into a theater, which is understood to be a temple of art; Baucis and Philemon even discover their own artificiality and learn that they are really actors.

times occupied itself with its distance from the classical world. The connection to the classical world and, simultaneously, the vigor of that world have been very much attenuated.

It is not, then, a matter of great effort to destroy it. Baucis and Philemon are destroyed, of course, by Mephistopheles. But Goethe's devil and his magic so consistently symbolize man's own creative power that we must hesitate to place the emphasis on any moral failure of Faust's. Rather we must consider the context closely. Faust occupies yet again the central position in the familiar triad of Part II. He stands between Mephisto and the three mighty men on the one hand (Greed/Caliban), and Lynceus on the other (Boy-charioteer/Ariel). As we have already seen from the original context in the *Argonautica*, Lynceus is Faust's "eye" for antiquity. Here in Act V he describes and mourns the destruction of Baucis and Philemon, the last vestiges of the classical world. But antiquity in this play is beauty, the embodiment of the ideal in the world. It is not smugness in Lynceus, then, when he sings,

> You fortunate eyes,
> Whatever you've seen,
> Whatever it was,
> It was so beautiful!
> [ll. 11300–303]

Rather it is his vocation, indeed his very nature, always to see "the eternal design" (l. 11297; cf. Fletcher's "kosmos"). Lynceus is the last vestige of what Faust has brought with him from the fulfillment of Act III, the capacity to perceive beauty, vision. But the last trace of classical beauty is destroyed in this act. So, too, is the capacity for vision. Faust is first disappointed that the trees in which he had hoped to build a platform have been destroyed, but he soon comforts himself that a watchtower can be built instead "to scan the infinite" (l. 11345). But almost immediately Faust is blinded by one of the four crones who materialize from the smoking ruins. What has really been destroyed is Faust's capacity to "see" the Absolute anywhere, even indirectly.

How is this loss seen in the play? Clearly there is considerable nostalgia here; it turns out, in fact, to be traditional nostalgia. In the *Argonautica* Lynceus is searching for Hercules in the first place because the Greeks have just learned from the Hesperides that the great hero had been there only the day before. On that visit Hercules plunged the three nymphs into mourning by killing their guardian serpent and by taking their golden apples, which he had been ordered to fetch. The moment the Argonauts come upon the nymphs, they turn to dust and earth. This episode is the climax of a series of disappearances of numinosity from the world of the *Argonautica*. The heroism of Hercules (and, by implication, of the entire Homeric world) turns to dust and earth in the hands of later generations.[3] When Baucis and Philemon become dust and ashes, then, Goethe repeats a gesture that itself comes down to us from antiquity. Our literature has always mourned the passing of the past.

Mephisto and the three mighty men also help us to understand that the emphasis here is once again on temporality, the passing of the past. When Mephisto and his mighty men arrive from their pirate expedition, Mephisto instructs them to arrange their treasures on display in the palace. This is, we remember, precisely what Lynceus does for Helen in Act III. In both cases the issue is the thematics of grasping. Lynceus' treasures were the plunder of war; Mephisto's, the plunder of piracy. Piracy is, however, only a step removed—"illegitimate" war as opposed to "legitimate" war. Shall we say that Mephisto perverts Lynceus' earlier position, or only that he shows us the same position from a later, more modern perspective? In Act III we were in the midst of Faust's great classical synthesis, which controlled and validated violence. There theft was associated with poetic power. This creative appropriation generated, we saw, an implicit theodicy. But in Mephisto's postclassical, Christian world (his biblical references return, l. 11287) the violence persists without the legitimation. The accumulated context of Act IV here shows the forces of history grimly at work.

Nevertheless, however grim they may seem, the context reiterates the need to accept these forces and to function within their frame-

---

[3]The pattern runs all through Apollonius' poem. Jason is consistently portrayed as a timid, inadequate, unheroic leader. Indeed, the destruction of the Hesperides invites comparison of Jason's theft of the golden fleece. Jason obtains it because Medea magically lulls the guardian serpent to sleep; Hercules, by contrast, heroically kills the serpent of the Hesperides by his own prowess. In Book II, Apollo passes away over the heads of the band and they are terrified; Homeric heroes, by contrast, rejoiced in contact with the immortals.

work. The heavy emphasis on the natural aging process—in people, in the world, in the culture—as well as the recollections of the march of history from Act IV and the *Argonautica* allusions, which demonstrate the awareness of history even in the supposedly timeless ideality of antiquity—all make the same point. Baucis' naive mistrust of Faust's dikes—"For the whole business / Did not proceed by honest means" (ll. 11113–14)—makes the same point at the psychological level. It seems profoundly improper to her that Faust should interfere with the natural boundary between land and sea and between human and supernatural spheres; but it is at least as improper to resist the more fundamental law of subjection to the temporal flux. There is no room either in the world or in human memory to preserve the past indefinitely; what resists the law of transformation into something new must pass, however tragic the consequences. The terms of the pact challenged Faust to accept and understand his location in time; all of Part I challenged him to accept his place in the world. Act V offers the final statement of this theme: man in the world is man in time, and this is the only place that he can *be,* however destructive or "tragic" that may seem. This is our implicit theodicy at a more abstract level.

Once we can see the first scene of the act as a reiteration of the rest of Part II, not as a taking back, the dialectic or the apparent reversal in the later scenes becomes a reversal of tone and perspective, but not of basic themes. And as we shall see, these same points will be repeated over and over in the final moments of Faust's life in the world—in his confrontation with the allegories from the smoking ruins, in his renunciation of magic (ll. 11433–52), and in his final speech.

Perhaps the four gray crones, whom Faust dismisses with such vigor, should really be seen as the last shred of antiquity, as infinitely aged and weakened Furies. They arise as the immediate consequence of Faust's crime, and following Euripides, Goethe had long since psychologized them as figments of the criminal's own imagination.[4] Whether we are to view them in this light, or as a quadrupling of the witch prologue from "Witch's Kitchen" and thus as a Shakespearean effect—or, indeed, as both, a doubling we have so often seen before—they mediate in the same way as all of Goethe's other classical figures. On the one hand, they appear as the limitations imposed on

---

[4]In *Iphigenia in Tauris,* 1787. Goethe would have known from Hederich that some mythographers knew of four furies. Similarly, there are effectively four witches in *Macbeth* because of the addition of Hecate.

life in the world—Want, Debt, Care, Need—and they first introduce themselves in this concrete sense. But on the other hand, it is impossible not to hear their names figuratively, as existential limitations as well.[5] This is most strongly the case with *Debt*, which has a double meaning in biblical English; the German *Schuld* is the usual word for guilt as well as for debt. With Baucis and Philemon barely dead this is surely the meaning that must be foremost in our minds. It is all the more astonishing, then, that of the four only Care can gain access to Faust. Guilt, we are told virtually in passing, still has no relevance to *Faust*. And this being so, the whole concept of retribution represented both by the Furies and by the witches in *Macbeth* no longer applies; once again the past is put behind us.

Care is the only figure who can get in. Why? The answer comes once again from the larger context of the play. Until now the play has been well insulated from poverty and need; nevertheless, from Gretchen's surprisingly anguished cry over Faust's casket of jewels—

> Everyone contends for gold,
> Everyone loves gold,
> Everyone. Alas, poor us!
> [ll. 2802–4]

—we have been conscious of the importance of gold in the play. Act I showed us that the economic theme was significant in its figurative aspect, as a metaphor for spirit. In its literal aspect gold burned the fingers of those who snatched at it, resulting in conflagrations and explosions. Want, Debt, and Need are none other than the plagues of the empire, which the gold from the depths was to eliminate; they are the newer and negative perspective on the economic theme. They embody this theme, furthermore, on the literal level; they are objective categories applied according to external, concrete measures. Care, by contrast, is a subjective, psychological category, for care is generated by the attitude of its victim, not by external circumstances. Act I, we saw, established the priority of subjective mental constructs over literal reality, and this priority still obtains. Once embodied from the smoke of the cottage, the first three crones apparently remain

---

[5]This argument is strengthened by the substantial possibility that Goethe wrote this scene as early as 1800, the evidence for which may be found in the notes in the Norton Critical Edition, 289.

trapped in their literalness and must leave the stage like ordinary figures; but Care, like the disembodied spirit that she is, reiterates the triumph of the figurative and whisks through the keyhole to approach Faust.

If Care is the one figure who can get in, it is important to understand her capacities. These are twofold: to deny her victim access to the world—"nothing earthly will avail him" (l. 11454), "he must famish in abundance" (l. 11462)—and to deny him access to time—"Eternal gloom descends, / Sun goes neither up nor down" (ll. 11455–56). This is, of course, the central problem for Faust. Even in "Night" he had described the dangers of care as an aspect of his rejection by the earth spirit (ll. 643–51).[6] The pact scene, again, turned on offering Faust access to the world—the totality of human experience—and to time. Faust would lose the bet, we remember, when he asked for time to stand still. But Care wants to make time stand still. She is the same danger that has confronted Faust all through the play, but now seen in a more threatening, modern perspective commensurate with the changed times of the play. Temptation has become threat, but Faust's reaction, his commitment to the temporal flux, remains constant.

There is only one way in which this commitment has changed at all: it has become increasingly visible and articulate. Nowhere is this clearer than in Faust's renunciation of magic. Threatened with a visit from the four crones and their brother, Death, Faust renounces magic in order, as he says, to stand before Nature only as a man (ll. 11406–7). Magic is now seen as demeaning and destructive in a reversal that closely approximates Enlightenment attacks on superstition (especially ll. 11414–19). The Proctophantasmiac from the "Walpurgis Night" would doubtless approve. Is this the great moment of peripety, a repentant turn from the evil of his ways? Hardly, when we consider Faust's next speech:

> The circle of the earth is familiar enough to me,
> The view into the Beyond is blocked for us;
> He's a fool who turns his squinting eyes that way,
> Invents his like above the clouds.
>
> [ll. 11441–44]

---

[6] In a later passage, probably written in 1799 or 1800, which would strengthen the argument that this part of Act V was written or at least conceived this early.

This is the most emphatic rejection of direct transcendence in the entire play, but by no means the first. In a train of thought familiar from "Charming Landscape," Faust continues to define the place of man.

> To the able man this world is not mute;
> Why does he need to roam through Eternity?
> [ll. 11446–47]

All that has really changed in this speech is the tempo. Once, he says at the beginning of the speech, he "raced through the whole world" (l. 11433); now he proceeds more prudently and sedately (l. 11440). Faust has long since renounced transcendence; this renunciation is but the last step in the process begun so much earlier. Now he renounces his impatience with Nature, his need for magical shortcuts. In effect, he is at long last ready to move at Nature's pace. He no longer wishes even to transcend time but to enter fully into the temporal flux and to be a part of it.

Nevertheless, as a way to transcend time, magic has been associated in the play with art as a metaphor for man's creative gifts. This theme has been particularly emphasized by the association of Faust with that theatrical magician Prospero. But Prospero, too, renounces his magic in a famous speech in the first scene of Act V of *The Tempest*. The parallels are telling. In *The Tempest* Prospero uses his magic to restore order in his family and to regain the dukedom from which he had been driven. Once these purposes are fully achieved, he renounces his magical powers and plans to return to the world, where he will spend much of his time in religious meditation. However, he renounces these powers only when he has achieved his purpose, and even after his great renunciation speech, he retains his control over Ariel. Ariel's freedom is repeatedly deferred until he shall have executed a series of "posthumous" orders, so to speak. Indeed, Prospero's very last speech in the play is yet another order to Ariel. Thus the renunciation of magic is at best ambivalent and not at all comparable to the pressing need to renounce perceived in Marlowe's *Dr. Faustus*, where the hero teeters on the verge of damnation. Prospero recognizes the sinful aspect of his magic only superficially; in fact, as he well knows, he has used it to good purpose, to recreate society. And Faust in Act V has done the same thing. His magic has created a new and prosperous community on a former swamp. The parallel to Prospero emphasizes, therefore, the positive and metaphoric significance of the magic that is here renounced. There is a certain playfulness to this "high point," as there necessarily is to all fulfilled moments in *Faust*.

And indeed, how does this speech differ from the position of "Charming Landscape" or the beginning of Act IV? Or even, in fact, from the pact scene? Only, I think, in being an even more emphatic statement of the necessary orientation of Faust's striving in the world. The language of all these passages recurs here. Faust's eternal dissatisfaction (l. 11452) echoes the pact, seizing (l. 11448) the end of the spirit song. Most interesting are the echoes from Act IV. We are not to look *beyond* the clouds that Faust established as a self-conscious metaphor for the ideal in his monologue. But even as he turned there into the world, nature remained for him "nobly mute" (l. 10095); now it is no longer so (l. 11446). Anything in the world can become the mediating metaphor; rainbows are no longer necessary. Faust now does what the clown admonished the poet to do in the "Prelude": "Just reach into the fullness of human life! / . . . And wherever you grasp it, it's interesting" (ll. 167–69). Faust substitutes for magic concrete activity in the world, what the play has long since approached with the concept of "deed." In his social engineering projects Faust imposes order upon the sea. But order has been the quality of the Absolute since the macrocosm, and the sea has embodied the chaos of nature (even the invocation of the earth spirit [l. 467] refers to shipwreck). In Act III, Faust created Arcadia "in play"; we recognized this as an artistic act. Now he creates his Arcadia in the world. To the extent that both temporarily impose a vision on the raw stuff of nature, they are the same. To the extent that Faust's utopia exists in the real world, it is not perfect, it destroys the Arcadia of Baucis and Philemon; for if it is to exist really in the world it is of necessity imperfect and transient, "tragic." In his last speech Faust recognizes that his real achievement is to have opened the opportunity to millions to engage in the creative act with him, to create each day their Arcadia anew in the midst of chaos ("surrounded by danger," l. 11577). "The act of creating," not "art," is the true mediation; this insight validates finally the equivalence of Nature and art in the play. Creation is the act that turns the moment into the highest moment out of time, the act that validates human existence. But it is, as Act I had explicitly shown, something that comes from within. It is something, this final speech says, that each individual must do for himself. The Absolute is, ultimately, perceived in the order projected by the human mind. Faust had to learn to read shows, then how to create them. Now he recognizes that his own shows are the only representations there will ever be for him of the force that inspired them.

In this moment of insight Goethe lets his hero die. It is hard to imagine what more he might have said. Mephistopheles offers us, of course, the negative perspective on Faust's last moment; we must remember that he introduced himself long since as the spirit who denies the creation (ll. 1338–40), but is always defeated by the creative power of life (ll. 1365–76). He cannot be expected to speak directly for the creative power, the life force that we have been calling spirit. As the embodiment of world he is more accurate when he says "Time triumphs" (l. 11592), for the ultimate triumph of time is Faust's recognition that every single moment can be a moment of revelation.

Faust's moment of greatest insight comes after Care has blinded him—perhaps *because* she has blinded him. At first his loss of vision would seem to relate, like the silencing of Lynceus, to the loss of eternal embodiments of the ideal, the subjection of everything toward which one looks to the passage of time. But this is precisely the point. Deprived of the ability to look to things outside of (and especially above) himself, Faust finds the light within. Since the very beginning of the play, memory and introspection have been the sources of poetic inspiration. Now, that theme is tied firmly to the epistemological core of the play. The inspiring ideal is something within us constructed from memories of interaction with the world and that ineffable something above ("above the clouds"), below (the gold of Act I), and inside of us. Thus the loss of vision constitutes only the loss of visible correlatives for the Absolute in the world. Faust turns in reaction not to speculation but to his own creative act. To the extent that this creative act is mistakenly assumed to be fully realizable in the world it may appear to be a tragic failure, but properly understood it is indeed Faust's ultimate—only—salvation. This is the tragedy not only of Faust, but of man.

What, the wary reader may well ask, prevents the play at this point from collapsing into a solipsism far worse than that of the Baccalaureus in Act II or, more important, that of Rousseau? Once again, the context of the play must determine our reading. The Absolute manifests itself in time in the creative urge of the self. When we say this we must remember what time means in the play. It is not inchoate, unstructured reality but a line along which stations can and have been marked. The most important way such stations have been marked in this play is by the literary tradition. Ultimately the extraordinary allusiveness of Goethe's style, the parodistic style we saw defined as the ideal of poetry, thus grounds the subjectivity of the poet in something outside himself—however individually perceived that something must be, as Act II showed. Faust's final line—"Now I savor the highest moment" (l. 11586)—is a pun in German. *Augenblick* is the usual word for moment, but as we have already seen, its component roots translated separately mean "the glance of an eye." The meaning of these roots communicates with particular force here as the blind Faust looks out over his handiwork. Thus the pivotal concept of temporality in the play, *Augenblick,* is a word that doubly reinforces the concept of vision. The representatives of the opposing poles of the dialectic, time (object and world) and vision (self and spirit), become infinitely reciprocal here as they are joined by the central word in the play. To live in time is to connect the self to the world with the glance that goes out from the self and the eye that receives the impact of the world.[7] In this identity of time and vision, real and ideal, world and spirit thus come together in Faust's last word. The nature of this ultimate synthesis, through pun—word *play*—shows that it resides not in the world but in the capacity of the human mind for play. The synthesis is accessible to Faust only in the double attitude that he is able to take toward it. The play has not and never will change the world; it can only make us understand it "playfully."

The synthesis here is truly dialectical; while the opposing poles become infinitely reciprocal, they do not lose their polar individuality. Faust does not confuse the real and ideal, nor does he mistake the real products of his eternally to be repeated creative acts—the dams, dikes, new farmlands, new communities—for the creative acts themselves. In the terms of the earlier parts of the drama, he does not

---

[7]On the fundamental importance of this reciprocity of vision and also of the mediacy of vision in Goethe's thought, see the fine analysis of the *Wilhelm Meister* novels in these terms by Ilse Graham in "An Eye for the World: Stages of Realisation in *Wilhelm Meister*," in *Goethe: Portrait of the Artist* (Berlin: de Gruyter, 1977), 182–226. In "The Grateful Moment: The Element of Time in *Faust*," ibid., 313–48, Graham stresses the basic importance of temporality in the drama.

confuse the play (now become creative activity) for reality. This is the insight that was denied to Euphorion. Faust, accordingly, will be granted a full-scale apotheosis in the last scene. Because of the now long-standing link in the play between art and Nature, human creativity may serve as an analogue for the creativity of Nature, of the (we now remember) heavily anthropomorphized earth spirit. This is the unity with Nature that Faust sought at the beginning of "Night," the fulfillment promised him by Mephistopheles in the pact scene. We immediately recognize, of course, the language of the bet in Faust's last speech, "Tarry awhile, thou art so fair" (l. 11582). And yet Faust has not lost the bet. Since he has now substituted process for goal, all moments are equally fulfilled. Because the richness of this moment is determined only by Faust's will to act, Faust can recreate the fulfilled moment whenever he likes. He now has full control of the rainbow by affirming its impermanence.

The blindness motif places us squarely in a tradition critical for the self-definition of the play, the mainstream of tragedy. It is impossible to overlook the parallel between Faust and Oedipus who both move from metaphorical blindness to literal blindness, from literal sight to higher insight.[8] Sophocles' *Oedipus the King* has always been the model tragedy for Aristotelian theory, so that the relation of Faust to Oedipus articulates Goethe's final position with regard to the theory. Another indication that the definition of tragedy is at issue here is the song of the lemures, which is adapted from the song of the gravediggers in *Hamlet;* for *Hamlet,* as we already saw in our discussion of the Gretchen tragedy, was the archetypal Shakespearean tragedy for the eighteenth century. In his blindness Oedipus recognizes the fundamental irrationality of the universe. Faust's persistence in his activity in the tragic delusion that he continues to achieve something would at first appear to follow and even heighten Sophocles. But in fact, Faust lives in a rational universe; his tragedy follows from the ineffability, from the unfathomable order, of the universe, not from the lack of order. Furthermore, blindness is directly associated with vision of this unfathomable order. Earlier in the play blinding was the danger of looking at the sun ("Charming Landscape") or Helen ("Inner Courtyard") directly. In the final scenes of the act the roses of divine love

---

[8]Commentators usually refer here to the parallel to Milton's *Samson Agonistes,* which itself plays on the Oedipus motif. Here is yet another example of the typical double determination of the later parts of *Faust.*

and the new day into which Faust is reborn will be "blinding." For Renaissance Neoplatonists blindness was the precondition for seeing God.[9] Thus once again Goethe has anchored himself to an earlier tradition only to subvert it. His tragedy has nothing to do with the isolation of the individual in an unjust or irrational universe or, as the neoclassicists would have it, with a flawed individual in a rational universe. It has rather to do with the fundamental limitations that prevent the human mind from comprehending the ineffable rationality of the cosmos celebrated by the archangels in the "Prologue in Heaven."

With "Entombment" the act again seems to reverse itself.[10] As in so many other places in the play, Faust's "tragedy" is followed by Mephisto's travesty. For "Entombment" is nothing other than operatic burlesque of the most extreme sort. The lemures, ghosts of those who led evil lives in Roman mythology, function here as Mephisto's equivalent to the late, elderly remnants of the classical world in the first part of the act. Mephisto, too, has adopted a querulous, elderly stance.

> We're in a bad state altogether!
> Traditional customs, old rights,
> You can't depend on anything anymore.
> [ll. 11620–22]

Once before, during the "Walpurgis Night," he parodistically adopted this stance with the old men around the fire (ll. 4092–95); now he parodies Faust. His fantastic gesturing and the dreadful jaws of hell— a puppet-play motif as well as a favorite in medieval drama and painting—emphasize the deliberate staginess of the episode. The flying machines for the angels confirm once again that this is an operatic realm. Act III defined opera as the modern successor to tragedy. The opera in Act III was stage-managed by Mephistopheles/Phorcyas, and since then all of the explicitly operatic moments in the play have been associated with Mephistopheles. Opera is thus the dramatic mode of

[9]See "Orpheus in Praise of Blind Love," in Edgar Wind, *Pagan Mysteries in the Renaissance* (New York: Norton, 1968), 53–80.

[10]Pietro Citati juxtaposes the positive and negative viewpoints—Faust's and Mephisto's—on Faust's death with particular effectiveness in *Goethe*, trans. R. Rosenthal (New York: Dial Press, 1974), 398. Altogether Citati's discussion of the final scenes of the play is full of wonderful observations.

the modern, fallen world, and thus an imperfect mode; this is an important point to remember in reading the final scene.

The parody in this scene is, however, for the first time in the play, actually beyond Mephisto's control. He cannot even control his own devils, who huff and puff too vigorously and so ignite the angels' roses of grace. Soon enough the devil suffers the pains of the burning roses just as the audience in Act I suffered from the trinkets of Boy-charioteer. He even addresses the flowers in his powerless rage as "will-o'-the-wisps" (l. 11741); the will-o'-the-wisp, we remember, once occupied the spirit pole in the trio of Part II. This is indeed a comic battle between the ideal and the real, the spirit of divine love and the principle of the world. Mephisto loses, finally, because he joins the opposing side; he falls in love with the angels. Until now fire has consistently symbolized the Absolute in the play; now it is also the element of love. But love—we think of Gretchen, of Galatea, of Helen—is nothing other than the tendency toward embodiment in the play, the force of Nature. Thus these angels—"messengers" and thus mediators, also hermaphrodites—are allegories of the synthetic act in the play. In every respect Mephisto is defeated in his own terms. He tried to trap Faust in carnal love; now he himself is trapped. Faust escaped Mephisto's "snares" by his capacity to read higher meaning in physical love and by understanding the metaphorical significance of the fire. But Mephisto is defeated precisely by the literal power both of the fire and his love. In a last ironic twist, the angels carry off Faust's immortal essence, that bit of divine spirit we have come to see was within Faust all the time, now literalized as a concrete object. Faust's salvation turns on his ability to distinguish the literal from the figurative; Mephisto is defeated because for him the two are the same.

The underlying—or perhaps complementary—seriousness of this scene is implied by the return to the cosmic context of the "Prologue in Heaven" as well as to the baroque operatic context of the high points of Part II. At the end of Calderón's *Great Theater of the World* the actors climb up to the upper stage to approach the table of God. The equivalent happens here. Thus it is not surprising that the tone should suddenly become serious in the final scene, "Mountain Gorges," even though the setting remains the same. Like everything else in this play the cosmic framework can appear positive or negative, profound or ridiculous, depending on the point of view. The reader must be prepared to encompass both points of view.

"Mountain Gorges" returns to this serious point of view with a fully allegorical restatement of the basic issues of the first part of the act. Here, too, the emphasis is on submergence into the temporal flux, this time in the aspect of living and growing nature. The chorus and the fathers, especially the Pater Profundus, describe this world in loving detail; it is not simply there to be transcended. The setting is reminiscent of "Forest and Cavern," the "Walpurgis Night," or the finale of the "Classical Walpurgis Night." In that respect it is the ultimate fulfillment of the desire to be out in nature that Faust expressed in his first speech to the moon back in "Night." The chorus of blessed boys emphasizes the importance of this world. These children died before they really lived, but even in death, Goethe insists, they need to enter into one who has lived in order to *see* the world; thus the Pater Seraphicus offers them his eyes (ll. 11906–7), reminding us of the connection of time and vision at the end of Faust's last speech. Furthermore the boys need to continue growing, the Pater Seraphicus tells them (l. 11919), and Faust is given them as a teacher. They are thus, as commentators have pointed out, the exact counterpart in the eternal realm to Homunculus in Act II, spirits who need to become, and who, for that purpose, are placed in the charge of old men. Goethe's eternal realm is subject to the same laws of growth and development as the natural realm. In other words, there really is no eternal realm, only the eternally varying flux of temporality.

In this eternally temporal realm we have access to the same synthesis of the real and ideal articulated by Faust in his last speech. There we saw that Faust could "eternalize" any aspect of the world by making it into a metaphor for the Absolute; here the Absolute is "temporalized" to make it a legible metaphor for our worldly eyes. The Mater Gloriosa, based as she obviously is on baroque Assumptions of the Virgin, is the same kind of mediated representation of the Absolute—now the Eternal Feminine—as the Lord of the "Prologue in Heaven." And even she is an eternally receding ideal. Furthermore, she is repeatedly reflected and fragmented into more mediate manifestations—the Magna Peccatrix, the Mulier Samaritana, the Maria Aegyptiaca, the chorus of penitents, and finally, Gretchen. Gretchen's specific function as embodiment of the Eternal Feminine for Faust—and apparently for Faust alone—demonstrates once again how much the mediation depends not on the mediator but on the projecting, creative mind of the individual seeker. We must each create our own rainbows. The ultimate mediacy of all understanding is finally articulated as explicitly as such an assertion ever can be in the final Chorus Mysticus. All experience is only reflection or allegory of an ineffable something that attracts us to strive after it, a something that can be played or presented but not articulated. If the chorus of boys are an analogue for Homunculus, the Mater Gloriosa is another Galatea, triumphant embodiment of love, accessible only as she glides past, eternally transient source of all being.

The synthesis takes place on other levels as well, on levels which again emphasize its instability and transience. The more perfected angels complain about carrying Faust's immortal essence, because it is impure, it is "two natures fused in one" (l. 11962). One of Faust's earliest formulations of his problem was his two souls (l. 1112), one of which clung to the earth and the other of which strove to transcend. Faust—or is it Goethe?—has spent the entire play reconciling those two souls, and now the angels complain! This is both a measure of the achievement of the drama and, at the same time, a clear warning that no reconciliation can or should be permanent, for they conclude, "Eternal love alone / Is able to divide it" (ll. 11964–65). All through the play eternal love has been an agent for synthesis. But as the force of nature it is also the agent for separation. In Act II that other aspect of the Eternal Feminine, the sirens, lured sailors to their deaths.

The constant movement in the act repeats this complexity. The primary axis of motion is vertical. The Pater Ecstaticus moves up and down; the sequence Pater Profundus, Pater Seraphicus, Doctor Marianus moves us from the bottom to the top of the landscape. The angels and women float above them and recede upward. This is, of course, the direction of Faust's striving from the early part of the play, and the direction of transcendence. How is it suddenly possible, after all the insistence on the need to move out into the world? It is moderated, first of all, by the chorus of blessed boys, who, we are repeatedly told, move in circles, the movement of nature from the "Prologue in Heaven" on. Surrounded by the circling boys the rising Faust will combine the two opposing movements in the play. In addition Goethe has subverted the significance of the upward movement in two ways. First of all, in his upward surge Faust transcends neither his own individuality nor his earthly concerns. The way he sinned against Gretchen becomes his special claim upon her; that is, one of his most world-oriented acts is the instrument of his transcendence. And surrounded by the boys, who are to learn from him about the world, he carries, in effect, his earth with him to Heaven. Second, let us consider the content of the speeches of the various fathers in praise of eternal love. They are, it turns out, all ecstatic descriptions of nature—rocks, forest, sea, beasts of the earth, streams, storms, lightning and thunder, clouds. This paean to eternal love is a paean to Nature. For the last time we are told that nature is the place for man to seek the Absolute. Faust will never reach the eternally receding Mater Gloriosa, who is herself but a representation.

If the impact of Faust's transcendence is so blunted, we must ask after the significance of his apotheosis. It is, clearly, modeled at least in part on baroque Assumptions, in which the triumphant Virgin, accompanied by choirs of angels, floats away from adoring humans on earth. Goethe quietly eliminates the traditional symbols of purity, the white lilies, one often finds in such paintings. This is only proper, for to the extent that we think of the scene as Faust's apotheosis, it is the apotheosis not of the Virgin but of the seducer. Seen this way, the motif is so wonderfully inappropriate that it reminds us again of the necessarily artificial and temporary nature of this triumph. It is, after all, "play." But the motif also recalls the not quite apotheosis of Euphorion at the end of Act III. Faust is accorded the full operatic apotheosis that was there denied his son, presumably because he has achieved more insight about the relation of real and ideal. Yet the parallel to Euphorion inevitably reminds us of the transience of all moments of triumph. It further reminds us that we are in the realm of the operatic, nonillusionist tradition in which the prologues had originally located the play. And here the most fundamental aspects of the nonillusionist mode are crucially important. It must be understood in no sense as a copy of but everywhere as representative of higher truth, and it generates that understanding by its very distance from the appearance of reality.

One might at first argue that the extensive use of Catholic "mythology" serves the equivalent function. After Goethe has so thoroughly undermined the Christian fundament of the Faust legend and presented the Christian postclassical world with such evident hostility in Act IV, the imagery cannot be meant seriously in the last scene. This must be true, but the implications extend further, I think. First of all, the Faust legend was Protestant, not Catholic. To end in a triumphant burst of Catholic imagery is to emphasize the distance of this play from the original legend. Then, partly, we might see it as a reversal of the perspective of Act IV like the many other reversals of perspective late in the play. And partly it shows—parallel to Faust's insight that any and all moments are fulfilled moments—that in the hands of the gifted poet any and all points of the tradition can be equally suitable vehicles of revelation. In the first three acts of Part II, antiquity was a privileged period in this regard; now the play has transcended its classicism. Finally, the very multitude and range of sources for this imagery—not only medieval, Renaissance, and baroque painting but also the Bible, the lives of the saints, Dante, and Emanuel Swedenborg, to name some of the major ones mentioned by commentators—suggests that Goethe intends to underline in a final pyrotechnic display the necessary allusiveness of literature and the extent to which this play is a summa of the European tradition.

In this view the final chorus constitutes, in a sense, the sum beneath the line, a final statement. It is not hard to pursue this line of reasoning and find multitudinous examples of closure in the final scene. In the Swedenborg allusions we see a return to the tradition of Protestant mysticism, the tradition from which the Faust legend grew. In "Entombment" Mephisto compared himself to Job in his torment (l. 11809). The last scene completes this return to Job by making the ultimate revelation of divinity a hymn to nature; this was precisely the reading of Job implied by the "Prologue in Heaven." Altogether, as we have seen, this part of the play returns to the scale and context of the prologues. The motif of rebirth returns us to the fundamental rhythm of "Night," while the return of Gretchen closes off the open-endedness of Part I. Nevertheless, closure must not be confused with finality. Goethe had a very strong sense of formal closure. The essay on Aristotle, for example, goes so far as to define catharsis as simply the closure basic to all drama.[11] Nevertheless, the poem—or drama, or whatever—is not life. Because it is artificial it needs, like Homunculus, to be enclosed, but this is not true of what it represents. In *Elective Affinities*, one of Goethe's characters ruefully comments that no one ever thinks about how life continues after the curtain falls on the marriage at the end of a comedy.[12] But the eternal recession of the ideal at the end of *Faust* makes precisely this demand

[11]"Supplement to Aristotle's Poetics," in *Goethe's Literary Essays*, ed. J. E. Spingarn (New York: Ungar, 1964).
[12]Bk. I, chap. 10, par. 6.

on us. The act of articulation, as the final chorus suggests, requires closure. But what that act attempts to represent is anything but closed. In the discrepancy between the statement and its meaning is room enough for all the varying readings of *Faust* as triumph or as tragedy of the human mind.

Reversal and discrepancy constitute the essence of this act. If it achieves moments of synthesis, it yet constantly shifts the terms. Synthesis is only momentary, here as everywhere else in the play. Formally, too, the act plays off the more "serious," more classicizing *Faust* section against Mephistopheles' modern operatic burlesque, "synthesizing" the two in a Renaissance-baroque operatic finale. Yet here, too, something remains unsatisfactory; the promising historical development is short-circuited. Here, if anywhere, the play should progress to modern drama, to whatever was to fulfill the promise of the Renaissance pastoral opera in Act III. But instead the drama reverts to the structure and mode of Act III, rather than moving forward. What, ultimately, is the new literature to look like? *Faust* is to be a Renaissance rather than a Reformation text, Catholic (in the broadest sense) rather than Protestant, allusive rather than exclusive. Nevertheless, in the turn to a particular allusion at the end we cannot help but see that Goethe refuses to establish a readily imitable modern masterpiece of either the German or the European tradition. In some sense the play ends by denying its own program, which indeed it must. For if *Faust* shows us anything on which we can agree, it is that there is no one form in which to fix the transient moment, the ineffable play that constitutes literary achievement.

14

Epilogue: *Faust* for Ourselves

So ist es mir, so ist es dir gelungen;
Vergangenheit sei hinter uns getan!

The ending of *Faust* is profoundly ambivalent; readers' responses to it have traditionally been polarized according to which parts of the play they connect it to. What I have tried to show is that there is a point of view from which all the parts of the play appear in a sensible, coherent relationship to one another. Given the complexity of the play, such a point of view or, as I have called it until now, underlying structure, must be formulated in fairly abstract terms to maintain its broad applicability. This is what I have tried to achieve with my formulation of Goethe's dialectic and its resolution in play. This structure has proved helpful in organizing my more specifically literary argument about the play. I would hope that it might prove equally fruitful in organizing other kinds of more topical readings of the play as well. I have tried to focus the thrust of my argument in my subtitle, "The German Tragedy," and perhaps I can best articulate the ramifications of my argument by elaborating that title. For ultimately I have attempted to render both terms in it problematic in their application to *Faust*.

The word *tragedy* cannot, I hope it is now clear, be applied to *Faust* in any unreflected sense. It has little to do in the play with the way Aristotle's *Poetics* was read in Europe in Goethe's own time or in ours. Rather, to the extent that it functions in Goethe's subtitle as a generic distinction, it attempts to recover an indigenous Western European tradition of ritual cosmic drama. Given the historical circumstances in which the text was composed, the play constitutes a polemic against the neoclassical use of the term *tragedy* and identifies a broader tradition of drama for German writers. But Goethe was much more interested in addressing readers than writers; cosmic drama in *Faust* repeatedly confronts readers with the basic issues of Goethe's poetics—the autonomy of the literary text, its fundamentally nonmimetic and nonaffective nature. The ramifications of this "lesson" extend beyond reading *Faust* to the ways in which we read, and the grounds on which we reject, a great many other works in our tradition.

But *tragedy* must be understood here in a sense broader than the specifically generic sense, as an ethical category. In arguing consistently against an ethical reading of the play I have really been arguing against a judgmental ethical reading. The play specifically and consistently denies us the possibility of judging Faust's behavior by telling us from the start that God will forgive whatever sins he might commit and by structuring the pact so as to subvert the Christian ethics of the Fall. Nevertheless, the destruction of Baucis and Philemon raises the moral question with special urgency at the end of the play and has been a traditional focus for moralist critics. It would be as naive to think that Goethe condoned the crime as it would to think that he was such an absolutist as to make Faust's last moments outweigh the earlier substantially positive ones. The whole point of the play, after all, is that there is no highest moment that takes priority over all the rest. *Faust* is ambivalent because it tries to take account of the totality of human experience, which is in itself a morally complex phenomenon, not reducible to a "ruling passion" or a moment of anagnorisis. The repeated occasions on which I have had to justify the moral stance—in discussing the "Prologue in Heaven," the Gretchen tragedy, the poet as thief in Act III, Mephistopheles as pirate in Act V—show the significance of the moral problem for Goethe. The very fact that Goethe would raise the moral issue with such urgency at the end shows that he was neither trying to avoid its complexity nor simply to gloss over it. Indeed, it might well be argued that Act V deliberately complements the "Prologue in Heaven" in this regard. There, we remember, the specifically moral issue was defined out of the play. In a sense, Act V readmits morality in order to contextualize it; within the epistemological concerns of the play, morality functions as a significant counterweight.

We might compare one of Goethe's particularly notorious "immoral" utterances from a late autobiographical work, *The Siege of Mainz*

(1822): "I prefer committing an injustice to putting up with disorder."[1] The situation appears to be parallel to the last act of *Faust*. To complete the order of Faust's engineering projects—to complete God's order of the perfection of human striving—it is "preferable" to murder the old couple. But if we consider the context of this apparently grotesque remark, it takes on a different cast. After the fall of Mainz to the allies in 1793, Goethe and a friend were watching the defeated French and their German sympathizers leave the city. Their vantage point was a window in the headquarters of the Duke of Weimar. At one point, bystanders interrupted the procession in order to lynch a particularly notorious sympathizer who was now leaving— legally, according to the terms of the surrender—with the ill-gotten gains of his collaboration. Goethe interfered to prevent the lynching and the wanton destruction that would certainly have ensued, and justified himself by saying, "I prefer committing an injustice to putting up with disorder." The disorder he feared included not only the litter that would have defaced the square under the duke's windows but also the disturbance of the peace guaranteed by the presence of the duke's headquarters on the square, the violation of the treaty guaranteed by the duke (among others), and thus, finally, the disruption of the legal order represented by the person of the duke. In this context, *order* is virtually a metaphysical term, while *justice* means "punishment for particular crimes" and is executed by mob rule. Properly understood, Goethe's position is thus comparable to that of many liberals today, who prefer that individual criminals perhaps escape justice rather than that the fundamental guarantees of legal order be infringed.

Morality seen from the point of view of the individual (justice) is set in the cosmic context (order). This is precisely the situation in Act V. What happens to Baucis and Philemon is without doubt unjust; that Faust is excused from the consequences of his part in their murder is also unjust. But it is equally without doubt that their deaths are demanded by the cosmic order portrayed in the play, whose historical aspect requires that Faust put antiquity behind him. Tragedy in Goethe, we might say, originates in the fact that order and justice are not synonymous. There is, to be sure, a difference in degree between

---

[1]"Ich will lieber eine Ungerechtigkeit begehen als Unordnung ertragen," from *Belagerung von Mainz,* in *Gesamtausgabe,* 10 (Stuttgart: Cotta, 1960), 517.

The Siege of Mainz and *Faust*. Releasing a collaborator is different from murdering the innocent. Given the intense nationalism prevalent in Germany when Goethe published *The Siege of Mainz*, however, there was less difference for Goethe's audience than for us; his refusal to hate the French was ill taken for decades afterward. There is still a significant difference, but this difference only points up the intensity with which Goethe himself perceived the tragic discrepancy between the fundamentally rational order of the cosmos and the necessary limitations of the human condition, which render that order inscrutable and even apparently malicious where it impinges upon human limitation. This is, finally, Goethe's theodicy, which we saw developing in the Gretchen tragedy and in Act III.

Here we must return again to generic concerns. I have been arguing throughout that the conception of tragedy in *Faust* is not Aristotelian but have barely touched on the Aristotelian focus upon the tragic hero and his suffering. The peculiar thing about Goethe's hero is that he does not suffer, either innocently or deservedly. After the death of Gretchen he is healed by the elves; after the murders of Baucis and Philemon he is translated to Heaven. Tragedy is not something that happens to the hero; it happens, rather, to those around him. This is the difference between the Aristotelian anthropological focus and Goethe's cosmological focus. To focus exclusively on the moral situation of the individual (justice) is the neoclassical stance; this is the position Goethe rejected. Similarly, to see the individual situation in its cosmic context is the stance of the earlier dramatic modes *Faust* attempts to recover. Thus the ethical dilemma—tragedy—and the generic aspirations of the play—also tragedy—imply one another. The discussion has concentrated more on the generic aspirations of *Faust*, but the formal and moralist readings are in fact complementary.

This combination of the various senses of tragedy extends finally to the epistemological and interpretive concerns of the drama. Tragedy arises in the discrepancy between justice and order, in the discrepancy between the world and the cosmic order. But this discrepancy exists as well between the cosmological vision of the text and its reader, who can approach it only from an individual point of view. For as we have seen, *Faust* requires the reader to perform the same kind of creative mediation between himself and the text that the artist performs between the world and the cosmic order. Thus it is that the interpretive endeavor itself is always tragic, at least in its limitation, if not in more disastrous ways as well. This burden of limitation—"renunciation" Goethe would have called it—is one that all of us as interpreters share, and there is perhaps no text in our tradition that presses it upon us so totally as Goethe's tragedy.

That *Faust* is German hardly needs to be justified; my point is that *Faust* is in significant respects less German than it is often taken to be. The Faust legend is quintessentially German and Protestant; the Reformation originated, we remember, in Germany and had most impact in the non-Romance cultures of northern Europe. But the Faust legend is consistently undermined in Goethe's play, which in fact affirms the Catholic cosmic dramatic tradition that the Reformation did much to destroy. Even in Part I, Goethe can be seen to be writing an explicitly European rather than specifically German work. Not only his sources and allusions but also his contexts of discussion cross national boundaries. This is the poet who in his later years was to assert, "The Germans were well on the way [to a great national literature] and will get back on it again, as soon as they give up the destructive endeavor to set the *Nibelungen* equal to the *Iliad*."[2] *Faust* is self-consciously and assertively a work of world literature.

And yet not only is Goethe's *Faust* the undeniable masterpiece and centerpiece of the German literary tradition in a way that no single text in English is for us, but for much of the first half of this century the text was made to embody the aspirations of a German nationalism that, I have argued, the text opposes and that Goethe in his own time is certainly known to have abhorred. It is difficult to explain this irony, or even to know what kind of statement would constitute an explanation. Nevertheless some brief narration of what happened to *Faust*, however simplified, seems necessary for American readers, who will otherwise have difficulty relating my reading of the play to what they may have known about *Faust* and Germany.[3]

When *Faust, Part II* was published, after the poet's death as he had

---

[2]"Urteilsworte französischer Kritiker" (French critical terminology [I]), in *Über Kunst und Altertum* (1817), 1:3; *Gesamtausgabe*, 15 (Stuttgart: Cotta, n.d.), 928–29; translation mine.

[3]The full history of Goethe's and *Faust's* reception in the nineteenth century is complex and beyond the scope of this chapter. A history of Goethe's reputation in Germany may be found in Wolfgang Leppmann, *The German Image of Goethe* (Oxford: Clarendon Press, 1961). A fairly detailed discussion of the reception of *Faust* may be found in Hans Schwerte, *"Faust" und das Faustische: Ein Kapitel deutscher Ideologie* (Stuttgart: Klett, 1962).

insisted, it was clear that this completion of the great German tragedy was neither what was expected nor what was wanted. In England and America, as well as in Germany, Goethe was rejected on moral grounds as a pagan (in the most literal and pejorative sense) and as an aesthetic egotist with no concern for his fellow man or society at large.[4] But an even more pervasive, though less articulately presented, concern in Germany was the violation of ideological expectations. If Faust was Germany, as writers were fond of asserting in the 1820s and 1830s, so too must Faust be German; he must be the Faust of the chapbook. This belief is reflected in the "Goethe should have" syndrome. (He should, for example, have involved his Faust in the Peasant Revolts.)[5] It is reflected in nineteenth-century treatments of the Faust theme, which revert to the chapbook pattern of Faust's damnation.[6] It is reflected in the Faust operas, which lay heavy emphasis on the demonic aspects of the story and also often revert to the chapbook conclusion.[7] It is reflected, finally, in popular usage, where Faust is as often "Dr. Faustus," the man who sold his soul to the devil.[8] Goethe

[4]The history of Goethe's reception in England is currently being rewritten by David J. DeLaura. See his "Heroic Egotism: Goethe and the Fortunes of *Bildung* in Victorian England," in *Johann Wolfgang Goethe: One Hundred Years of Continuing Vitality* (Lubbock: Texas Tech Press, 1984), 41–60. A tradition of religious objections to Goethe's text as unchristian, as too Catholic, as too Protestant continued into the twentieth century and underlies much of the confused discussion of the morality of the text.

[5]Argued repeatedly by Friedrich Theodor Vischer. See, for example, his "Zum Zweiten Theile von Goethes *Faust*," *Kritische Gänge*, n.s. 3 (1861): 135–78. An abridged version of this essay may be found in *Faust, ein deutscher Mann: Die Geburt einer Legende und ihr Fortleben in den Köpfen*, ed. Klaus Völker (Berlin: Wagenbach, 1975), 147–60.

[6]The major German ones are Nikolaus Lenau's *Faust* of 1836 and C. D. Grabbe's *Don Juan und Faust* of 1829. Grabbe's play owes more to Byron's *Manfred* than to *Faust*. It is symptomatic that the only treatment of the "titanic" theme in the period at all compatible with the spirit and mode of Goethe's work is by a relatively unpopular foreigner: Shelley's *Prometheus Unbound* (1820).

[7]The most cursory glance at the popular Faust operas of the century shows that it was the demonic and destructive aspect that was attractive. Weber wanted to compose a *Faust*, but did not; the demonism of *Der Freischütz* (1821) shows what its appeal would have been. Charles Gounod's *Faust* (1859) is a saccharine treatment of the Gretchen tragedy that ignores the metaphysical implications of the text. Ludwig Spohr (1814) and Hector Berlioz (1846) both send Faust to hell with great gusto. And Arrigo Boito, who follows Goethe's text more faithfully than any of the others, nevertheless titled his version *Mefistofele* (1868).

[8]The poet Levin Schücking, for example, wrote to his fiancée on March 8, 1843, "Just as Dr. Faust sold his soul to the devil, so Heine sold his attitudes, his honesty and all higher humanity to his style" (*Briefe von Levin Schücking und Louise von Gall*, ed. R. C. Muschler [Leipzig: Grunow, 1928], 206; translation mine).

was thus widely perceived in Germany to have failed, or refused, to represent German aspirations; even Goethe's defenders, whether tactfully or unwittingly, overlooked Goethe's subversion of the Faust legend and discussed only those parts of the play that seemed to fit traditional moral patterns.[9] While it would be incorrect to say that Goethe was not recognized as the great poet of Germany between, say, 1820 and 1870, his cultural significance can be read more in the vigor of the attacks upon him than in either the unstinted admiration or intelligent appraisal he received (although both existed to a small degree).

During this period Goethe's less profound admirers tried to present him as truly German and as moral in some orthodox sense, but their arguments fell on deaf ears until about 1870, when the cultural establishment of the new empire suddenly legitimated Goethe as the father of German culture. Goethe's *Faust*, which had been rejected as un-German, *was* after all the embodiment of Germany and its aspirations; suddenly the text once descried as immoral and pagan guaranteed the morality of the nation. *Faust* could now be referred to publicly as "the second German Bible."[10] The Goethe idolatry of the period is notorious, and still makes Goethe suspect to many Germans. This reversal was accomplished by overlooking as much as possible any differences between Goethe's *Faust* and the legend. Not until the appearance of a book titled *Faust, the Unfaustian* in 1933 was any substantial scholarly attempt made to distinguish Goethe's treatment from the context of the legend, which in the meantime had truly become the German myth and had swallowed up Goethe's play.[11] This is important be-

---

[9]Such eminent early enthusiasts as Madame de Staël, A. W. Schlegel, and George Henry Lewes, while assuring readers that the play was a series of disorganized scenes, sovereignly dispensed their own inaccurate summaries of the text. Madame de Staël, *De l'Allemagne*, pt. II, chap. 23 (Paris: Garnier-Flammarion, 1968), 1:343–67; A. W. Schlegel, *Vorlesungen über dramatische Kunst und Literatur*, Lecture 36 in *Kritische Schriften und Briefe*, ed. Edgar Lohner, 6 (Stuttgart: Kohlhammer, 1967), 278–79; G. H. Lewes, *The Life of Goethe* (New York: Ungar, 1965), 451–86, 545–54.

[10]By Franz Dingelstedt, director of the Vienna Burgtheater. See Schwerte, *"Faust" und das Faustische*, 161. Clearly Dingelstedt is more concerned here with national ideology than with religion; nevertheless the metaphor is striking in the extreme.

[11]Wilhelm Böhm, *Faust, der Nichtfaustische* (Halle: Niemeyer, 1933). By that time *Faustian* had become the ideological justification of German expansionism (see Schwerte, *"Faust" und das Faustische*, 148–90). And Oswald Spengler had made it synonymous with the rapacious but melancholy West in *The Decline of the West* (1918), where *Faustian*, with specific and repeated reference to Goethe's *Faust* (reduced to "Night" and the engineering projects of Act V), identifies Western man. Indeed, Spengler attributes the fundamental methodology of his book to Goethe.

cause the basis of the modern *Faust* scholarship was laid in this period, especially in a series of major commentaries, whose influence is still widely pervasive. [12]Despite Thomas Mann's efforts to reidentify Goethe as a cosmopolitan, nonnationalist writer, *Faust* remains the focus of ambivalence among German speakers even today.[13]

Thus throughout the history of its reception the "German-ness" of *Faust* has been an issue in an unremitting series of efforts to connect the text directly and unambiguously to the real world in precisely the way that Goethe denied was possible for literature. Goethe's image for the result of such abusive misunderstanding of the nature of art was the explosion when Faust tried to rescue Helen. The validity of his insight is borne out by the fate of the German ideologues who embraced his Faust.

Goethe has often been criticized for ignoring political and social issues; my reading of the play will be criticized on the same grounds. But I have been trying to show that those issues are not ignored in the play. The ideological abuse of the text for the last century and a half testifies to its social vitality, but the way in which the text addresses these issues has, I would argue, been misread. They must be seen as special cases of larger, more abstract issues; they must also be seen as issues that cannot be addressed directly and explicitly by a work of art, which by its nature does not deal directly with the real world. Such issues are addressed indirectly, as the play has forced us to see over and over. They are addressed by making the reader confront his own reactions to the complex, often paradoxical, situations the drama poses. This is the aspect of the text I have endeavored to uncover.

---

[12]Nicholas Boyle documents this continuity in the Reclam commentary to *Faust* (the least expensive and most widely used commentary) in " 'Du ahnungsloser Engel du!': Some Current Views of Goethe's *Faust*," *German Life and Letters* n.s. 36 (1982–83), 116–47, esp. 116–26. Ehrhard Bahr argues convincingly that no significant change in German understanding of Goethe took place until the late 1960s ("Die Goethe-Renaissance nach 1945: Verspieltes Erbe oder verhinderte Revolution," paper presented at the national convention of the Modern Language Association of America, December 1981; I am grateful to Professor Bahr for making the manuscript of this talk available to me).

[13]The novel *Lotte in Weimar* (1939) (published in English as *The Beloved Returns*) directly presents the resentment of Goethe's contemporaries that he was "un-German." In *Dr. Faustus* (1947) Mann personifies Germany in a hero modeled on Nietzsche and stylized in terms of the Faust legend. Goethe's *Faust* is conspicuously marginal in Mann's treatment: the Gretchen and Helena episodes are trivialized, an Ariel figure who recalls the Boy-charioteer/Ariel/Euphorion group from Part II is brutally destroyed by Mann's devil.

So sind wir nicht am rechten Ort
Und ziehen unseres Weges weiter fort.

Index

Index

Index

Library of Congress Cataloging-in-Publication Data

Brown, Jane K., 1943–
  Goethe's Faust.

  Bibliography: p.
  Includes index.
  1. Goethe, Johann Wolfgang von, 1749–1832. Faust. I. Title.
PT1925.B76   1986   832'.6   85–17149
ISBN 0–8014–1834–8 (cloth) (alk. paper)
ISBN 0-8014-9349-8 (paper) (alk. paper)